PSYCHOLOGICAL FACTORS OF PEACE AND WAR

PSYCHOLOGICAL FACTORS OF PEACE AND WAR

Edited by

TOM HATHERLY PEAR

Contributions by

G. W. ALLPORT

J. COHEN

H. V. DICKS

H. J. EYSENCK

J. C. FLUGEL

HILDE HIMMELWEIT

MADELINE KERR

T. H. PEAR

L. F. RICHARDSON

Essay Index Reprint Series

Originally published by
HUTCHINSON & CO., LTD.
London

BOOKS FOR LIBRARIES PRESS
FREEPORT, NEW YORK

INTERNATIONAL STANDARD BOOK NUMBER:
0-8369-2290-5

LIBRARY OF CONGRESS CATALOG CARD NUMBER:
76-156703

PRINTED IN THE UNITED STATES OF AMERICA

CONTENTS

PREFACE

Because wars begin in the minds of men it is unnecessary to apologize for adding another to the huge pile of books about the causes of war. Even in this era of psychology, little has been written about the mental factors involved in peace and warfare. It might be argued that all causes of war are ultimately mental, since if not experienced by someone, they do not exist. Who experiences them, and how; these are all-important questions.

The whole of Part I can be read without technical knowledge. Part II, though of general interest, requires some familiarity with the methods of psychological investigation.

Thanks are offered to Mr. W. T. Kimber for encouragement at an early stage, to Mr. Andrew Boyd of the United Nations Association and to Dr. J. C. Flugel for advice concerning publication, to Mrs. Nancy E. Lingard for help with the typescript and index, to Mrs Gartside, Mrs. C. H. Foster and Miss Nora M. Williamson for typing and indexing.

Grateful acknowledgments for permission to reprint Chapters II and X respectively are due to the late Dr. Henry Guppy, of the John Rylands Library, Manchester, to Dr. Jerome S. Bruner, editor of the *Journal of Social Issues*, and to Professor T. H. Marshall and Mr. Geoffrey Gorer for allowing the use of certain quotations from their work in *The Listener* (1947), and in an unpublished address to the British Association (1947) respectively. Dr. Dicks's chapter appeared originally, in slightly different form, as a privately circulated document prepared in 1947 for the Royal Institute of International Affairs, London.

The University,
Manchester,
    July 1950.

T. H. PEAR.

FOREWORD

"Peace must be founded, if it is not to fail, upon the intellectual and moral solidarity of mankind."

The United Nations Association, which, together with its sister associations in over thirty other countries, is seeking to influence men's minds in the cause of peace, is all too aware of the formidable psychological factors which make the path of peace so difficult.

In this book a number of eminent psychologists have set down the results of their inquiries into some of these factors. The United Nations Association strongly commends their findings both to students of psychology and to the wider public which realizes the importance of these studies. Individual views expressed are naturally those of the contributors and not necessarily of the association; but UNA is proud to have the privilege of introducing this distinguished team, and grateful to the House of Hutchinson for its ready co-operation in putting their work before the world.

C. W. JUDD,
Secretary, UNA.

July 1950.

PART I

CHAPTER I

INTRODUCTION

by T. H. Pear

THE title of Chapter II, "Peace, War and Culture Patterns," is almost self-explanatory. Most social psychologists and sociologists ought to examine the idea expressed in Dr. Ruth Benedict's *Patterns of Culture*, that war is a social theme which may or may not be used in any culture.

This assertion is especially true of today's and tomorrow's developments. Who, today, suggests that the atom bomb was the result of simple aggressive tendencies, or even of an 'instinct' of curiosity?

It is here suggested that since culture-patterns not dominated by the idea of 'naturalness' of war still exist, they can be studied with profit. Definitions of warfare and peace, both in our time, are given in modern terms. The almost obsolete idea of war as a biological necessity is examined, as well as the belief or slogan that modern warfare (the significance of the adjective is often neglected) is due to human aggressiveness.

Dr. Cohen's theme in Chapter V, "Women in Peace and War," is almost unexamined by social scientists, though it has not been neglected by dramatists, poets, novelists and anthropologists. Is modern warfare the expression of the male against the female element in society? Do wars occur nowadays because of the dominating influence of men in administration and government? Would a fuller emancipation of women promote a more peaceful social order?

Dr. Cohen asserts that the elaborate effeminacy of women in some classes of society today may be largely a product of civilized life, and there is no good reason to suppose that such a practice is closely connected with female biological functions or that it satisfies any inborn mental disposition of woman.

Dr. Eysenck's Chapter III, "War and Aggressiveness," surveys studies of social attitudes, especially of aggressiveness. He shows the limitations of such investigations; they deal with conscious ideas verbally communicated, not with unconscious ideas issuing in non-verbal behaviour. Since people's opinions about war and peace are conscious and usually verbalized, such studies are valuable. But they are more than thermometers, registering the momentary variable 'temperature' of the individual's mind, for recent extensions of such studies show that attitudes towards certain aspects of war are related to social stratum and to political affiliation, and that within the single person, there is an organization of social attitudes related in interesting ways, and this affects his conservative, radical or liberal leanings.

Equally thought-provoking is the statistical demonstration of a dangerous lack of agreement between the view of expert students of the causes of war (who, contrary to popular belief, show few serious divisions of opinion) and voters. This leads one to reflect upon the unsatisfactory number and nature of the channels of communication between students of social behaviour and the public.

Dr. Himmelweit's Chapter VIII, "Frustration and Aggression," should be considered in conjunction with Dr. Eysenck's. She points out that a strange aspect of man's behaviour is his relative readiness to accept the idea that war is inevitable, and in times of war to become an active member of a belligerent force, though this involves heavy personal sacrifices, even death, an overthrow of many standards and values which in peacetime he considered important, and acceptance of new standards hitherto regarded as highly undesirable or abhorrent. To accept any simple concept of an 'instinct' of self-preservation, roused by some real or imagined threat to the individual's group, involves a difficulty usually evaded—why is man so ready to believe in the existence of such external threats?

Psycho-analysts have postulated some positive force within the person which welcomes the occurrence of war, and with it the removal of inhibitions that exist in times of peace. (It would be interesting, however, to know how many of these theorists actually fought in a war as distinct from serving as medical officers.) For Freudians this positive force is conceived as pent-up aggression, seeking a socially approved outlet, and due to frustration. Later, Freud postulated an aggressive instinct *per se*, which was not solely a reaction to frustration.

Dr. Himmelweit reviews experimental studies of aggression. The situations involved in these inevitably stimulate and frustrate conscious rather than unconscious needs, and more work is necessary to bridge the gap between laboratory situations and those of real life. She pleads for clarification of the concept (or concepts) of aggressiveness, and points out the necessity of considering a person's social status in relation to the degree and kind of aggressiveness he shows, and, if adult, is allowed by his culture pattern to show. She concludes that 'frustration' has a different, perhaps even a unique, meaning for different persons, that it must be considered in a physical and social context, and that its quality and intensity depend upon each individual's 'picture of himself'.

In view of the widespread interest in discussions of national character, and of the popular tendency to beg most psychological questions arising out of this concept, Dr. Henry V. Dicks's Chapter IX, "Some Psychological Studies of the German Character," is particularly apposite.

Recently there have been three—not always unrelated—lines of attack upon problems of national character, by cultural anthropologists, statisticians and psycho-analysts. A combination of their techniques makes possible an attempt to discover whether in a given community there exists a 'basic personality'; the sum of characteristics found to recur regularly in representatives of a given cultural group, and caused by similar influences. The result is a 'behavioural shorthand' of custom and accepted practice; of typical ways of dealing with members of the group; these, inside the group, are taken for granted.

In 1942, Dr. (then Lt.-Col.) Dicks worked in a transit camp for recently captured prisoners of war. Here he made a running survey of enemy morale, using interviews (according to schedule), informal conversations and a kind of mass-observation technique. His psychiatric status was not disclosed; he was represented as a welfare officer interested in the prisoners as men. Their political and religious affiliations, rank and age group were carefully studied. Accordingly he presents a most interesting picture of the typical character-structure of five classes (with transitions between them): whole-hearted Nazis, believers with reservations, 'unpolitical men,' the divided, and the active convinced anti-Nazi. No women could be studied by Dr. Dicks in similar circumstances. The whole chapter implicitly criticizes many writers on national character who have made no such intensive and extensive study of their subject-matter.

Dr. Richardson reminds us that general statements can be examined, verified or refuted, "by collecting the facts from the whole world over a century or more". Chapter X, "Threats and Security," points out that a threat from one group of people to another may produce reactions of contempt, submission, negotiation, avoidance or retaliation. Examples, in the memory-span of many readers, of all these causes and effects are examined, and stress laid upon the disastrous stimulation of war efforts which threats and counter-threats inevitably produce.

Chapter XI, "Statistics of Fatal Quarrels," examines data collected by Professor Quincy Wright and by Dr. Richardson, who have studied the distribution of wars in time. It discusses whether wars have become more frequent, and shows which nations have been most involved in wars of late.

Dr. Madeline Kerr's Chapter IV, "Personality and Attitudes Towards Warfare," is related to Chapters II and III. She inquires how people make the personality adjustments enabling them to cope with the changed social relationships in war conditions: even to acquiesce in their own destruction. She employs Moreno's concept of 'social roles'. The child at first, unable to understand what is going on around him, acts out the roles which the adults play: later he assimilates a role through conditioning, perception and objectification.

Personality, she holds, is not a relatively unchanging unit, but in great part a product of the behavioural environment. It is composed largely of 'projections' about ourselves and others. The individual chooses certain roles under the stresses of his 'social field'; life is made considerably easier (to put it mildly) if he accepts the culturally approved way of living. The child is taught, implicity and explicitly, that he 'ought' to play, on appropriate occasions, certain roles. Those which are over-learned may become stereotypes.

Dr. Kerr urges further studies of societies in which prestige is important, and of the relation between economic factors and psychological events.

In Chapter VI Dr. Flugel expounds and clarifies some neglected aspects of psychological problems of world integration. To them there are three approaches; moral, political—these date back to antiquity—and psychological; the last-named so novel that it still produces characteristic reactions of surprise, even of derisive humour, in many people who find themselves confronted with unexpected situations or ideas.

Among the sparse blessings of today we may count the majority opinion that war is undesirable. Yet one obstacle to preventing it is the fact that to large numbers of people it gives real, short-term emotional satisfaction. Dr. Flugel shows why the reliance of the League of Nations, and later the United Nations, upon a purely intellectual appreciation of their necessity accounts for much of their lack of success.

Moral and religious approaches to these problems are seriously weakened by the fact that they customarily appeal to the individual's conscience, which in wartime he is likely to delegate, often with relief, to his group leader.

The problem of the gross immorality of the mutual behaviour

of sovereign states has never been squarely faced. A serious cause of our modern troubles is that while inventions have shrunk space and time—so that, whether we like it nor not, in the physical sense, we are 'One World'—there has simultaneously been a recrudescence of a vigorous sense of nationhood. Yet a successful federation or integration of smaller units into a larger whole is already a common social pattern—as seen in the large business concerns, in the older English Universities, in Switzerland, in the British Commonwealth. In wartime, creation of loyalty to a large group is relatively easy; why not in peace?

Finally, he poses a major philosophical problem: Is man to regard himself as fighting against and trying to control Nature, or as himself a part of Nature's purpose in moulding her to his will?

In Chapter VII Professor Allport appeals eloquently for international co-operation. He points out the vagueness of saying that our international troubles are 'moral' or due to the 'lack of religion'. The great moral creeds of the world, taken in their purity, would probably help to control the ravages of technology, but how, in an age of great industries, bureaucracy, instant communication and atomic energy shall one effectively love one's neighbour? Only social research focused upon overlapping problems of nations will give the answers.

"Since wars begin in the minds of men it is in the minds of men that the defences of peace must be constructed." Yet too often political expediency, power-politics, self-national purposes have conspired to overlook, to 'place on file', counsel which might well have been heeded.

He gives valuable advice to social scientists and reminds them that to be effective their science will have to be international. We should study the procedure of conferences of all kinds, to see how they can be made more effective. Our efforts should be focused on child welfare, education, health. "Adults are the bigots."

Propaganda we have with us, whether we like it or not, so its strategy and tactics merit more study. Until recently, anthropologists have accentuated the differences that divide the families of mankind, and have relatively ignored the common considerations of justice and morality, identical over vast areas of the earth. An encyclopaedia of cultural uniformities and similarities should be compiled, and study of national character should be undertaken with this in mind.

B

CHAPTER II

PEACE, WAR AND CULTURE-PATTERNS

by T. H. Pear

PSYCHOLOGISTS ought to examine or extend the idea in Dr. Ruth Benedict's *Patterns of Culture*[1] that war itself "is a social theme that may or may not be used in any culture" (p. 30). The purpose of this chapter is to discuss this suggestion.

In the limited space, I can offer only brief definitions of terms and they will be used in order to focus our minds. Complete and formally satisfactory definitions would be far from brief, but in partial compensation references will be given.

Today I ask, "Can *modern* war (the adjective is emphasized) and the types of warfare, if indeed they can be so called, which now threaten us, be understood better by the aid of the culture-pattern theory in some form? May not warfare only, but the state of uneasy peace which we have suffered since 1910 be the expression of a vast culture-pattern, or a relatively minor pattern, superimposed upon a major one, in which the many varieties of behaviour called war have grown, slowly or quickly? If so, to what extent may even recent psychological, sociological and ethnological attempts to explain war be already out of date? And if the culture-pattern theory is helpful, then since culture-patterns can be changed quickly (cf. the Maoris, the Japanese, the Russians) there may either be hope that the next war could be postponed indefinitely, or fear that it may come sooner even than most people expect. Moreover, since culture-patterns not dominated by the idea of the 'naturalness' of war still exist, can we study them with profit? For reasons I have never quite understood, certain expounders and students of religion in this country also delight to describe and study sordid crimes: could militarist-nationalists be persuaded to examine non-warlike cultures in a similarly ambivalent way? The experiment seems worth trying.

Let us consider a brief definition of 'culture-pattern' (fuller accounts are given in two Rylands lectures).[2] Culture-pattern is the general principle of integration by means of which the customs,

[1]New York, Houghton Mifflin Co., London, Methuen, 1934.
[2]"Psychological Implications of the Culture-Pattern Theory," and "Personality in its Cultural Context," *Bulletin of the John Rylands Library*, XXIX, 1945 and XXX, 1946.

institutions and dogmas, the sentiments, interests and values of a culture are woven into a more or less coherent 'pattern'. As Dr. R. H. Thouless writes:[1]

"The motives to which men may respond and the goals towards which their behaviour may be directed are multitudinous, and every society makes use only of a certain selection of these. The particular selection of potential human purposes that any particular society employs may be said to give it its characteristic 'pattern'. Different cultures may differ both in the extent to which their activities are subordinated to a single pattern of motivation, and in the kind of pattern they have adopted."

We may focus attention upon this last description, especially upon 'selection' and 'pattern'. The pattern may be woven about different 'centres', such as the ego, age, sex, property or power. Possibly many of the inter-weavings that an arm-chair theorist's ingenuity could suggest may be found working fairly well in some part of the world. After all, a female film-star functioning as colonel of a regiment of fighting men might seem too fantastic to have been invented by any sane person.

As time (about fourteen years) has gone on, the concept has taken more complicated forms, some of which are due to psychological re-thinking of implications of the original idea. A useful distinction is between explicit and implicit culture. To borrow from Dr. Clyde Kluckhohn,[2] explicit culture comprises "all features of a group design for living which might be described to an outsider by participants in the culture".

To illustrate this from war, a Bren gun is an object of explicit culture. The uniform of a unit of the fighting forces might suggest itself as another, were it not for the fact that combatant officers sometimes suddenly refuse to recognize certain uniforms, and 'execute' —using whatever euphemisms may occur to them; to be vehemently rejected by their enemies—certain wearers of explicit badges. This ambiguity in practice, attached to a distinction understood and accepted in theory, strengthens my central argument: that war is rapidly ceasing to have rules.

[1] In *The Study of Society*, ed. by F. C. Bartlett and others, Kegan Paul, 1939.
[2] "Patterning as exemplified in Navaho Culture," *Language, Culture and Personality*, Menasha, Wis., U.S.A., pp. 109–30, 1941. "Covert Culture and Administrative Problems," *American Anthropologist*, XLV, pp. 213–27, 1943. C. Kluckhohn and William H. Kelly, "The Concept of Culture," in *The Science of Man in the World Crisis*, ed. by Ralph Linton, New York, Columbia University Press, 1944.

Implicit culture is "that section of behaviour of which members of the group are unaware, or minimally aware". In many countries the connection of the churches with warfare shows both explicit and implicit elements. A British Army chaplain may wear combatant officer's uniform with a priest's collar. The first of any letter-group which may follow his name, signifying special distinction is 'C.F.' 'D.D.' would, I believe, come second. These are explicit, but there are implicit features of the culture-pattern. Presumably no clergyman is explicitly bound to hold a sacred service to bless a lethal weapon: while some willingly do this, others probably have declined. To many, perhaps to most educated people, the long-standing tendency of our ruling families to put their sons in the Navy, Army or Church, often in this order of preference, is known or acknowledged implicitly rather than explicitly. The custom, up to 1939, that great armament firms appointed to their boards of directors combatant officers of high rank immediately upon their retirement, is implicit to many people; but explicit to students of the international arms trade. The present-day link-up of many physical and biological scientists with preparations for war is implicit to most men in the street—even to a certain number of social philosophers.

Two kinds of *patterns*, distinguished from *configurations*; to be explained in a moment, are defined by Kluckhohn:

"A sanctioned pattern, if described, would convey to the hearer or reader an idea of what, in a defined situation, people would do or say if they conformed completely to ideals accepted in the culture."

For example, in stating an ideal English sanctioned pattern, "more than three people at a bus-stop form a queue," the degree of deviation of actual instances of relevant behaviour from the ideal does not matter, but in a behavioural pattern, the attention is focused upon some mode of what people in fact do.

The expression in behaviour of a sanctioned pattern is to shoot an enemy in uniform unless he surrenders, but the behavioural pattern of bombing Hiroshima has been described by Group-Leader Chester and Dr. J. Bronowski,[1] and by John Hersey in the famous special edition of the *New Yorker*, 31st August, 1946. And this, though speakers in Parliamentary debates in the House often seem studiously to avoid mentioning it, is likely to be the behavioural pattern in future warfare.

Let us distinguish between *pattern* and *configuration*:

[1] *The Listener*, XXXVII, No. 946, 13th March, 1947.

"Pattern is 'a structural regularity . . . to which there is some degree of conformance on the part of a number of persons', 'a . . . generalization of behaviour or of ideals for behaviour'."

Configurations are Edward Sapir's "unconscious systems of meanings" and Benedict's "unconscious canons of choice". Perhaps 'minimally aware' or 'unverbalized' are better descriptive terms than 'unconscious'. These configurations are not unconscious in everyone and are not necessarily unconscious in the sense used by Freud or Jung, though to explain the attitude of some persons, the action of such mechanisms might be postulated with advantage.

Let us take an example which illustrates all these points, and is now sufficiently 'distanced' in time to be discussed coolly. Between 1930 and 1933, the presence and the activities of the Officers' Training Corps in English schools were matters of active discussion. Critics were not necessarily pacifists—in fact, many supported the League of Nations. Some, quoting published opinions of army officers, said that the Corps was not preparing schoolboys for the next war, and while not criticizing the infantry training, cited the absence of instruction in gas warfare, or about tanks, though these were certain to play a great part in any war. Others focused upon the overt aim of the Corps, to train officers, not soldiers in general, and asserted that if no elementary and few secondary schools had O.T.C.s, the army would be undemocratic. Some pointed out that unless a public school was powerful enough in numbers, prestige or both, to flout the Headmasters' (self-elected) Conference, it would not be recognized as 'public'.

A psychologist who asked his friends for their frank opinions might receive answers like these:

1. If war breaks out, I don't want my son to serve in the ranks.
2. I expect him to be commissioned; that is one reason why I made sacrifices to send him to a public school.
3. Officers ought to be gentlemen.
4. I wish my boy to be trained to lead others (this often went with an overt assumption that a complementary class existed, fitted to be led, and not attending public schools).

Any or all of these arguments were often combined. It might too have been possible to find an ambitious schoolmaster who said frankly that promotion depended in part upon being a keen O.T.C. officer, and that therefore this consideration guided him. So anyone who writes a social-psychological account of British officer-selection between

1927 and 1947 might usefully draw a distinction between pattern and configuration. In 1940 this distinction might have been easier to explain to some generals than to others. As our configurations turn into patterns we become sophisticated.

What is modern warfare, regarded from the social psychologist's point of view? We may begin with Professor Lasswell's "Violence directed against people outside the community, justified in the name of the community, and accepted by the community".[1] One may ask, "Who and what is the Community?" If mass-observers had recorded what thousands of people in this country said at 11 a.m. on 3rd September, 1939, would this, even if the sample had been 'representative', have really represented the community? Would it have corresponded entirely with what its members thought? And since no plebiscite was held, how could the community have nullified or rejected the Cabinet's decision? Certainly different levels of public and private opinion[2] might be distinguished in one and the same person. A definition of war becomes even more difficult if we ask whether the present events in Palestine (April, 1947) are to be called war, for the soldier there feels that the absence of rules causes many conflicts in deciding how to behave.

We pass to the definition of Doctors E. F. M. Durbin and J. Bowlby:[3] "War is organized fighting between large groups of adult human beings". Yet the Second World War blurred distinctions between adults and non-adults. In many countries, children helped valuably in the war. Our own Government spoke of 'men' of eighteen, but considered them too immature to vote, and in law they were 'infants'. When a handful of uniformed adults dropped an atom bomb, devised by civilians, which annihilated tens of thousands of adults and children, was this warfare or did it symbolize the end of war as historians and lawyers knew it? In any case, a definition which includes the term 'fighting' is only with difficulty applicable to conflicts in which atomic bombs and bacteria may be used, since the counter-attack, if any, is not made by the persons attacked, and bacteria will probably harm both sides.

As recently as 1941, Professor D. W. Harding wrote[4] "A surprising feature of much social violence, including war, is its moderation (p. 13). There is in fact extraordinarily little cool extermination

[1] *World Politics and Social Insecurity*, 1935.
[2] Cf. Tom Harrisson, "What is Public Opinion?" *Political Quarterly*, XI, 1946.
[3] *Personal Aggressiveness and War*, Kegan Paul, 1939.
[4] *The Impulse to Dominate*, Allen and Unwin, 1941.

of other people" (p. 15). So even recent definitions of warfare require re-phrasing.

What are the rules of warfare today? Do they exist anywhere, codified and accepted even by the Great Powers? Could students like ourselves ascertain these rules if we tried? Some American physicists who worked upon the atom-bomb disagreed with both President Truman and the Navy about the way in which the bomb was to be employed. It is relevant to mention that the chief argument put forward for its use was that it would shorten the war against Japan, not that it was allowable by the rules of warfare. Matters had already got past even that stage of mental tidiness.

A definition to which we shall return is that of Emery Reves:[1] "War takes place whenever and wherever non-integrated social units of equal sovereignty come into contact".

Is there any agreed definition of peace other than the purely negative one of absence of war? By many the absence of such a positive concept is tacitly accepted, yet to a peace-lover it would seem that just as the absence of a satisfactory agreed definition of love does not prevent him from experiencing and knowing that he experiences it, so there can be positive experience of peace, even if it 'passeth understanding'. That such mental conditions may bore some people is beside the point. But the war-lover may ask: "How do people behave peacefully?" The answer is that people are behaving peacefully most of the time.

Dr. Lewis F. Richardson[2] has suggested as a criticism of a peaceful attitude *vis à vis* another group, 'proved readiness to co-operate'. We may leave the matter there: towards people who say they don't know what peace is, I feel like the professor of philosophy who in anguish of spirit said to an unusually persistent questioner: "You know damned well what the mind is, so shut up!"

Let us look at a few recent contributions from specialists on the subject of war.

A monumental pair of volumes by Professor Quincy Wright on *The Causes of War*[3] have recently appeared. He classifies and summarizes recent contributions.

Biologists emphasize the impropriety of analogies between animal and human warfare. The chief contribution to our knowledge of the

[1] *The Anatomy of Peace*, Penguin Books, 1947.
[2] "Generalized Foreign Politics," *British Journal of Psychology, Monograph Supplement*, No. 23, 1939.
[3] Cambridge University Press, 1942.

causes of modern war have been made by psychologists, particularly the analysts and the attitude-measurers. All consider war to be a function of social customs and institutions.

Anthropologists emphasize the conventional and customary nature of war, and regard it as an invention, widely diffused in the world.

While the older sociologists assumed the correctness of the analogy between international conflict and the biological struggle for existence, and therefore tended to regard war as 'necessary' for human progress, their successors regard it as a species of the genus conflict, applicable to strife between classes, in industry, in the family and civil strife. (The attitude of the social psychologist makes him doubt the usefulness of calling these war.) All the above investigators tend to insist that the factors causing war are extremely complex but inherently controllable.

Wright asserts that most publications about the 'economic causes' or determinants of war have been by historians or publicists rather than by professional economists. He says that in text-books of economics studied at present, war hardly figures at all. Thorstein Veblen in *The Theory of the Leisure Class* and the Marxists mention and discuss war.

He is optimistic about the contributions of those social psychologists who employ the concepts of personality and culture, combining the data of psychology, sociology and anthropology. They, he thinks, may be able to suggest cures.

It is not irrelevant to interpolate the suggestion that since for centuries it has been easy to make a profession of writing about war (the ability has been known to run in distinguished political families) and after every war leaders usually write their memoirs, war themes form a powerful vested interest. Writing about peace is less esteemed socially, less popular, less lucrative—and less easy. Such facts may deter the spread of thinking about peace.

A point made by Wright is that the waging of war by the political leaders occurs in a highly symbolic form. Until recently, they and the masses led had no acquaintance with the actual conditions of war 'behind' the symbols, and this is still true of many Americans. Mr. Asquith as Prime Minister declared "We shall not sheathe the sword" before entering upon a war in which probably nobody who mattered, including himself, believed that the sword would be used. Blockade and propaganda were in fact the knock-out blows of the First World War. The orators employ easily understood symbols, or abstractions which are not understood. Both these forms of expression may be seriously misleading, and not always by accident. Yet as Wright puts it, the muscle-movements which actually declare war "must occur in a context of verbal legitimacy".

He suggests that the concepts of psycho-analysis and of relativity have helped to promote a general feeling of insecurity in the post-war world.

Much remains to be done by psychologists if they wish to reduce the threat of war for, as he says:

"Arguments which influence opinion often have little support in social science, and truths affirmed by social scientists often have little influence upon the movements of opinion in contemporary societies. This suggests that little should be expected from studies of the statistics of populations, commerce, finance and armaments or the technicalities of law and procedure in explaining war. It is only as such matters affect opinion that they cause war, and opinion is moved by symbols of such vague meaning that no precise correlation with statistical series or refined analyses is to be expected. The causes of wars must be studied directly from indices of opinion, not indirectly from indices of conditions, even though the two have an overlapping vocabulary."

This points to the necessity of studying today's channels of communication, particularly the Press, radio and films, to see how this state of affairs can be improved. As an example may be quoted the publicity given by the B.B.C. to Hersey's account of Hiroshima, and a whole week's broadcasts upon the uses and abuses of atomic energy.

Wright points out that while, in the past, small wars had localized effects, like small eruptions on the skin, the events of the last two wars have been comparable to the outbreak of a general fever, seriously involving the whole organism, i.e. the whole world.

Perhaps it is now unnecessary to spend much time in refuting the belief that war is a biological necessity, a universal law of Nature, though the assertion, in one of its many forms, that war is 'due to human instincts' needs more consideration. Yet it should be noted that recently throughout a whole week, experts tried to explain on the radio how the next war might be fought. And it is hard to conceive anything less instinctive than the behaviour of the atomic scientists and of their thousands of helpers who telescoped fifty years into four as the result of super-human efforts of thinking, experimenting and organization at the very highest level. Yet we still read certain 'explanations' of warfare by writers who seem not to have noticed even the last stages of the First World War.

In his article "The Nature of War and the Myth of Nature"[1] reprinted as a chapter of his book *Man's Most Dangerous Fallacy: the Myth of Races*, Professor M. F. Ashley Montagu points out the very different types of conflict between organisms which some writers term 'fighting'. He writes:

"The illegitimate use of such terms as struggle, fighting, force and so on, when applied to plant and animal life, and the deliberate confusion of these terms with war, is too often made and far too often allowed to pass unchallenged. I cannot resist quoting Professor Pollard in this connection, who entertainingly remarks of this confusion:

'The sun and the moon, we suppose, declare war with great regularity because they get into opposition every month. Parties in the House of Commons are perpetually at war because they are opposed. The police wage war because they are a force; for *naturally* if we use force against a criminal, we must needs make war upon other communities. War, indeed, will last for ever, because men will never "cease to struggle". So the League of Nations has obviously failed whenever a stern parent is caught chastizing a peccant child: and "fighting" will go on without end because drowning men will fight for life, doctors will fight disease and women will fight for places at drapery sales. And this is war![2]' "

Professor Bryce is quoted as asserting that until the days of the French Revolution, men never fought to impose their own type of civilization upon others. Professor Montagu argues that war did not arrive until men reached the agricultural state of development, not more than 20,000 years ago. Then came property, then industry, then wealth, power, ambition and finally the desire to acquire additional property, including slaves, in war. "The modern most potent cause of war is economic rivalry—a purely cultural phenomenon having no biological base whatsoever."

Recently Dr. Ruth Benedict's article, "The Study of Cultural Patterns in European Nations,"[3] approximates two concepts; one ancient, and, some would say, shaky, the other new, plastic and perhaps untried. The first is National Character, the second Culture-Pattern.

She says, "Every nation in Europe and Asia has simultaneously

[1]*Scientific Monthly*, LIV, pp. 342–53, 1942.
[2]*Vincula*, London, 1925.
[3]*Transactions of the New York Academy of Sciences*, Series II, Vol. 8, pp. 274–9, June, 1946.

denied and boasted that it had a National Character". It has been called a myth in an eloquent book by Mr. Hamilton Fyfe[1] and has been carefully examined from the sociologist's standpoint by Professor Morris Ginsberg[2] who shows that much of what is called 'national character' is national reputation. In a slightly different form the valuable concepts, that a community may have a 'modal personality-structure' or 'basic character-structure' have been put forward by Erich Fromm,[3] Abram Kardiner,[4] and Ernest Beaglehole.[5] They are all developed from ideas closely related to those of culture-patterns.

"To the anthropologist, the study of national character is a study of learned cultural behaviour. For several decades before the war, anthropologists had done pioneer work, in this field, in compact primitive communities. During the last decade, theoretical points made by anthropologists about cultural conditioning had been widely accepted. Anthropologists had presented their case convincingly enough so that there was wide agreement that social arrangements are of fundamental importance in shaping any people's tenets about life, whether they are assumptions about the function of the State, economic motivations, relations between the sexes, or dependence upon the supernatural. The forms these tenets take in our own cultural background were no longer generally considered to be direct consequences of human biology, and 'human nature' was no longer considered as a sufficient explanation of them. Behaviour, even in civilized nations, was increasingly understood as ways of acting and thinking which developed in the special kind of social environment characteristic of that part of the world."

Dr. Benedict makes the point that an anthropologist, asked to describe a *primitive* society, will focus upon certain features which he has been trained to regard as especially important, yet so far few or no European nations have been studied in this way.

"Habit formation in a special social environment; the rewards and punishments bestowed by society; the praise allotted to certain kinds of achievement; the connotations given to exercise of authority, and to submission to it, in day-by-day living; the degree to which responsibility for his own conduct was entrusted to the

[1] *The Illusion of National Character.*
[2] "National Character," *British Journal of Psychology*, XXXII, pp. 183-204, 1942.
[3] *The Fear of Freedom*, Kegan Paul.
[4] *The Individual and Society, and Psychological Frontiers of Society*, Columbia University Press, 1945.
[5] "Character Structure," *Psychiatry*, VII, No. 2, 1944.

individual—all such questions had been regarded as essential in cultural investigations of behaviour in primitive societies, and had hardly been raised in studies of European nations. In classic studies of civilized countries, the approach is, ordinarily, either historical or economic, or political."

Such segmental approaches are valuable and necessary, yet they need much supplementation. Let us look at the questions which an ethnologist might ask about a simple community, and suggest examples bearing upon war and peace in our own English culture-pattern.

1. *Habit formation.* Consider the public school and the elementary schools. How far do they respectively induce in later life, anxiety to find and then to follow a leader, a readiness to lead or a love of independence? Are early habits of obedience implanted in the home— if so, is this done by parents or nurses? Or in schools for the young; if so, in nursery schools or 'prep.' schools? Are some habits of obedience to verbal commands or precepts grafted on to earlier conditionings, connected with feeding, weaning and elimination, and therefore possibly supported by intense unconscious feelings of guilt? Professor Kimball Young's *Handbook of Social Psychology*[1] gives a set of tables comparing the early education of various nations, e.g. the Americans, Marquesans, Balinese, the Nazis, Japanese, etc.

2. *Social rewards and punishments.* What is the social and financial value attached to rewards for prowess in war and in peace respectively? Note, for example, in our country the surprise with which some older M.P.s greeted Parliament's recent decision not to reward the leaders in the Second World War with money, and the differences of opinion, possibly following an 'age-line', concerning the cessation of the nation's pension to the Nelson family. Compare this with the present difficulty in finding incentives for certain kinds of necessary or dangerous work like house-building, coal mining and nursing.

3. *Degrees of individual responsibility for one's conduct.* In peacetime it might be said that the individual is held completely responsible; in war, as Professor J. C. Flugel says,[2] he may delegate his conscience, unless he is a conscientious objector. The position was not always clear here, but it was far simpler than in Nazi Germany. Whether the majority in a country thinks war to be 'natural' or not depends largely upon such facts, as dictators know well.

One may ask whether civilized nations are not too complicated to study by methods which may be sufficient for small communities.

[1]Kegan Paul, 1946.
[2]Chapter XIX of *Man, Morals and Society*, Duckworth, 1945.

Dr. Ruth Benedict answers that partly offsetting this defect are certain great advantages; the multiplicity of the facts known and recorded about Western nations; the historical research, the statistics, the many available records of personal experience, the novels and the fact that civilized languages are recorded and ordered in grammatical categories.

4. *Social stratification and attitudes towards property and authority.* There has been little attempt in England to investigate class differentiation and attitudes towards property and authority in the detached way in which they would be approached by an anthropologist studying a primitive tribe.

The relation of warfare to property is strikingly illustrated in this country: note, for example, the willingness to conscript life but not property, shown in the last ten years. The attitude to property depends only in part upon whether one is rich or poor. Dr. Benedict says:[1]

"Property may be, as in Holland, something which is an almost inseparable part of one's own self-esteem, something to be added to, kept immaculately, and never spent carelessly. This is true, whether the individual belongs to court circles or can only say in the words of a proverbial expression: 'If it's only a penny a year, lay it by'. Alternatively, the attitude toward property may be quite different, as in Roumania. An upper-class person may be, or become, a pensioner of a wealthy man, without loss of status or self-confidence; his property, he says, is not 'himself'. And the poor peasant argues that, being poor, it is futile for him to lay anything by: 'he would,' he says, 'if he were rich'. The well-to-do increase their possessions by other means than thrift, and the traditional attitude toward property differences associate wealth with luck or exploitation, rather than with assured position as in Holland. In each of these countries, as in other European nations, many of which have deeply embedded special attitudes toward property, the specific nature of these assumptions can be greatly clarified by study of what is required of the child in his handling and ownership of property, and under what sanctions and conditions expanding opportunities are allowed in adolescence, and at his induction into full adult status."

I leave to experts the task of framing answers to Dr. Benedict. As a social psychologist, I anticipate that to be valuable, these replies should be thought out with particular reference to the sub-culture

[1] *Loc. cit.*

pattern of the writer. For example, the relation of warfare to social stratification is complex but its importance is undoubted. And many historians themselves are part of a fairly homogeneous social stratum. The theory of Elliot Smith and Perry,[1] relating the early cause of war to social stratification has not been properly discussed. (*See* also J. Cohen.[2])

Let us turn to the definition of warfare already given by Emery Reves in his book *The Anatomy of Peace*. Presumably it will be criticized on the ground that Reves, like so many of his predecessors, attributes war to one cause only. Yet probably few will disagree with his tenet that today the main stumbling-block to world peace is national sovereignty.

Can insistence upon national sovereignty, and the actions which accompany it, be regarded as derived from a culture-pattern which dominates and integrates almost all other designs for living? It is clear that belief in national sovereignty does not arise out of original 'Human Nature', but is a very recent development.

Without mentioning the culture-pattern theory, so far as I can ascertain, Reves gives some excellent examples. He mentions that educated people have abandoned the idea that their planet is the centre and the most important part of the universe, and that the Copernican theory is generally accepted by them. Yet

"nothing can distort the true picture of conditions and events in this world more than to regard one's own country as the centre of the universe, and to view all things solely in their relationship to this fixed point. It is inevitable that such a method of observation should create an entirely false perspective. Yet this is the only method admitted and used by the seventy or eighty national governments of our world, by our legislators and diplomats, by our Press and radio. All the conclusions, principles and policies of the peoples are necessarily drawn from the warped picture of the world obtained by so primitive a method of observation.

"Within such a contorted system of assumed fixed points, it is easy to demonstrate that the view taken from each point corresponds to reality. If we admit and apply this method, the viewpoint of every single nation appears indisputably correct and wholly justified. But we arrive at a hopelessly confused and grotesque over-all picture of the world."

[1] W. J. Perry, *The Growth of Civilization*, Methuen, 1926; G. Elliot Smith, *Human History*, Cape, 1934.
[2] *Human Nature, War and Society*, Watts, 1946.

C

Our Government and all the other national governments construct round our own centre a mental pattern which we regard as the only 'real' ones. So Reves quotes, in ways which in turn would be supremely irritating to an Englishman, a Frenchman, a German, etc., different national accounts of international events between the two world wars, looked at from some of the major national vantage-points.

The Englishman may read about America's point of view, which perhaps he has never seen stated as a whole, with some sympathy, some scepticism and, as he reads further, with not a little irritation. The same twenty years looked at from the fixed point of the British Isles is described in a way which will seem only natural and right to a British reader, but reassuring in a queer way which might suggest a few problems to a questing mind. The account from the point of view of France may stun him. The Italian apologia will annoy and the German infuriate him. From 'the vantage-point of Moscow' comes a summary of 'events' which may split his mind. The Swiss, the Swedish, the Japanese accounts are not given. Whom should you chose to write the Spanish one?

"The dramatic and strange events between the two world wars could be just as well described from the point of view of any other nation, large or small. From Tokyo or Warsaw, from Riga or Rome, from Prague or Budapest, each picture will be entirely different and, from the fixed national point of observation, it will always be indisputably and unchallengeably correct. And the citizens of every country will be at all times convinced—and rightly so—of the infallibility of their views and the objectivity of their conclusions.

It is surely obvious that agreement, or common understanding between different nations, basing their relations on such a primitive method of judgment, is an absolute impossibility. A picture of the world pieced together like a mosaic from its various national components is a picture that never and under no circumstances can have any relation to reality, unless we deny that such a thing as reality exists.

The world and history cannot be as they appear to the different nations, unless we disavow objectivity, reason and scientific methods of research.

But if we believe that man is, to a certain degree, different from the animal and that he is endowed with a capacity for phenomenological thinking, then the time has come to realize that our inherited method of observation in political and social matters is childishly primitive, hopelessly inadequate and thoroughly wrong.

If we want to try to create at least the beginning of orderly relations between nations, we must try to arrive at a more scientific, more objective method of observation, without which we shall never be able to see social and political problems as they really are, nor to perceive their incidence. And without a correct diagnosis of the disease, there is no hope for a cure."

So Reves argues, there are different patterns in the minds of observers in different countries. To make or to alter such patterns is the aim of the modern propagandist, who is immensely powerful in these days of the Press, films and radio. But the concept of national sovereignty dominates all these patterns, and seriously menaces the continuance of civilization. Perhaps President Truman, Mr. Churchill and Mr. Molotov would not agree. Yet how can there be world peace if there are eighty different national sovereignties?

Only a few years ago it was common to hear, "What has world peace to do with psychologists?" Now the question seems oftener to be, "How can psychologists help to make world peace a reality?" Probably no serious psychologists doubt that great psychological issues are involved, whatever can be done about them, now or later.

It might be useful for those of us who are connected with universities to ascertain if recently there has been a closer link between scientists' activities and considerations of national 'welfare'.

After any victorious war many people feel a strong upsurge of national sentiment, for a variety of reasons. It is, however, obvious that this is likely to happen in the defeated countries too. But while between the wars we used often to hear, "Science is international", in 1947 we hear with increasing frequency that in the 'national interest' (not 'in the interests of national security', the phrase during the war) this or that ought to be done. And whether the action in any particular instance is morally desirable or not, the fact of the increase in the nationalization of science is a matter of special psychological interest, in that it has now spread to psychology itself. We frequently read of psychological reforms urged to increase our national prosperity.

A considerable part in forming this nationalistic-intellectual culture-pattern is played by scientists of different kinds. The activities of scientists will be considered instead of 'Science', a misleading word, which can even be used deliberately to mislead unphilosophical thinkers. But, for reasons not difficult to discover, though seldom sought, it is impossible to trace and record all the behaviour of present-day scientists in a scientifically satisfactory way. Not only is there deliberate concealment, or a ban by 'M.I.5' upon knowing what is done: there is also the difficulty that some of the scientists' researches—atomic energy perhaps being the most overt—are being developed simultaneously for both peaceful and warlike purposes. It is no secret that an important task of the American scientists in the last year of the war, as well as today, was to 'handle' psychologically and administratively, their military colleagues. This and many other signs show that scientists are deeply involved in the military machine. Many physical scientists may now be working in an organization for whose members the immediate prospects of national strife seem much more probable than those of even long-distant international peace.

Is this position of being 'caught up', however, peculiar to the physical scientists? Is not some important bacteriological research governed entirely by considerations of unrestricted germ-warfare? Moreover a few psychological writings seem coloured by similar assumptions. I am merely recording this fact in the positive, i.e. non-normative, manner that psychologists desire.

The title of an oft-quoted book is *The Fight for Our National Intelligence* (Professor Pollard might wish to add this to his list of uses of the word 'fight'). In a recent article its author remarks: "The greatest amount of work on intelligence tests has been done with school children, *but fortunately the needs of the Services during the war* (italics mine) have greatly stimulated the development of intelligence tests appropriate for adults". The article quotes a psychologist as saying (in March 1939) in an address to educationalists, "This part of the nation's capital (i.e. highly intelligent children) must not be wasted by failing to provide education for those able to profit by it. In the fierce competition of today between national groups, no nation can hope to survive if it persistently ignores these considerations". One nation, which perhaps before 1939 ignored them less than we did, was Germany. Still, she ignored others much more important, and paid for it.

The possibility that a branch of psychology may be developed and used by the British as a means of fighting for their national intelligence, or upholding it against all comers, is fairly new. Yet why try to increase the use of our national intelligence unless one of its most important functions will be to preserve a state of affairs in which intelligent people of all nations can co-operate to prevent the destruction of civilized man? Half a dozen atom bombs dropped upon the English cities would render the intelligence of most inhabitants useless.

The statement sometimes made, both here and in the U.S.A.,

that the Second World War put psychology and ethnology on the map might suggest that some who helped in this operation are illustrating the functional autonomy of untransformed motives. A demonstration of this possibility appears in Chapter XIV of Professor Kimball Young's *Handbook of Social Psychology* (1946). Though entitled "The Psychology of War and of Military Moral," the chapter opens at the point where war is supposed to have been declared: "We shall begin with the selection and training of military personnel". Professor Young then proceeds to describe in detail what psychologists, under direction from the Government, do. Yet this may cast little more light upon the really important and difficult question, why wars occur nowadays, than would accounts of the activities in wartime, of manufacturers of uniforms or of patriotic songs—for these practitioners, too, are put on the map by wars. There is really little about the causes of war in Professor Young's book.

With a closely reasoned argument Dr. R. H. Thouless, in his *General and Social Psychology*,[1] attributes warfare, at least, perhaps, as we knew it up to about say, 1930, to our aggressive-acquisitive culture-pattern, coming into conflict with rather similar ones. Were this a discussion at a popular level, I might be strongly tempted to assent, probably with approval from very many professional colleagues. A book often quoted is Durbin and Bowlby's *Personal Aggressiveness and War*, which, however, has been criticized by Dr. J. M. Blackburn in his *Psychology and the Social Pattern*.[2]

Criticism of their explanation of war in terms of human aggressiveness is chiefly along the lines that though their book contains much (usually uncritically quoted from the Freudians) about human aggressiveness, there is in it little about war, as it actually happened, even in 1914-18.

I should like, however, to begin my examination of this view of aggressiveness by going back further than is customary. The subject-matter of science is of two kinds: phenomena or 'appearances' (not to sight only) and concepts, or patterns in someone's mind, made in order to subsume the experiences into comprehensible schemes. You and I may have no doubt that light is falling upon this desk, yet the concepts introduced to explain 'light' will vary with the progress of physics, often usually becoming more complicated and difficult to grasp as the science progresses.

We begin with phenomena to which the name 'aggressive action'

[1]University Tutorial Press, London.
[2]Kegan Paul, 1945.

is given. It will conduce to clearness if we confine ourselves at present to recordable acts and postpone the consideration of alleged or imputed experiences. Let us then speak of acts of aggression rather than of 'aggressiveness'.

What does aggression mean? A dictionary, citing as sources of its derivation *ad* and *gressus*, suggests that it means 'taking a step towards'. With what purpose, it may be asked? One human being (and it is human aggressiveness we are considering) might take the first step towards another with intent either to help or to injure. Perhaps any behaviour, whether consciously or unconciously motivated, which alters or interferes with another person's complete freedom of action, thought or feeling, is aggressive in this 'pure' sense. Yet, does a parent who succours a child commit an act of aggression?

To write like this is not to indulge in quibbles or mere word-spinning; a phrase occasionally used by people who dislike having their verbal habits upset. Apparently, for some psychologists, if A does anything which modifies what B was doing or intending to do, since A 'takes a step towards', his action is aggressive. He may touch your arm to deter you from walking into the traffic, or save you from a fit of depression by offering a loan—is this aggressive? A phrase sometimes used in psychological writings is 'aggressive love-making'. Apart from the possible and frequent confusion, common in these writings, of love with sexual desire, the consideration may be omitted that any expression of love for another involves taking a step towards him or her, literally or metaphorically.

If, however, we allow that aggression nowadays means 'step-taking with intent to hurt', we now come up against the problem "Is aggressiveness a human instinct?" I have discussed this at length in a previous Rylands lecture,[1] and will not repeat the argument here. But since the word 'instinct' may have been ambiguous from the start, and many years have been necessary to tease out all the possible meanings of Freud's term 'sexuality'—if indeed the task is yet complete—so perhaps 'aggressiveness' will be analysed into simpler concepts. It is not irrelevant to mention that if its use by English-speaking psychologists owes anything to the fact that it arrived in our text-books *via* German and Latin, the circumstance that both these languages belonged to culture-patterns in which militarism or intent-to-hurt were dominant, might be taken into account. It would be interesting to know the number and range of synonyms for aggressiveness in the languages of gentler peoples who yet take steps towards others.

[1]"Are There Human Instincts?" *Bulletin of the John Rylands Library*, XXVII, 1942.

Clearly too, Gordon W. Allport's theory[1] that motives may be transformed, especially through fusion with others, and that these transformed motives may become functionally autonomous, may alter the whole picture. The best type of school prefect who seeks for and enjoys taking responsibility is aggressive in a loose sense, but his aggressiveness can be very complex and subtle.

It is difficult to decide whether to spend much time upon the next hypothesis, but since it seems to be accepted by many psychologists (certainly not by all) it should be mentioned. It is that we possess a reservoir of unconscious hatred and destructive impulses, constantly replenished. What, we may ask, is the evidence, except that some leading thinker said so? This is not the place to argue in detail the view that Freud's use of pictorial analogies, obviously useful and perhaps necessary in developing an entirely new concept, has retarded progress in psychological thinking. As a constant visualizer, I must confess that I find the greatest difficulty in imagining both the reservoir and its contents. I constantly ask myself, "Does this assumption make sense, psychologically, physiologically, neurologically or metaphysically?" Many psychologists including some, like Professor Flugel, deeply influenced by psycho-analysis, are far from dogmatic about this. They, with Professors W. McDougall[2] and J. Drever,[3] point with much more justification to the fact that whether a human tendency towards aggression, pugnacity or self-assertion (for they use different terms) is innate or not, it will have plenty of chances to arise during life as a result of the thwarting of other impulses, either by the physical environment or by other people. Professor Dollard and others[4] have studied extensively the conditions of such thwarting and the different types of behaviour which result from it. This naturally leads to psycho-analytic explanations, e.g. often the aggressive impulse is repressed into the unconscious or the repressed person is ambivalent, i.e. feels emotions of opposite tendency towards the thwarting cause.

Perhaps a little re-examination is allowable. In particular one wishes to know if this concept of ambivalence is believed to be applicable to all love. Is there no perfect love, free from any admixture of hate? Fortunate people who believe this are unlikely to seek the professional services of psycho-analysts, or indeed of psychotherapists at all.

[1] *Personality*, Constable, and Henry Holt, New York.
[2] *Introduction to Social Psychology*, Methuen.
[3] *Instinct in Man*, Cambridge University Press.
[4] *Frustration and Aggression*, Kegan Paul, 1944.

It is fair to speculate, as Dr. J. Cohen does in his unusually penetrating analysis of this subject in reference to warfare, that inferences are possible from the fact that Freud developed his later ideas of human aggressiveness and hatred during the most depressing time in Vienna. He never rose mentally above the sub-culture-pattern in which he lived, and as Professor Harding suggests, Freud's ideas on government were not far removed from Hitler's. Writers like Christopher Caudwell, Karen Horney and Erich Fromm have made this point. It is time that social psychologists defined their attitude towards such criticism of what by some Freudians seem to be regarded as axioms, and in doing so, assessed the significance of the possibility that at least for a short time, they may expect professional advancement in a society which puts hatred and malice before friendliness, dominance before co-operation. Until recently almost all doctors made their living from disease and disability, not from health, yet the concept of social medicine is rapidly developing.

Nobody will deny that aggressiveness played a great part in waging the last war—even to write this might seem a blasphemous use of understatement—but while in wars centuries ago a very high percentage of the armies was aggressive, and the civilians kept out of the fighting, it cannot be emphasized too often that in the Second World War a high percentage of people participated unaggressively, including many in uniform. It is perhaps significant that recently an otherwise undistinguished examination script contained the not entirely muddled query, "If this war is due to instinct, why must we have a large Pay Corps?"

Recent criticism of the aggressiveness theory of war is along the following lines. It fails to distinguish between the aggressiveness of the war-makers, which can be very real indeed (though frequently personal greed, still socially disapproved if found out, masquerades as socially approved aggressiveness) and the attitudes of the general population, many of whom may not know of the impending war, of the combatant, semi-combatant, and non-combatant soldiers, and of the victims. In a war involving more than half the population of the world, a vast number of people who had nothing to do with declaring war suffered passively. Often aggressiveness had to be stirred up and intensified even in the fighters (we have recently read about the experimental army 'hate schools', abolished as a result of psychiatrists' reports), in the uniformed sections many people of both sexes lived an unaggressive life and yet helped to win the war, 'back-room boys' and scientists are unlikely to have done their best thinking if viscerally stirred; 'beating the enemy' cannot have been a constant day-and-night goal giving incentive to all non-combatants, as the excellent book *War Factory*[1] among others, showed. Primitive aggressiveness—if one can use such a term, would probably become transformed and fused with other 'drives'. As a result, the fusion may be more correctly described by another name and perhaps by that of another drive with which it has become fused. A man might have enlisted to beat the enemy, then have become fascinated by a new mechanical means of doing so, have found that he could improve it and conduct important research, rewarded by promotion, and eventually have enjoyed ordering people about. His final experience will be far removed from primitive aggressiveness.

Yet if the kind of culture-pattern in which Freud, we, and many Americans have been brought up is to be described as 'aggressive-acquisitive', and if we assume that this fact has played a great part in causing wars in the past, the main thesis of this lecture is unaffected —that war is the expression of a culture-pattern.

Positive criticism of the culture-pattern theory has taken directions like the following:

1. Is the pattern which one observer 'perceives' in a community (the verb is used vaguely) likely to be 'perceived' by others, expert and inexpert? An account of 'the Germans' by someone who is at present on the Continent primarily as a soldier in the army of occupation, and speaks little German, would obviously differ from that by an English observer who spoke German fluently and had lived there between the World Wars. Such a person is Lord Vansittart, though in his accounts of the Germans he seldom or never mentions that he had talked to, to say nothing of sympathizing with, German working-men and women. Elsewhere I have pointed out the tendency, at one time, for writers and speakers to be content with comparing the alleged mentality of nations with the alleged mentality of animals— dogs (preferably mad), bees, wolves, vampires. Later, perhaps, came the custom of applying one adjective to a whole nation—at the moment the fashionable one, both in politics and in psychology, appears to be 'aggressive'.

Is it completely fatuous to apply an adjective to the observed behaviour of a social group? Perhaps not, if the group is small enough to be really observable, if all reporters attach the same meaning to the word and if translated from one language to another, this fact is stated, together with some indication whether the word 'dates' in

[1] By Mass Observation, Gollancz.

the first language. Lastly, it would be good if users of the borrowed term really understood both languages.

Here the distinction between 'pattern' and 'configuration' is useful. The number of instances in which the pattern was observed, and their statistical significance, should be stated.

People who have lived all their lives in England, with its very striking varieties of behaviour characterizing different geographical areas, its distinctions between urban-residential, urban-industrial and rural life, and its complicated and ever-present social stratification, occasionally raise a quizzical eyebrow when our national character is confidently described by the stranger within our gates. But the English ought to admit that their own views of other nations are open to the same criticism.

Perhaps the comment has not been made often enough, that several different patterns may be perceived in the same culture, by people especially prone through temperament, training or education to notice them, and again the 'pattern-configuration distinction' should be remembered here. Very complex patterns appear to be perceptible at present in the French nation (cf. Phyllis Bottome's *Individual Countries*[1] and *Faith in France*,[2] with preface by Professor D. W. Brogan). I offer a concrete example. English people who have merely spent holidays in France sometimes ask, "How can a nation claim to lead the world's culture when one goes about its country in imminent risk of contracting typhoid fever?" The answer that culture must not be confused with plumbing comes readily to the intellectual's tongue, yet I remember the look of baffled amusement with which it was received by members of an American Air Force unit stationed in England.

It might be possible to employ another method of investigation, to inquire into the factors 'beneath' the culture-pattern which so to speak, push up one piece of the fabric as in a relief, or (to mix metaphors) may stain parts of it so that the pattern is more easily visible. Perhaps, too, antagonistic sets of forces may be discovered tending to make different patterns—themselves antagonistic.

Little has been written about how it feels to be part of a well-marked culture-pattern; though presumably a good deal of the work carried out under the titles of 'mass-observation', and 'participant observation' might be re-examined with this in view. Certain autobiographies might also be studied. Dr. Marie Jahoda once suggested

[1]Allen and Unwin, 1947.
[2]*Faith in France*, Sherratt and Sons, Manchester, 1947.

to me that social psychologists in training might undertake a 'social analysis' of themselves and their colleagues. This would be different from Freudian psycho-analysis, which seems sometimes to create a special culture-pattern grafted on to Freud's.

Let us consider a way in which this might be attempted. After preliminary talks and discussions, and reading of books by writers like Margaret Mead's *Growing Up in New Guinea*[1] and *Coming of Age in Samoa*,[2] articles by Marie Jahoda[3] and Florence Kluckhohn[4] and selected publications of 'Mass-Observation', the investigator-in-training might be asked to write an account of his or her own growing up in Great Britain, with special reference to social stratum, religious and political affiliations and the attitudes inculcated towards parents, siblings and the opposite sex. Certain parts might be marked 'Confidential', to be read only by selected persons. As a result of comparing the accounts in class discussion, a picture of the general culture-pattern and of its sub-patterns might be drawn. Help could be obtained from schemes of investigation used by Kardiner, Beaglehole and from studies made by Dr. J. A. Waites.[5]

Of particular interest might be a detailed account of the 'subject's' attitude to parents, to authority in general, to religion (both as experience and as a formal frame for behaviour) and to social strata 'above' and 'below' him, with special reference to the degree to which he 'knows his place' and accepts it, considers himself movable or immovable in the social scale of his own country, or estimates that he would be socially happier in another.

It might be possible to study by questionnaires and interviews the nature and the relative strength of sentiments connected with parents, religion, social stratum and country, to see how their relative strength compares in different people of apparently the same culture-pattern. Protestants, Catholics and Jews living in the same town and of similar economic status might be compared. The mutual relationships of sentiments might be studied. To what extent are certain

[1]Penguin Books.   [2]Penguin Books.

[3]"Some Ideas on Social and Psychological Research," *Sociological Review*, XXX, 1, pp. 63–80, 1938. "Incentives to Work," *Occupational Psychology*, Vol. XVI, No. 1, pp. 20–30, January, 1942.

[4]"The Participant Observer Technique in Small Communities," *American Journal of Sociology*, XLVI, No. 3, November, 1940.

[5]"An Inquiry into the Attitudes of Adults towards Property in a Lancashire Urban Area," *British Journal of Psychology*, XXXVI, pp. 33–42, 1945. Also "Attitudes towards Property", and "Property: A Study in Social Psychology," theses deposited in Manchester University.

types of sentiment bound up with each other, and has the degree of intimate interlocking varied as years went on? In parts of England there is a strong tendency for land-owners to be Church of England and Conservative, and in the Fens at least, agricultural workers tend to be nonconformist and non-Conservative. Attitude measurement and factor analysis may throw light upon this (a possibility suggested in an unpublished paper read by Dr. H. J. Eysenck to the British Psychological Society on 11th April, 1947).

Since sentiments are more easily developed around persons and things than around ideas, it might be possible to examine whether there is a significant correlation between lack of 'intellectual' education, and the tendency to think of abstract political and moral issues primarily in terms of persons (leader, Führer). Does the person of the Archbishop of Canterbury, for example, exert such an influence on the Church of England as that of the Pope on the Church of Rome? Can workers for peace hope to weave a sentiment around any living leader comparable to that which existed for 'Monty' in the war? If not, what can be done?

The investigator's complexes, both in the psycho-analytic sense and in the sense of 'untidy' or unformed sentiments should also be studied. 'Uprooted' or 'displaced' persons are unlikely to be free from complexes about both their native country and the land or lands in which they are guests.

But if, as seems possible, a sentiment in its early formative stages may resemble a complex, in its 'untidiness' and lack of understandable inner structure, that this too may be true of the late stages of its decay and that repression may also occur in the formation of a sentiment, these possibilities seem important in the study of one's own culture-pattern.

In this connection, the recent rapid development of methods and channels of communication (Press, radio, film)[1] is very important. By presenting ideas visually to millions who cannot read or write (cf. the early film instruction methods of the USSR) or even to those who can, but 'only just' (cf. many films shown in Great Britain and America) a powerful impression can be made, and quickly. So a new culture-pattern can be built up, perhaps deliberately 'contrived' out of an old one. And the films and radio have made the phrase the 'inevitability of gradualness' almost obsolete.

Many questions remain. Do the various uses of the term 'culture-pattern' mean the same thing? I doubt it; further agreement about

[1]Footnote of *Made for Millions* (ed. F. Laws) 1947, London. Contact Press.

terminology is urgently desirable. Is a culture-pattern judged by reference to the common people, to their leaders, especially those who speak and write with authority, to their heroes or to their ideal personalities? Presumably different judges may employ any or all of these criteria, and this is a source of ambiguity.

But upon one thing students of culture-patterns all seem agreed: modern warfare is not due to simple instincts, nor is it inevitable.

CHAPTER III

WAR AND AGGRESSIVENESS:
A SURVEY OF SOCIAL ATTITUDE STUDIES

by H. J. Eysenck

1. *Introduction.* A complex phenomenon like war has obviously so many facets—sociological, anthropological, ethical, psychological—that there are great difficulties in assessing the relative importance of any particular point of view. Yet it may perhaps be claimed with some degree of justice that ultimately all causative influences must find themselves reflected in the individual attitudes towards war and personal aggressiveness which are built up by social pressure, by teaching and propaganda, by personal precept, by childhood experience, by parental emotional conditioning, and the thousand and one agencies which determine our outlook. Consequently the experimental study of the origin, growth, and structure of these attitudes represents an important contribution of social psychology to the investigation of the complex phenomena of war and peace.

Certain limitations are implied in the method of experimentation used in these studies, and must be fully realized before the conclusions can be adequately judged. In the first place, social attitude measurement deals with *conscious* ideas, opinions, emotions, and sentiments; it does not claim to uncover the secret processes of the 'unconscious mind', or to reveal the remarkable activities of the 'id'. As will be shown later on, the social psychologist may subject psychoanalytic doctrines in this field to the experimental test whenever they are definite enough to allow of actual prediction; prediction, to be scientifically and socially useful, must be of actions and of conscious attitudes, and so is capable of being tested. To the psychoanalyst, for whom conscious motives play a very minor role, this restriction may appear so serious as to make any possible contribution of little consequence.

But the general consensus of opinion in modern psychology deprecates this exclusive insistence on unconscious motivation, and maintains firmly a balanced attitude which refuses either to deny the reality of certain Freudian mechanisms, or to extend their province so far as to engulf the whole of normal psychology. While the occurrence of sadistic feelings and other abnormal emotional manifestations during war is acknowledged to occur in a number of neurotic and psychotic persons, modern psychology refuses to erect an imposing

49

theoretical edifice regarding the nature and derivation of 'aggression' on the extremely subjective interpretations given by a number of psycho-analysts of the dreams, free associations and other productions of their patients, who cannot by any stretch of the imagination be called a representative sample of the normal adult population.

A second characteristic of the material with which we are dealing in this chapter is that the attitudes measured are *verbally communicated*. There is much room for falsification of a conscious kind here, as well as for misunderstandings, wrong emphases, and carelessness. Yet in actual practice we find that when the ordinary precautions of scientific attitude-testing are followed, there is very considerable agreement between the attitude a person records in his questionnaire, and that which he is known to hold (25). This general finding applies in the main to matters in which neither blame nor praise attaches to the direction of his choice; when social evaluation enters strongly, falsification of responses has been shown to take place. But the conscientious experimenter is fully alive to this possibility, and attempts to avoid the difficulty by anonymous returns, suitable indirect wording of the questions, and various other methods.

A third characteristic of these studies is that they deal with relatively large-scale investigations, carried out inevitably in a somewhat superficial manner. The main reason for this state of affairs is that social psychology at present is at a stage where it is looking for worth-while hypotheses to investigate; large-scale attitude studies are conceived of as providing clues which may then be followed up by more detailed and profound investigations.

2. *Aggressiveness*. Discussions of the contributions which psychology can make to the understanding of war almost invariably centre around the problem of aggressiveness. Writers of the psycho-analytic school, like Hopkins (39), Glover (36), and Durbin and Bowlby (19), take the view that the ultimate origin of the aggression which finds expression in war and other types of social conflict is to be found in childhood experiences of the individual; much play is made with such concepts as the 'unresolved Oedipus conflict'. Followers of the frustration-aggression hypothesis, like Dollard, Miller and Hovland (14), take a somewhat wider view and believe that frustration in any field serves as a source of aggressiveness, a view adumbrated by McDougall and Drever. They also, however, recognize that conflict in the family may have a powerful part to play in the creation of frustration and aggression.

Isolated attempts have been made by Lasswell (50), and by

Krout and Stagner (48), to discover if emotional experiences of childhood influence adult attitudes towards a variety of issues. Thus it
was shown that attitudes favourable to revolt against established
institutions were found more frequently in subjects who had repressed
aggression against the father, a parent-child relation not so frequently
found in conservatives. Similarly, radicals[1] were found to show more
frequent feelings of rejection by their parents, and more unhappiness
in childhood. Other studies also show significant correlations between
radicalism and antagonism to the father (66). Respect for law and
education were found to be more marked in subjects whose home life
had been satisfactory (79).

Another study deserves mention. As part of a general investigation
carried out for the Society for the Psychological Study of Social
Issues Committee on the Psychology of War and Peace, Stagner
(98, 99, 100) gave to various groups of students, scales measuring
attitudes towards war, force, nationalism, fascism, intolerance, capital
punishment, as well as towards father antagonism and childhood
satisfaction. The results showed that in general, antagonism to parents
correlated *negatively* with all the social-aggressive attitudes mentioned.
A more detailed breakdown of results showed that the subjects who
liked the father and did not like the mother scored highest on many
of the aggressive scales; this result is, of course, well in line with
our cultural stereotype of the stern, aggressive father and the gentle,
yielding mother. Preference for mother, dislike for father, showed an
anti-aggressive pattern, as might have been expected.

It was also found that on contrasting students satisfied and dissatisfied with their childhood, those who were satisfied tended to be
much more nationalistic/capitalistic than the other group.

Interpretation of these results is difficult because they are all
derived from a single culture-pattern; that of American capitalism.
Thus it might be inviting to speculate that radical attitudes towards
social issues are founded on parent antagonism, but it must be remembered that the correlations apparently supporting such a belief were
obtained in a society in which radical beliefs are ostracized, where
even mildly liberal attitudes are considered 'subversive', and where
organizations such as the Dies Committee flourish. Where the great
majority of parents of all classes, and particularly of college students,
share a capitalistic outlook, the rising generation's disagreement with

[1]The term 'radical' in psychological literature denotes the person occupying the
opposite pole of an attitude continuum to the 'conservative'; it is roughly synonymous
with 'progressive', signifying 'advanced' opinions.

their parents on emotional grounds may easily make them critical of social and political beliefs held by the parents, thus inevitably leading them to the only alternative social and political outlook. (Republican and Democratic partisanship, of course, does not provide such alternatives, being merely a game of Box and Cox with political patronage as its basis.) The crucial test would be a repetition of the experiment in a socialist country; would children of socialist parents, who are antagonistic to these parents, develop a conservative outlook? If so, the alleged affinity between childhood antagonism and radical attitudes would be shown to be merely an instance of a more embracing generalization of the linking up of emotional antagonisms with cognitive disagreements, a generalization which in other circumstances would lead to a correlation between childhood antagonisms to parents and conservative political attitudes.

We have spoken hitherto as if 'aggressiveness' constituted a general factor, i.e. as if there were a marked tendency for a person who was aggressive in one set of circumstances to be aggressive in others also. This belief is by no means universal. Beginning with William James, psychologists in search of a 'moral equivalent for war' have thought that aggressive impulses might be sublimated through sport, physical exercise, the conquest of disease, etc. Writers of the psycho-analytic school in particular have made much of this concept of sublimation, and have often added the view that persons who express aggressiveness freely in personal relationships have less hostility which can be 'displaced' on to 'out-groups'. This belief, indeed, lies at the basis of some modern therapeutic tendencies of the 'group therapy' kind.

Evidence regarding this important point is furnished by Stagner (98), who showed that students who evinced aggressive attitudes in one direction also tended to show them in other directions, the average intercorrelation being as high as $+0\cdot4$ for various groups. This work is particularly convincing because extensive questionnaire studies were supplemented by personal interviews and other special observations, such as thematic apperception tests, free association, reaction time and galvanic measures. Stagner also inquired into certain alleged 'sublimating' activities, such as playing football, expressing annoyances openly, and so forth. If the 'sublimation' theory were correct, we should expect that students who had 'sublimated' their aggressive impulses would be less aggressive on the various scales (capital punishment, war, fascism, etc.) than those who had failed to 'sublimate'. In actual fact, exactly the opposite was observed; all instances and expressions of aggressiveness showed positive correlations. While we must recognize that only verbal behaviour is involved in these tests, the onus of proof would seem to lie definitely on the proponents of the 'sublimation' theory; the results quoted are plainly incompatible with that theory. The same might be said of correlations reported by Eysenck (24, 25) and by Ferguson (31) in a series of articles, in which a consistent tendency was found for persons aggressive in one context to be aggressive in another context.

We may conclude this brief review by saying that it has been established that aggressive attitudes tend to be general, extending over large areas of belief and conduct; that no evidence has been found in favour, and much evidence against, the 'sublimation' type of theory; and that work on the genesis of aggressive attitudes is inconclusive in virtue of being restricted to a single culture-pattern.

3. *Primary Social Attitudes.* In a recent Gallup Poll in this country, the question was asked: "Do you think that another world war is likely during the next twenty-five years?" Forty-eight per cent of the respondents thought it likely, 31 per cent unlikely, with 21 per cent undecided. Great differences were found between the well-to-do, 61 per cent of whom thought war likely, and the poorer classes, only 39 per cent of whom thought so. Conservatives and Liberals were more convinced of the likelihood of war than were Labour voters.

These results show that attitudes towards certain aspects of the problem of war are related to social class, or to political affiliation. The question inevitably arises: Are there certain persistent, all-embracing groupings of attitudes, to which isolated opinion statements such as the above can be related? What light has social psychology to throw on the organization of social attitudes, with particular reference to the place of attitudes towards war and peace in this scheme? Much evidence is available in this connection through the work of Thurstone, Ferguson, Carlson, Eysenck, and others, and it is believed that an understanding of the underlying issues will throw some light on the general problem.

Attitude structure may be conceived as having four distinct levels. At the lowest level we have haphazard, isolated statements of opinion which may or may not represent accurately a person's views on a given subject. When the same statement is made repeatedly, we may say that here is evidence that it represents more than a passing fancy, without deep roots in the general matrix of the person's mind. Statements such as: "War is often the only means of preserving the national honour," or "War is a futile struggle resulting in self-destruction" were shown by Stagner (95), to have repeat reliabilities of between +0·85 and +0·96; we may take this fact as evidence that over a period of several months opinion statements of this kind remain remarkably steady.

So far we are still on the level of opinion measurement. When it can be shown that a number of statements dealing with one and the same issue—war, or anti-semitism, or religion—tend to correlate highly together, so that they can be arranged on a uni-dimensional scale for the measurement of attitude toward that particular issue, then we can claim to have isolated an *attitude*. Below is given a brief scale of this kind measuring the relative favourableness towards war of the respondents. The statements were derived from a larger number by means of the Thurstone technique; the scoring is based on the Likert method, however, as in our experience this combination of techniques gives a higher reliability than either alone (Eysenck and Crown, 27).

The score on the scale is simply the sum of the numbers printed against each answer underlined by the subject; these numbers were derived by multiplying an item's scale position by the numerical value of the chosen answer, dividing by a constant, and rounding off.

Questionnaire Used in Measuring Attitude Towards War

Underline the answer which in each case agrees most with your own opinion on the issue in question; underline the '?' only when you find it impossible either to agree or disagree with the proposition. Disregard the numbers written against the answers.

1. Certain issues are so vital for a nation that war is preferable to submission.

Strongly agree.	Agree.	?	Disagree.	Strongly disagree.
−2	−1	0	+1	+2

2. In war, even the winner loses more than he can hope to gain.

Strongly agree.	Agree.	?	Disagree.	Strongly disagree.
+4	+2	0	−2	−4

3. War is an important factor in progress, eliminating the unfit.

Strongly agree.	Agree.	?	Disagree.	Strongly disagree.
−6	−3	0	+3	+6

4. Under no circumstances can war ever be justified.

Strongly agree.	Agree.	?	Disagree.	Strongly disagree.
+8	+4	0	−4	−8

5. War brings out virtues in people which in peace lie undetected.

Strongly agree.	Agree.	?	Disagree.	Strongly disagree.
−4	−2	o	+2	+4

6. There is no such thing as a 'righteous war'.

Strongly agree.	Agree.	?	Disagree.	Strongly disagree.
+2	+1	o	−1	−2

7. War is a glorious adventure.

Strongly agree.	Agree.	?	Disagree.	Strongly disagree.
−8	−4	o	+4	+8

8. War never settles the problems at issue between the nations involved.

Strongly agree.	Agree.	?	Disagree.	Strongly disagree.
+6	+3	o	−3	−6

Detailed results regarding the reliability and validity of this questionnaire are given in a paper by Eysenck and Crown (28); here we may just note certain points. A factorial study of the intercorrelations between the eight items disclosed the existence of a strong factor of militarism or war-mindedness, which accounted for 38 per cent of the variance. Question 1 had the highest saturation with this factor (·94), followed by Question 4 (·80). The index of reliability for the scale was found to be ·83. Further points from this study will be noted later, particularly the correlation between militarism and conservatism, and the correlation between militarism and neuroticism; here our main insistence is on the demonstration that different statements dealing with attitudes towards war display a certain amount of functional unity.

When the existence of a definite attitude has been demonstrated, the question arises whether concepts of a higher order may not exist which are based on the intercorrelation of several attitudes. For instance, may not militarism, anti-semitism, nationalism, religionism, and pro-capitalism intercorrelate and define an attitude of 'conservatism'? This type of higher-order concept constitutes the fourth and highest level in the hierarchy of attitude structure, and may justly be called a 'primary social attitude'.

Large-scale correlational studies, involving widely differing groups of students, middle-class adults, Liberals, Conservatives, Socialists, Englishmen, Americans, men and women, old and young, Eugenicists, Fabians, and various others, have given us a picture of these Primary Social Attitudes which is presented diagrammatically in Fig. 1. It will be seen that two orthogonal (uncorrelated) factors are involved, and that a large number of different social issues are shown in their relation to these two primary social attitude factors. The nature of the factors can easily be determined by inspection of the issues which define them. The first factor is clearly a radicalism-conservatism one, as has been proved independently by showing that the items which

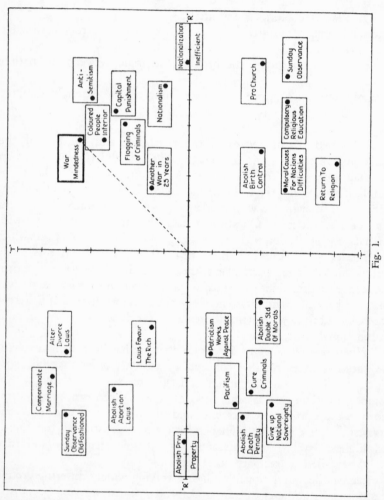

Fig. 1.

define this factor also show large differences in endorsement between Conservative and Socialist groups equated for age, sex, and education (24, 25).

The second factor is perhaps less easy to label; it has been variously called 'practical-theoretical' and 'tough-minded v. tender-minded'. That it is more than a statistical artefact, and has a very real existence, has been shown elsewhere (25). These two, the 'R' and 'T' factors, as they have been called, will be seen to influence and determine the attitude to about an equal extent; when correction is made for the unreliability of the scale used for measuring this attitude we find that over 50 per cent of its variance is accounted for in terms of R and T, leaving some 40 per cent to be accounted for in terms of more specific factors.

We can now see that the items in the conservative-tough-minded quadrant are essentially similar to the items which were used by Stagner to define his 'aggressiveness' factor; our analysis shows that this is not a simple factor but a composite one which may be reduced to a combination of the two primary social attitudes. This is an important discovery, because we know a great deal about the distribution and the correlates of these two factors, while our information about 'aggressiveness' is very meagre; thus we can bring a much wider range of knowledge and information to bear on our topic. It is also important because the correlation between 'war-mindedness' and 'conservatism' is apparently not conditioned by the specific American or British culture-pattern, but comes out quite clearly in samples of various kinds drawn from both nations. Again, it would be most desirable to repeat investigations of this kind in culture-patterns even more unlike each other than American capitalism and British social-democracy; it may be predicted that much might be learned regarding the nature and structure of attitudes from comparative studies in Germany, Italy, Poland, Russia, India, Mexico, etc.[1]

4. *Correlates of War-Mindedness.* We may study the correlates of war-mindedness either directly, or by reference to the two primary social attitudes which give rise, in combination, to this quality. In one study of the 'direct' type (95), a questionnaire somewhat similar to the one printed in the previous section was used with various adult and college groups in the southern states of America, during the academic year 1937-8. Age was not found to be of great importance, but women tended to give less militaristic replies; this difference, however, was much smaller than might have been expected. Republicans were significantly more militaristic than Democrats, but again the difference was slight. Jews were considerably less militaristic than Protestants or Catholics; there was no significant difference between

[1]Such studies are in progress at the moment.

these two religious groups. Men having had fighting experience, and/or some military training, or who were members of a veterans' society, scored significantly more militaristic than people without any military training, and members of a labour union.

As regards occupational differences, professional and labour groups were less militaristic than the average, while clericals and business men were more militaristic. Children of business men and of labourers have shown a similar difference, according to a report by Porterfield (73). These results all fit into the radical-pacifist v. conservative-militaristic pattern discussed in previous sections.

Militaristic and pacifist groups, as measured by the questionnaire, also differed profoundly with respect to beliefs about methods of keeping out of war. Organizations approving of 'complete military preparedness' often claim that this policy is intended to keep the peace; yet persons holding this view were found much more militaristic than the other groups. On the other hand, those who believed in 'united action of workers, farmers, and consumers', in 'taking profits out of war', in 'socialism', and in the 'League of Nations' tended to be less militaristic than the average. These results again appear to fit in well with our general picture. Lastly, it may be noted that personal willingness to fight (as verbally asserted, at least) is related to militaristic attitudes.

Other studies by Pintner (72), Turteltaub (109), Lundberg (56), Smith (89), Droba (15, 16, 17, 18), Pihlblad (71), Farnsworth (29), Jones (41), Stump and Lewis (105), Page (68) and many others give results similar to those quoted above. There is a general tendency for respondents to be pacifistic rather than militaristic; parents tend to be more militaristic than their children; males tend to be more militaristic than females; the influence of college education tends to be in the direction of lessened militarism, except for students at military academies. Jews, Christian Scientists, and Methodists tend to be more pacifistic than Lutherans, Catholics, and Congregationalists; Republicans are more militaristic than Democrats, while Socialists are much less militaristic than either group. Mutatis mutandis, these results would appear to be broadly true of British respondents also.

Parent-child correlations in attitude toward war tend to be roughly similar to correlations found for other social attitudes (cf. below). In one of the best controlled studies, Newcomb and Svehla found that mothers and sons, mothers and daughters, fathers and sons, fathers and daughters, and mothers and fathers all agreed in their war attitudes to about the same extent; coefficients of correlation varied from ·43 to ·46 for these different pairs (cf. 50). The same investigators also found that parent-child relationships varied more definitely and more consistently with socio-economic status than with age, correlations being higher for the lowest occupational levels, and lower for the highest occupational levels. This generalization was derived from studies of different attitudes; the figures for attitudes toward war read as follows:

Parent-child Correlation in Attitude Towards War

Age of child	High	Medium	Low
	OCCUPATIONAL LEVEL		
19 and under · ·	·24	·45	·66
20—23 · · · ·	·26	·21	·54
24 and over · · ·	·27	·40	·32

These figures are of absorbing interest; they also point up the importance of further research into the reasons why parent-child correlations are higher in the working-class than in the middle-class groups, and into the relation between attitude-formation and the dynamics of the family situation. They also suggest national comparisons—does a similar law hold true in England, for instance? And are there systematic differences in the size of parent-child correlations between different nations—are correlations higher in Germany, for instance, than they are in less autocratic countries? These are questions which urgently call for an answer if we are to understand the genesis of war-minded attitudes.

We have shown that parental influences determine to some extent the individual attitudes which children exhibit; does parental influence also condition the patterning of attitudes in children? If certain children resemble their parents with respect to one set of attitudes, will they also resemble them with respect to other attitudes? A group of 220 parents was selected whose attitude toward the church correlated very highly with that of their children; another group of 227 parents was selected who correlated very highly with their children on attitude toward communism. For these two groups, the parent-child attitude correlation of war-mindedness was ·41 and ·35, as compared to a correlation of ·44 for an unselected group of 1,090 parents and children. This suggests that the attitude correlations between parents and children are relatively specific to the issue involved, and that there is no tendency for certain children to agree or disagree in general with their parents.

Again, if parents are selected in such a way that they show high agreement between two attitudes, say towards communism and towards the Church, will the children also show unusually high agreement on these two issues? For unselected parents, this particular correlation was found to be ·48; the selected group showed a correlation of ·96. Unselected children showed a correlation of ·43; the children of the selected parents showed a correlation of ·60. As Murphy (66) points out "what might be called a cluster effect is thus passed from parents to children to the extent of the difference between coefficients ·600 and ·430". But this patterning does not seem to be particularly strong in its influence, and it does not seem to extend to other issues: the unselected group showed a correlation of ·26 between attitudes towards church and war, while the selected group of children showed a correlation of ·31.

In none of these studies is there an attempt to show correlations between an attitude such as militarism and the personality of the individual holding the attitude. A direct attempt to link up the study of social attitudes with work on the measurement of the main *Dimensions of Personality* (23) was made by Eysenck and Crown (28). Using the Crown Word List (13), an objective word association test which had been shown to measure validly and reliably a person's standing on the 'neuroticism' continuum, i.e. on the line leading from emotional stability to emotional instability, a significant relation was found between 'neuroticism' and 'militarism' (the latter being measured by means of the scale quoted earlier in this chapter). This relation between neuroticism and militarism was somewhat curvilinear; in other words, people who were strongly pro-militarist or strongly anti-militarist tended to: be significantly less well-adjusted, stable individuals than were those who tended towards less extreme opinions. A similar tendency for extreme views to be related to lack of emotional adjustment was found in a study of anti-semitic attitudes (28); here also a significantly curvilinear relation with neuroticism was found. While these findings are only preliminary, they suggest that much interesting and valuable material may be unearthed by a study of the correlations between personality traits and social attitudes.

These are direct studies of 'war-mindedness'; do indirect studies, by way of the conservative-radical dichotomy, or the tender-minded v. tough-minded factor, throw any additional light on our problem? Detailed discussions and bibliographies will be found in Murphy (66), or in Bird (6); here we can only sum up the main findings. Morgan and Remmers (64), Stagner (100), and Allport (1) show that parents and children tend to have similar attitudes (r = ·6 to ·7; mother-father correlation only ·4), but there is a regular tendency for parents to be less liberal. Liberalism and intelligence are often found to be correlated in college populations, the average coefficient of correlation being about ·3 to ·4; Carlson (8), reports a specific correlation between pacifism and intelligence of ·402 for 215 students. Liberal students are also usually found to be better educated and better informed on social questions, as shown by Jones (42), Vetter (110), Symonds (106), and Allport (1). In England, little work has been done along these lines; in one study, age and sex were shown to have little importance in deciding the relative radical-conservative attitudes of 750 middle-class adults, while college education tended to be associated with a certain amount of radicalism (25).

5. 'War-mindedness' and Stereotypes. A militaristic or aggressive attitude seldom exists in vacuo; it is likely to be related closely to some object or class of objects. In thus becoming attached to a nation, or a race, our adient or abient reactions tend to become rationalized into consistent and meaningful systems of ideas regarding the object in question; such systems are called 'stereotypes'.[1] They have their origin in feeling, emotions, and 'intuitions' rather than in fact. The individual who holds stereotyped views is often entirely unaware of the part played in their creation by preferences or aversions, rationalizing and emotional reactions. Such views are evidence of uncritical accept-ance of unanalysed circumstances; they may be true in isolated cases, they may apply to a limited number of members of the group to which they are referred, but on the whole they confuse thinking by always introducing the 'class-error',[2] and by failing to stress the importance of individual differences.

[1]In classifying stereotypes in terms of pleasant (adient) and unpleasant (abient) reactions, the writer wishes to bring the whole concept of 'stereotyped' attitudes into relation with the judgmental theory of affectivity as stated by Carr (1925) and elaborated by Peters (1935). According to this theory, Affection is a meaning; the meaning P (pleasantness) is a function of a normal reaction tendency to approach the object (ad-ire), the meaning U (unpleasantness) of a reaction tendency to avoid it (ab-ire). This way of looking at stereotypes is useful because it brings to bear on the discussion a whole mass of experimental and theoretical work done in connection with affective states generally. Summaries of this work, as well as a treatment of the judgmental theory of affectivity, will be found in McGeoch (1942), Rapaport (1942), Beebe-Center (1932), Young (1943), Gardiner et al. (1937), and Hunt (1939).

[2]Class error—judging the individual not in terms of his personal unique charac-teristic but only as a member of some class or group, i.e. a Jew, a Communist, an old maid, or a negro.

Stereotypes are legion—spinsters and Bolsheviks, Irishmen and professors, lords and cockneys, gangsters and senators, capitalists and journalists, actors and Jews, each word conjures up a caricature of a whole group of people, each a libel on the uniqueness of man. Experimental work shows these weeds in rich profusion—Rice (77), Farnsworth (30), Katz and Braly (43), Hartmann (38), Menefee (61), Fink and Cantril (32), Sherif (84) and others have demonstrated the wide-spread nature and the growth of stereotyped opinion. Eysenck (22) has shown in one particular example both the existence and the falseness of a well-known stereoptye, viz. that of national differences in sense of humour. Using humorous pictures with captions culled from such journals as *Punch*: the *New Yorker, Berliner Illustrierte, Lilliput*, the *Saturday Evening Post*. etc., he showed that not only did British people find it impossible to discriminate which were American, which British, which German, but they liked the products of all three nations equally well. They also tended, however, to ascribe German nationality to pictures which they did not like, on the basis of the false stereotype that Germans have no sense of humour. Other experimental approaches to this problem gave similar results.

While there is little doubt that stereotyped attitudes play a part in the opinions of people, social psychology is in danger of developing stereotyped views about the nature of this concept of 'stereotype'. Much of what is accepted as experimental evidence is in reality artefact produced by inadequate methodology. As an example of this danger, we may quote the investigation of Katz and Braly (43), in which 100 students were presented with eighty-four adjectives, with the request that they should pick out those characteristic of various nationalities. Considerable agreement was found among the answers— Germans are scientifically minded, methodical; Italians are artistic, musical; Negroes are superstitious, lazy; Americans are industrious, sophisticated; Turks are cruel, sensual. Attitudes were most stereotyped about Negroes, Germans, and Jews; least about Japanese, Chinese, and Turks.

Doubtful about interpretations of such data, Eysenck and Crown (26), repeated the investigations with slight modifications on an adult, middle-class, non-student population in this country. Results of the experiment were identical; much agreement was found in the adjectives used, and those most frequently employed with respect to the various nations were similar to those reported by Katz and Braly. Table 1 shows the results in an abbreviated form.

TABLE 1

Five adjectives most characteristic of each race.

GERMAN	Scient. minded	Industrious	Arrogant	Aggressive	Over-national-istic
ITALIAN	Musical	Lazy	Artistic	Religious	Unreliable
NEGRO	Superstitious	Religious	Lazy	Faithful	Happy-go-lucky
IRISH	Religious	Quick temp.	Happy-go-lucky	Witty	Superstitious
ENGLISH	Sportsmanlike	Reserved	Tradition loving	Conventional	Intelligent
JEW	Shrewd	Mercenary	Industrious	Intelligent	Loyal to family
AMERICAN	Boastful	Pleas. loving	Generous	Materialistic	Talkative
CHINESE	Industrious	Courteous	Meditative	Loyal to family	Intelligent
JAPANESE	Cruel	Fanatic	Treacherous	Imitative	Industrious
FRENCH	Sophisticated	Talkative	Artistic	Passionate	Witty
RUSSIAN	Industrious	Tough	Suspicious	Brave	Progressive

One modification was introduced into the experiment, however, which threw an altogether new light on the results: subjects were encouraged to introspect, and to write lengthy reports on their reactions to the tasks, amplifying the bare adjectival descriptions if they so desired. The result showed that 59 per cent of the subjects considered the tasks meaningless, as they did not know any representatives of these various nationalities;[1] they pointed out that only long residence in a country could enable you to say anything worthwhile about people there, and that even then "people everywhere differ among themselves". However, if the experimenter insisted on setting them a task, they had to fall back on what they had seen in motion pictures, or read in books, or heard vaguely in conversation; they were fully conscious that the qualities thus attributed to the various nations probably did not in fact portray anything but bias and prejudice.

Thus, in the majority of cases the written record does not indicate the existence of rationalized emotional reactions and unawareness of the pitfalls of 'group' thinking; the results are determined not by the presence among the subjects of stereotyped views on different nations, but by the experimental design which imitates the ancient Socratic method of argument: "Have you ceased beating your wife?" By not permitting the subject to answer in any but a pre-determined way the experimenter cannot fail to achieve his 'proof', but it may prove nothing but the artificial nature of the experiment. What applies to the one experiment analysed at length here applies also to the others quoted: the conclusions cannot be accepted without further proof of a more rigorous kind.

[1] Another 19 per cent refused to do the test, declaring it to be 'meaningless' and 'impossible'.

While the existence of stereotypes is undoubted, the tendency in social psychology to look for unconscious processes and 'rationalizations' in relation to all social thinking is open to criticism. Many people are rational in their views, and know full well how little they are qualified to judge such difficult questions as 'national character'; in a number of cases, no doubt, emotional and unconscious processes obscure this natural attitude, and lead to vehement anti-semitic or anti-negro attitudes (cf. Eysenck and Crown (28) for experimental proof). But such cases may only constitute a small percentage of the total population and it is dangerous to generalize from the exception to the rule. Experimental design will have to be much improved before we can claim to be fully informed on the subject of 'stereotypes'. In the absence of such knowledge, little can be said usefully about the relation of stereotypes to war-minded attitudes; the hypothesis frequently put forward that a positive correlation obtains between war-mindedness and stereotypy of attitude remains to be proved.

In thus stressing the fact that many recent writers have rather tended to over-emphasize unconscious, unreasonable and emotional factors, it has not been our desire to gainsay the existence of such motives, tendencies, and determinants. There is too much strictly experimental evidence regarding the importance of autistic factors for a generally negative attitude to be possible; our intention has been merely to plead for a less one-sided outlook. In their excitement about the discovery of the powers of 'emotion' over 'intellect', many psychologists have gone to extremes, portraying the 'man in the street' as the mere plaything of uncontrollable unconscious forces which cannot in any way be influenced by reason. Such a view is no less contrary to fact than the previous over-estimation of rationalistic influences; what is needed is a more realistic appraisal of the relative importance of these two factors in each individual case.

Much of the more impressive work along these lines has been in the interpretation of ambiguous perceptual stimuli, in which a conflict is precipitated between realistic and autistic tendencies (Sanford, 80, 81; Levine, 51, 52). Thus, for instance, a larger number of food interpretations were made of certain ambiguous pictures by hungry than by satiated subjects. Murray (67) found similarly that the induction of fear in his subjects made them attribute 'maliciousness' to faces in photographs. Sherif (85, 86) in his well-known work on the autokinetic phenomenon, showed the influence of the desire to conform, on judgments of the position of a point of light in a dark room. Proshansky and Murphy (75), and Haggard and Rose (37), succeeded in influencing perceptual experiences through arbitrary rewards and punishments; Schafter and Murphy (82), showed that the control of the figure-ground relation played an important part in this process.

This work on perceptual factors has been duplicated in relation to social attitudes.[1] Levine (51) caused students either very favourable or very unfavourable to the USSR to learn passages either pro-Russian or anti-Russian. Both as regards learning and forgetting, the material in accordance with the student's views was found superior to the material which was contrary to his opinions. Seeleman (83) and Allport and Kramer (2) showed that favourable and unfavourable attitudes to Negroes and Jews affect a person's powers of recognition of members of these two ethnic groups. Postman (74) found that when children were asked to learn pairs of words which embodied definite attitudes (Stalin—Devil), compatible pairs were learned and retained more easily than pairs of words incompatible with the subject's views. Hundreds of similar experiments are quoted by Rapaport, Sears, Sherif and Cantril, Murphy, and others.

In all these studies, what is most impressive is not so much the demonstration that cognitive and perceptive processes may be influenced by emotional and unconscious factors, but that such effects are relatively difficult to produce, and require a weakening of the forces of reality.[2] In other words, as Murphy (65) puts it, "we are . . . commonly capable of mobilizing our energies under frustration so as to move in the realistic direction". "We have . . . a variety of means for the perceptual handling of an affect-dominated situation, but we know very little about the factors that determine for the individual at a given time which of these means will be used." Thus we must conclude that social attitudes and social behaviour are undoubtedly affected both by realistic and autistic factors; much more thorough analysis is required before we can assess their relative

[1]The importance of perceptual elements in attitude formation is particularly stressed by Murphy (65) and by Sherif and Cantril (87), who point out that "the perceptual stage in the formation of attitudes is especially important in cases which do not have a motivational (instinctive) basis".

[2]As Luchins has shown experimentally, "the greater the ambiguity of the stimulus, the greater is the effect of attempted social influence". Cf. also Coffin (12a), Chapman and Volkman (10a) and, in an analysis of a complex social situation, Cantril (76). As Sherif and Cantril put it, "the role played by internal and social factors (in perception and judgment) decreases with the stability, clarity, or structuredness of the stimulus, and with the strength of frames or points of reference already established". Their 'internal and social factors' correspond to our 'emotional and unconscious' influences.

E

importance in any accurate fashion. In the absence of such information premature generalizations are to be deprecated.

It should be noted that in this discussion we have treated 'stereotypes' as unconsciously determined, emotionally toned caricatures of really existing objects or classes of objects; this is the original meaning of the term as used in social psychology. More recently, it has become fashionable to extend this meaning to cover all that is general in social attitudes. Thus Britt (7), quoting Vetter's (110) finding that people who endorse one radical opinion tend also to endorse other radical opinions, comments that "such studies demonstrate the psychological advantages of stereotyping. To know an individual's attitudes in certain situations may tell you a great deal about what attitudes to expect from him in other situations".

This extension of meaning is in our submission quite unwarranted. The word, as defined in its original meaning, is clear, unambiguous, and related to a set of well-known if ill-understood facts; in its wider meaning it is made to cover so vast an area that it becomes hazy, ambiguous, and ill-defined. There are clear differences between 'general' and 'stereotyped' attitudes, and there would appear to be little point in confounding these two terms.

5. *Changing War-minded Attitudes.* If attitudes arise through social learning, presumably they can be changed through the provision of novel educational or propaganda influences. The work of Arnett et al. (3), Barry (4), Knower (45), Kulp (49), Marple (58), Moore (63), Sorokin and Boldyreff (91), Wheeler and Jordan (111), as well as studies summarized below, go to show that this assumption is in fact true, and that the effects of oral and written argument, of film shows, of expert and majority opinion can be traced experimentally in the changing attitudes of the subjects taking part in these experiments.

Longstreet (53), gave a series of lectures on the facts of war to a class of schoolboys, changing their views (at least temporarily) in the direction of opposition to war. Kirkendall (44), showed that a class of seventy-five students, listening to a talk on "Investigations of War Profits and Munitions Manufacturing", became more strongly pacifist in their views. Charrington and Miller (12), showed the effectiveness on a group of 170 college students of a pacifist lecture; not only was their attitude at the time shifted strongly toward the pacifist end of the scale, but on re-testing after six months the group still showed a statistically significant shift from its original position, although a certain amount of regression had occurred. The same investigators showed that precisely similar effects followed reading the Eddy-Page pamphlet: "The Abolition of War". Stagner (96) showed the effect of a series of eighteen lectures on 140 summer session students.

Gardner's (35) results, obtained on some 850 school-children, are perhaps even more impressive. He used as propaganda devices (1) a rational lecture in favour of peace, (2) a persuasive-emotional lecture in favour of peace, (3) a talk dealing with the cost of war in terms of lives and money, (4) two emotional stories glorifying war, (5) the motion picture *The Valiant*, which stresses the emotional appeal of dying for one's country. Differences induced in various sub-groups exposed to various combinations of these stimuli are in the expected direction; the author draws particular attention, however, to the fact that changes are demonstrably cumulative—two or three lectures against militarism change opinions not two or three times as much as one lecture, but five to ten times as much.

This fact of cumulative influence of propaganda has also been reported on by other investigators, notably by Peterson and Thurstone (69). In their well-known studies on the effects of motion-pictures on the social attitudes of children, these two experimenters used films such as *Journey's End*, *All Quiet on the Western Front*, *The Valiant*, in order to investigate the changes in social attitudes towards war, capital punishment, etc., of the children who formed their experimental group. While single films usually showed only slight effects, several related films produced effects much greater than could be accounted for in terms of the summation of the effects of each by itself. This 'pyramiding stimulation' effect is a law of propaganda which is well enough understood by practical exponents of the gentle art of persuasion; its scientific demonstration should in time lead to a mathematical formulation of the underlying rules which might enable us to predict the effectiveness of propaganda more securely than can be done at present.

One other feature of propaganda may be briefly noted, as it has good experimental backing. The propagandist attempts to convert his victims to a general viewpoint; he inevitably does so by specific instruction and examples. Thus in attempting to convert people to socialism in general, he may discuss the iniquities of capitalist management of the coal mines, or the responsibility of capitalism for war, etc. Now Rosenthal (78) has shown that so far as his results are concerned the effects of specific stimulation are largely specific; no generalization of learning or 'transfer of training' takes place from the specific instance to the general principle. He showed the film *Capitalist World* to 100 students, measuring their opinions on forty-seven radical-conservative statements. Eight of these statements were closely related to the theme of the film, which is a socialist propaganda device, while ten had no particular counterpart in the film. On retesting the group after viewing the film, changes were significant on the 'related', but not on the 'unrelated' statements. As Bird (6) points out, "this study suggests that motion-picture propaganda exerts effects which are specific to their content. Whatever transfer occurs from related to remote attitudes is slight and seems due to identical elements in the movements and in the statements in the test". The application of this principle to propaganda against militarism is obvious.

We noted the fact of 'opinion regression' in connection with the Cherrington-Miller (12) study. Similar effects were noted by Peterson (69), and Thurstone (107) in following up the observations on the children whose attitudes had been changed by the films used in the various studies mentioned; after periods of delay varying from two to eight months, opinion had regressed toward the original point of view, but not all the way. Propaganda, even of so moderate a form, was still effective after this lapse of time. In these studies, counter-influences to the original propaganda film or talk were haphazard and unsystematic, and consequently not very effective over the period investigated. Regression, however, may be almost simultaneous, as when a 'pro' talk is immediately followed by a 'con' talk (88); in such a case cancellation of effects takes place in the majority of cases.

Such simultaneous regression is also reported by Cherrington (11) in his study of the effects of participation in conferences dealing with the causes of war and the cures for war. While participation tended to lead to well-structured, consistent attitudes, it did not lead to any changes on the Thurstone scales of attitude towards war.

The studies summarized in this section show that attitudes towards war are easily modified by various propaganda devices; recent history gives melancholy emphasis to this finding. As Bird (6) points out, "these results constitute a challenge to our educational procedures. Only as students are trained to relate fields of knowledge, to think critically in terms of facts rather than opinions and fictions, to question their own gullibility, and to have a fine regard for opposed points of view held by intelligent people will our educational system fulfil its function in the social sciences".

7. *Opinions on the Prevention of War.* Attitude studies do not extend

only to the measurement of opinion of certain issues, they may also legitimately cover views on the methods which ought to be adopted in order to change existing malpractices, or to prevent contingencies such as war from arising. Much important material has been collected in this sphere by Fletcher (33), Stagner (97), and others.

In one such study (102), (103), fifteen statements dealing with methods of preventing war were answered on a five-point scale by 1,240 men and 1,068 women; they had to indicate their agreement or disagreement with the propositions set out in Table 2. Also sampled were 129 experts from various fields of social science; many of these had done research on war. Historians, political scientists, and economists were about equally represented; sociologists and social psychologists almost twice as strongly as the others. The judgments (a) of the experts, (b) of all men, and (c) of all women were transformed into rankings to indicate the importance of each of the fifteen proposals in the opinion of the group; these three sets of rankings are given after each statement in the table. A number 1 indicates that the item was considered most important; a 15 that it was considered least important.

TABLE 2

We, the people of the United States, in order to preserve the peace, should:

1. Build up our military strength, on land and sea and in the air, so that no nation or combination of nations would dare to attack us. (11 : 8 : 11)

2. Join with other peace-loving nations in economic and other non-military measures to prevent further attacks by any country. (3 : 2 : 1)

3. Stop giving military protection to our citizens, or their trade, or their property, in other parts of the world. (7 : 10 : 9)

4. Establish higher protective tariffs, so as to build up American industry to a point of self-sufficiency where it will be independent of the entanglements resulting from foreign trade. (15 : 13 : 14)

5. Educate the American people to realize that strong labour unions are a great bulwark against war and fascist tendencies in the United States. (5 : 12 : 13)

6. Reduce our naval and air strength until it is only strong enough to defend our own shores and Hawaii—not the Philippines, nor our trade and investments in the Far East. (8 : 15 : 15)

7. Educate American children in the fundamentals of patriotism, making sure they realize that America has always stood for peace and justice among nations. (10 : 1 : 2)

8. Take the lead in reducing tariffs, with reciprocal treaties wherever possible, so as to lower the economic barriers which now separate nation from nation. (1 : 7 : 6)

9. Oppose socialism, communism, and other alien philosophies which threaten to make America more like the war-making dictatorships of Europe. (13½ : 5 : 5)

10. Make it perfectly clear that America is ready to defend herself— that anyone who attacks our honour or our vital interests must count on fighting it to a finish. (6 : 6 : 10)

11. Educate children to be international-minded—to support any movement which contributes to the welfare of the world as a whole, regardless of special national interests. (2 : 3 : 3)

12. Establish ownership of industry, in order to eliminate the autocratic power of the big business men who now profit from war, or from the policies which lead to war. (9 : 9 : 3)

13. Help to establish "United States of the World" in which America should be about as independent as the State of Illinois is now, in our present U.S.A. (12 : 14 : 12)

14. Keep out of alliances now, but support a League of Nations, with strong armed forces of its own, as soon as there is any prospect of establishing it on a world-wide basis. (4 : 11 : 8)

15. Permanently keep away from entangling alliances which might limit our national freedom of action or involve us in the quarrels of other nations. (13½ : 4 : 4)

(In the above table, five possible answers to each question have been omitted. In the original questionnaire, these are given as YES, yes, ?, no, NO, defined as emphatic yes, moderate yes, not sure, moderate no, emphatic no. The table is reproduced by permission of the Editor, *J. Soc. Psychol.* The numbers in parentheses refer to the rank position of each proposal for social scientists, and for men and women separately.)

It will be seen that there is no correlation whatever between the views of the experts and the non-expert men and women; men and women, on the other hand, correlate significantly.[1] Experts are less militaristic (items 3 and 6), more opposed to tariffs (items 4 and 8), less favourable to isolation and patriotic propaganda (items 7, 14,

[1]Rho=0.86.

15), and more 'radical' (items 5 and 9). In fact, when the replies are analysed it is found that on some items which the 'man in the street' endorses as likely to reduce the danger of war, the expert on the contrary holds that they actually increase the danger of war—item 15 may be quoted as an example.

In general, this survey shows that experts' opinions on the prevention of war are displaced towards the *radical* end of our R factor, while the man in the street's views are displaced towards the *conservative* end. It is possible that this tendency is peculiar to American capitalist society; other results might be found in this country.[1] Nevertheless, such lack of agreement between expert and voter is unfortunate and dangerous; it argues that there has been a failure of social communication. It is one of the tasks of the social psychologist to point out the existence of such failures; methods of remedying them cannot be usefully discussed in this context.

The finding that social scientists in general tended to advocate relatively *radical* policies for the preservation of peace seems to indicate that the view of those who advocate an instinctive basis for war is widely rejected nowadays. Certainly few psychologists believe in such a genetic basis of aggressiveness; of several hundred American psychologists polled by Fletcher in 1932 (33), well over 90 per cent rejected the view that human nature made war inevitable. As will be seen from Fig. 1, the view that war is inherent in human nature forms part of the conservative—tough-minded group of 'aggressive' beliefs and attitudes of which war-mindedness is one. This general view is not in accordance with scientific belief, and policies based on it are, therefore, hardly likely to find favour with social scientists.

What then are the policies which according to expert social psychologists would be likely to make a recurrence of war less likely?[2] A sample of fifty-two American social psychologists was queried in considerable detail by Stagner (97); these men represented an authoritative cross-section of the whole group. "They were unanimous on the need for both political and economic internationalism. They endorsed a democratically organized League with sovereignty above that of nations on specified issues. They advocated a 'reasonable'

[1]See, for instance, a study carried out in this country by Mass Observation (59) on an unstated number of persons in Hammersmith and Shrewsbury who 'looked as if they lived in the area'.

[2]In addition to the papers here discussed, the reader may wish to consult a symposium, "Psychological Considerations in Making the Peace," J. Abnorm. soc. Psychol. 1947, 38, 131–224.

rather than a 'vengeful' peace. They favoured an end to 'white imperialism'." "The chief obstacles to durable peace (on the American scene) were perceived as: economic nationalism; absence of loyalty to an international government; and fascist indoctrination of the Axis peoples." "A long-range programme was based on the assumption that uncontrolled aggression anywhere is a menace to the peace of the world. Some frustrations are socially necessary, but many frustrations of biological needs and of ego-values could be ended by the extension of political and economic democracy. Further, the aggression which results from unavoidable frustration can be handled realistically if we improve our mental hygiene practices, reduce scapegoating, and develop a scientific attitude towards human relationships."

8. *Retrospect and Prospect.* The studies discussed in this chapter are only a sample of what has been done in this field, but even a complete enumeration would add little to the light which this work throws on the relation of social attitudes to war and war-mindedness. In this last section, an attempt will be made to evaluate this contribution, and to discuss the conditions under which future progress is likely to occur in our understanding.

Social psychology as a whole has charted for itself a dangerous course, threatened by the Scylla of nebulous Freudian generalizing, and by the Charybdis of pointlessly amassing unrelated 'facts'. Thus we have two great groups of workers whose efforts bring extraordinarily little return for the labour expended: On the one hand the Neo-Freudian, Crypto-Jungian group of 'intuitionists' who scorn the pedestrian methods of scientific verification, who base their conclusions on very small, biased samples, and whose alleged 'facts' are themselves only interpretations according to very dubious canons of evidence; on the other, the mole-like calculators of innumerable correlations between measures taken without any theory or hypothesis capable of proof or disproof, who mistake the collection of a thousand unrelated 'facts' for science, who seek to atone for the scientific barrenness of their results by stressing the mathematical beauty and purity of the methods used, and who seem incapable of seeing the wood for the trees.

If, then, the present achievement of social psychology is well below its promise, let us seek to discover the reasons. Three main causes stand out above all others. The first of these lies in the present organization of research. A large part of the research in social psychology is done by Ph.D. students; it is inevitable that such research should fall short of the large-scale effort and team-work that are required to bring almost any topic to fruition. In two years, with six months spent on getting acquainted with the field, and another six months on writing his thesis, the student cannot be expected to do work that will genuinely advance science; his thesis will inevitably represent a *tour de force*, designed rather to show his command over methodology than to contribute to knowledge.

Related to this first difficulty is the second: the under-capitalization of social science. In its very nature, social psychology demands relatively large expenditure: libraries, Hollerith and calculating machines, field workers, investigators, and interviewers—a whole apparatus, a complicated machinery, is required for successful work. Just as in the physical sciences the days of the string-and-sealing-wax laboratory are gone, so in the social sciences too, work to be worth while has to be done on a large scale. To take but one example, the individual worker cannot possibly undertake to collect a proper random or stratified sample of the population for his investigation, just as little as the physicist can build himself a cyclotron for a particular investigation. As the one must have behind him the resources of a large laboratory, so the other should have at his disposal a well-organized opinion-poll type of organization. In the absence of the necessary funds for such organizations to be affiliated to University Departments, we should not be surprised that so much work in this field is valueless because of inadequate sampling, or because in the enforced absence of other human material only University students have been tested.[1]

These difficulties can be overcome by changes in the organization of University Departments, and by the proper endowment of social research. The third difficulty is perhaps even more crucial. The scientist, to carry on his investigation, must have access to the material he is studying, and he must be allowed to conduct experiments upon it. Yet the social scientist is frequently barred from making any such study, and is hardly ever in a position to conduct any such experiments.

To give just one example, social scientists are often asked what could be done to solve certain social problems, such as that of incentives in relation to coal output. Usually, an answer is expected, and when none is forthcoming social science in general (and psychology in particular) is arraigned for its failure. Yet in no other science would one expect an immediate answer to a difficult and novel problem.

[1]It is not always realized that there is no Chair of Social Psychology in this country, and no University Department primarily concerned with research in this field.

If the scientist is asked how an atom bomb could be produced he will reply, rightly, that given full financial and political support he may be able after several years of large-scale, intensive research to given an answer to the question. Similarly, the reply of the social psychologist must be that, given full financial and political support, and permitted to investigate the problem empirically, he may be able, after several years of intensive research, to give an answer to the question.

Yet almost invariably the position is such that the psychologist is kept away from the object of his inquiry. How can he answer questions regarding the psychology of war if he is not permitted to conduct research and experiments on those who have been engaged on war itself, victors and victims alike? Here, the writer would suggest, lies the main problem of social psychology. The social psychologist is often accused of carrying out 'trivial' experiments; the fault may lie with society for making it impossible for him to study the really serious and important topics by refusing him access to his experimental material.

When these difficulties are realized, the amount of knowledge already gained by social psychology appears rather more imposing than when viewed against the infinite possibilities of the subject. Realization of these possibilities depends on the removal of the obstacles enumerated on the preceding pages.

Even on the assumption that no great improvement is likely to take place in the organization of social science, it is possible to suggest certain directions along which psychology is most likely to see its efforts at research rewarded. In the present writer's view, there are three main topics which should be studied more intensively than hitherto.

The first of these is the study of the correlates of war-mindedness. We can, with a certain amount of accuracy, measure war-mindedness; what we need to know is the degree to which it is determined by such factors as sex, age, education, social class, rural and urban residence, job satisfaction, work history, and the thousand and one other factors that have been suggested as causative agents in the genesis of this particular social attitude. Is it true that frustration in the field of employment, or family life, or ambition, leads to aggression? Is boredom a factor in middle-class bellicosity? What are the factors which lead to 'sublimation' of aggressive tendencies, what are the factors which lead to open expression? How are verbal expression and actual behaviour related? So far we have only tentative answers to one or two of these questions; yet they can all be answered by the use of present-day methods.

The second topic suggested is the study of the genesis of war-mindedness. Taking samples of children at various ages, it should be possible to trace the growth of war-minded attitudes, determine the agencies such as school-teaching, parental instruction, religious education, etc., which favour or retard that growth and show to what extent these attitudes are related to familial patterns of sibling rivalry, Oedipus complexes, parental disharmony, etc. It should also prove possible to relate aggressive behaviour in the school, on the playground, and in the street to war-minded attitudes.

The third topic to be dealt with is the fundamental problem of the relation between social attitudes and personality traits. It is reasonable to suppose that a person's temperament and character, as well as his intelligence, will determine to some extent how he will respond to the relatively uniform matrix of instruction and indoctrination impressed on him and his fellows by society. Attempts to frame theories in this field have not been conspicuously successful; typical is the Freudian attempt to explain both pacifism and militarism in terms of the Oedipus complex (39). A theory which succeeds in explaining two contraries in terms of the same mechanism is obviously too successful to be very useful for social prediction; at least a supplementary principle seems to be called for to explain the causes determining the direction which the dynamic created by the Oedipus complex will take.

Along these three lines, then, successful research into 'war-mindedness' may be envisaged. But it should be stressed again that to be successful such research must get away from the all-too-frequent pattern of asking large numbers of people large numbers of questions in the vague hope of arriving at scientifically and socially important conclusions. The need is for single, clearly stated, verifiable hypotheses, supplemented by suitable, methodologically adequate investigations. Research to date has suggested many worth-while hypotheses, and has succeeded in clarifying the problem of methodology; it is doubtful if in the circumstances it could have done much more.

REFERENCES

1. Allport, G. W. "The Composition of Political Attitudes. *Amer. J. Sociol.*, 1929, 35, 220–238.
2. Allport, G. W., and Kramer, B. M. "Some Roots of Prejudice." *J. Psychol.*, 1946, 22, 9–39.

3. Arnett, C. S., Davidson, H. H., and Lewis, H. G. "Prestige as a Factor in Attitude Change." *J. Sociol. Soc. Res.*, 1931, 25, 373–81.
4. Barry, H. "A Test for Negativism and Compliance." *J. Abn. Psychol.*, 1931, 25, 373–81.
5. Beebe-Center, J. G. *"The Psychology of Pleasantness and Unpleasantness.* New York: Van Nostrand, 1932.
6. Bird, C. *Social Psychology.* New York: Appleton-Century, 1946.
7. Britt, S. H. *Social Psychology of Modern Life.* New York: Farrar and Rinehart, 1941.
7a. Cantril, H. *The Psychology of Social Norms.* New York: Wiley, 1941.
7b. Cantril H. *The Invasion from Mars.* Princeton: Univ. Press, 1940.
8. Carlson, H. B. "Attitudes of Undergraduate Students." *J. Soc. Psychol.*, 1934, 5, 202–12.
9. Carr, H. A. *Psychology: A Study of Mental Activity.* New York: Longmans, Green, 1925.
10. Carter, H. "Recent American Studies in Attitudes Towards War: A Summary and Evaluation." *Amer. Sociol. Rev.*, 1945, 10, 343–52.
10a. Chapman, P. V. and Voltman, J. "A Social Determinant of the Level of Aspiration." *J. Abn. Soc. Psychol.*, 1939, 34, 225–38.
11. Cherrington, B. M. "Methods of Education in International Attitudes." *Teach. Coll. Contrib. Educ.*, 1934, No. 595.
12. Cherrington, B. M., and Miller, L. W. "Changes in Attitude as a Result of a Lecture and/or Reading Similar Material." *J. Soc. Psychol.*, 1933, 4, 479–84.
12a. Coffin, T. G. "Some Conditions of Suggestion and Suggestibility." *Psychol. Mongr.*, No. 241.
13. Crown, S. "A Controlled Association Test as a Measure of Neuroticism." *J. Personal.*, 1947, 16, 198–208.
14. Dollard, J., et al. *Frustration and Aggression.* New Haven: Yale Univ. Press, 1939.
15. Droba, D. D. "A Scale of Militarism-Pacifism." *J. Educ. Psychol.*, 1931, 22, 96–111.
16. Droba, D. D. "Effect of Various Factors on Militarism-Pacifism." *J. Abn. Soc. Psychol.*, 1931–2, 26, 141–53.
17. Droba, D. D. "Churches and War Attitude." *J. Sociol. Soc. Res.*, 1932, 16, 547–52.
18. Droba, D. D. "Political Parties and War Attitudes." *J. Abn. Soc. Psychol.*, 1933–4, 28, 468–72.
19. Durbin, J., and Bowlby, E. *Personal Aggressiveness and War.* New York: Columbia Univ. Press, 1939.
20. Edwards, A. L. "Four Dimensions in Political Stereotypes." *J. Abn. Soc. Psychol.*, 1940, 35, 566–72.
21. Edwards, A. L. "Studies in Stereotypes: 1. The Directionality and Uniformity of Responses to Stereotypes." *J. Soc. Psychol.*, 1940, 12, 357–66.

22. Eysenck, H. J. "National Differences in 'Sense of Humour': Three Experimental and Statistical Studies." *Char. and Person.*, 1944, 13, 37–54.

23. Eysenck, H. J. *Dimensions of Personality.* London: Kegan Paul, 1947.

24. Eysenck, H. J. "General Social Attitudes." *J. Soc. Psychol.*, 1944, 19, 207–227.

25. Eysenck, H. J. "Primary Social Attitudes: 1. The Organization and Measurement of Social Attitudes." *Internat. J. of Opin. and Attit. Res.*, 1947, 1, 49–84.

26. Eysenck, H. J. and Crown, S. "National Stereotypes: An Experimental and Methodological Study." *Ibid.*, 1948, 2, 1–14.

27. Eysenck, H. J. "An Experimental Study in Opinion Attitude Methodology." *Int. J. Opin. and Att. Res.*, 1948.

28. Eysenck, H. J. "The Psychology of Anti-semitism." *Nineteenth Century*, 1948, 164, 277–284.

29. Farnsworth, P. R. "Changes in 'Attitude Toward War' During the College Years." *J. Soc. Psychol.*, 1937, 8, 274–9.

30. Farnsworth, P R., and Misumi. "1. Further Data on Suggestion in Pictures. *Amer. J. Psychol.*, 1931, 43, 632.

31. Ferguson, L. W. "Primary Social Attitudes." *J. Psychol.*, 1939, 8, 217–223.

32. Fink, K., and Cantril, H. "The Collegiate Stereotypes as a Frame of Reference." *J. Abn. Soc. Psychol.*, 1937, 32, 352–6.

33. Fletcher, J. M. "Verdict of Psychologists on War Instincts." *Sci. Mon.*, 1932, 35, 142–5.

34. Gardiner, H. N., Metcalf, R. C., and Neene-Center, J. G. *Feeling and Emotion: A History of Theories.* New York: American Book Co., 1937.

35. Gardner, I. C. "The Effects of a Group of social Stimuli Upon Social Attitudes." *J. Educ. Psychol.*, 1935, 26, 471–9.

36. Glover, E. *War, Sadism, and Pacifism.* London: G. Allen and Unwin, 1935.

37. Haggard, E., and Rose, G. S. "Some Effects of Mental Set and Active Participation in the Conditioning of the Autokinetic Phenomenon." *J. Exp. Psychol.*, 1944, 34, 45–59.

38. Hartmann, G. W. "The Contradiction Between the Feeling-Tone of Political Party Names and Public Response to Their Platforms." *J. Soc. Psychol.*, 1936, 7, 336–55.

39. Hopkins, P. *Psychology of Social Movements.* London: Allen and Unwin, 1938.

40. Hunt, W. A. "A Critical Review of Current Approaches to Affectivity." *Psychol. Bull.*, 1939, 36, 807–28.

41. Jones, E. S. "The Opinions of College Students." *J. Appl. Psychol.*, 1926, 10, 427–36.

42. Jones, V. "Attitudes of College Students and the Change in Such

Attitudes During Four Years in College." *J. Educ. Psychol.*, 1938, 29, 14–25, 114–34.

43. Katz, D., and Braly, K. "Racial Stereotypes of One Hundred College Students." *J. Abn. Soc. Psychol.*, 1933, 28, 280–90.

44. Kirkendall, L. A. "A Study of the Changes, Formation, and Persistence of Attitudes of Pacifism." *J. Educ. Sociol.*, 1937, 1, 222–8.

45. Knower, F. H. "Experimental Studies of Changes of Attitudes. 1. A Study of the Effects of Oral Argument on Changes of Attitudes." *J. Soc. Psychol.*, 1935, 6, 315–47.

46. Knower, F. H. II. "A Study of the Effect of Printed Argument on Changes of Attitudes." *J. Abn. Soc. Psychol.*, 1936, 30, 522–32.

47. Knower, F. H. III. "Some Incidence of Attitude Changes." *J. Appl. Psychol.*, 1936, 20, 114–27.

48. Krout, M. H., and Stagner, R. "Personality Development in Radicals." *Sociometry*, 1939, 2, 31–46.

49. Kulp, D. H. "Prestige, as Measured by Single-Experience Changes and Their Permancy." *J. Educ. Res.*, 1934, 27, 663–72.

50. Lasswell, H. D. *Psychopathology and Politics.* Chicago: Univ. of Chicago Press, 1930.

51. Levine, J. M., and Murphy, G. "The Learning and Forgetting of Controversial Material." *J. Abn. Soc. Psychol.*, 1943, 38, 507–17.

52. Levine, R., Chein, I., and Murphy, G. "The Relation of the Intensity of a Need to the Amount of Perceptual Distortion: A Preliminary Report." *J. Psychol.*, 1942, 13, 283–93.

53. Longstreet, R. J. "An Experiment with the Thurstone Attitude Scales." *Sch. Rev.*, 1935, 43, 202–8.

54. Lorge, I. "The Thurstone Attitude Scales: II. Reliability and Consistency of Younger and Older Intellectual Peers." *J. Soc. Psychol.*, 1939, 10, 199–208.

55. Luchins, A. S. "Social Influences on Perception of Complex Drawings." *J. Soc. Psychol.*, 1945, 21, 257–73.

56. Lundberg, G. A. "Sex Differences on Social Questions." *Sch. and Soc.*, 1926, 23, 595–600.

57. McGeoch, J. A. *The Psychology of Human Learning.* New York: Longmans, Green, 1942.

58. Marple, C. H. "The Comparative Susceptibility of Three Age Levels to the Suggestion of Group Versus Expert Opinion." *J. Soc. Psychol.*, 1933, 4, 176–86.

59. *Mass Observation. Peace and the Public.* London: Longmans, 1947.

60. May, M. A. *Social Psychology of War and Peace.* New Haven: Yale Univ. Press, 1943.

61. Menefee, S. C. "The Effect of Stereotyped Words on Political Judgments." *Amer. Sociol. Rev.*, 1936, 1, 614–21.

62. Menninger, K. *Man Against Himself.* New York: Harcourt, Brace, 1938.

63. Moore, H. T. "The Comparative Influence of Majority and Expert Opinion." *Amer. J. Psychol.*, 1931, 32, 16–20.
64. Morgan, C. L., and Remmers, H. "Liberalism and Conservatism of College Students as Affected by the Depression." *Sch. and Soc.*, 1935, 41, 780–4.
65. Murphy, G. *Personality.* New York: Harper, 1947.
66. Murphy, G., Murphy, L. B., and Newcomb, T. M. *Experimental Social Psychology.* New York: Harpers, 1937.
67. Murray, H. A. "The Effect of Fear Upon Estimates of the Maliciousness of Other Personalities." *J. Soc. Psychol.*, 1933, 4, 310–29.
68. Page, K. "19,000 Clergymen on War and Peace." *World Tomorrow.* 1931, 14, 138–54.
69. Peters, H. N. "The Judgmental Theory of Pleasantness and Unpleasantness." *Psychol. Rev.*, 1935, 42, 354–86.
70. Peterson, R. C., and Thurstone, L. L. *Motion Pictures and the Social Attitudes of Children.* New York: Macmillan, 1933.
71. Pihlblad, C. T. "Student Attitudes Towards War." *J. Sociol. Soc. Rev.*, 1936, 20, 248–54.
72. Pintner, R. A. "A Comparison of Interests, Abilities, and Attitudes." *J. Abn. Soc. Psychol.*, 1933, 27, 351–7.
73. Porterfield, A. L. "Opinions About War." *Sociol. Soc. Res.*, 1937–38, 22, 252–64.
74. Postman, L., and Murphy, G. "The Factor of Attitude in Associative Memory." *J. Exp. Psychol.*, 1943, 33, 228–38.
75. Proshansky, H. M., and Murphy, G. "The Effects of Reward and Punishment on Perception." *J. Psychol.*, 1942, 13, 295–305.
76. Rapaport, D. *Emotions and Memory.*
77. Rice, S. A. "Stereotypes." A source of error in judging human character. *J. Person. Res.*, 1926, 5, 267–76.
78. Rosenthal, S. R. "Change of Socio-Economic Attitudes Under Radical Motion Picture Propaganda." *Arch. Psychol.*, New York: 1934, No. 166.
79. Rundquist, A., and Shelto, D. *Personality in the Depression.* Minnesota: Univ. of Minn. Press, 1933.
80. Sanford, R. N. "The Effects of Abstinence from Food Upon Imaginal Processes: A Preliminary Experiment." *J. Psychol.*, 1936, 2, 129–36.
81. Sanford, R. N. A Further Experiment." *Ibid.*, 1937, 3, 145–59.
82. Schaffer, R., and Murphy, G. "The Role of Autism in a Visual Figureground Relationship." *J. Exp. Psychol.*, 1943, 32, 335–43.
83. Seeleman, V. "The Influence of Attitude Upon the Remembering of Pictorial Material." *Arch. Psychol.*, 1940, No. 257.
84. Sherif, M. "An Experimental Study of Stereotypes." *J. Abn. Soc. Psychol.*, 1935, 29, 371–5.
85. Sherif, M. *The Psychology of Social Norms.* 1936.

86. Sherif, M. "A Study of Some Social Factors in Perception." *Arch. Psychol.*, 1935, No. 187.
87. Sherif, M., and Cantril, H. *The Psychology of Ego Involvements.* New York: Wiley, 1947.
88. Sims, V. M. "Factors Influencing Attitude Toward the T.V.A." *J. Abn. Soc. Psychol.*, 1938, 33, 34–56.
89. Smith, J. J. "What One College Thinks of War and Peace." *J. Appl. Psychol.*, 1933, 17, 17–28.
90. Smith, M. "Spontaneous Change of Attitude Toward War." *Sch. and Soc.*, 1937, 46, 30–2.
91. Sorokin, P. G., and Goldyreff, J. W. "An Experimental Study of the Influence of Suggestion on the Discrimination and the Valuation of People." *Amer. J. Sociol.*, 1932, 37, 720–37.
92. Stagner, R. "Trends in Student Political Thought." *Sch. and Soc.*, 1936, 44, 602–3.
93. Stagner, R. "Fascist Attitudes: An Exploratory Study." *J. Soc. Psychol.*, 1936, 7, 306–19.
94. Stagner, R. "Fascist Attitudes: Their Determining Conditions." *J. Soc. Psychol.*, 1936, 7, 438–54.
95. Stagner, R. "Some Factors Related to Attitude Toward War." 1938. *J. Soc. Psychol.*, 1942, 16, 131–42.
96. Stagner, R. "A Note on Education and International Attitudes." *J. Soc. Psychol.*, 1942, 16, 431–5.
97. Stagner, R. "Opinions of Psychologists on Peace Planning." *J. Psychol.*, 1945, 19, 3–16.
98. Stagner, R. "Studies of Aggressive Social Attitudes: I. Measurement and Interrelation of Selected Attitudes." *J. Soc. Psychol.*, 1944, 20, 109–20.
99. Stagner, R. II. "Changes from Peace to War." *J. Soc. Psychol.*, 1944, 20, 121–8.
100. Stagner, R. III. "The Role of Personal and Family Scores." *J. Soc. Psychol.*, 1944, 20, 129–40.
101. Stagner, R., and Krout, M. H. "Correlation Analysis of Personality Development and Structure." *J. Abn. Soc. Psychol.*, 1940, 35, 339–55.
102. Stagner, R., et al. "An Analysis of Social Scientists' Opinions on the Prevention of War." *J. Soc. Psychol.*, 1942, 15, 381–94.
103. Stagner, R., et al. "A Survey of Public Opinion on the Prevention of War." *J. Soc. Psychol.*, 1942, 16, 109–30.
104. Stratton, A. M. *International Delusions.* Boston: Houghton Mifflin, 1936.
105. Stump, N. F., and Lewis, A. "What Some Ministers Think About War. *Rel. Educ.*, 1935, 70, 135–57.
106. Symonds, P. M. "A Social Attitudes Questionnaire." *J. Educ. Psychol.*, 1925, 16, 316–22.
107. Thurstone, L. L. "Influence of Motion Pictures on Children's Attitudes." *J. Soc. Psychol.*, 1931, 2, 291–305.

108. Tolman, G. C. *Drives Toward War*. New York: Appleton Century, 1942.

109. Turteltaub, D. *The Influence of Suggested Majority Opinion Upon Attitude Toward Prohibition and Militarism*. Minneapolis: Univ. Minn. Ph.D. Thesis, 1932. Quoted by Bird, C., q.v.

110. Vetter, G. B. "The Measurement of Social and Political Attitudes and the Repeated Personality Factors." *J. Abn. Soc. Psychol.*, 1930, 25, 149–89.

111. Wheeler, D., and Jordan, H. "Change of Individual Opinion to Accord With Group Opinion." *J. Abn. Soc. Psychol.*, 1929, 24, 203–6.

112. Wright, Q. *A Study of War*. Chicago: Univ. of Chicago Press, 1942.

113. Young, P. T. *Emotions in Man and Animal*. New York: Wiley, 1943.

CHAPTER IV

PERSONALITY AND ATTITUDES TOWARDS WARFARE

by Madeline Kerr

1. The old controversy, based upon an over-simple dichotomy: "is war engendered by psychological *or* economic factors?" can be dismissed as arising out of a false issue. Instead, it seems more feasible and useful to discuss different aspects of the socio-economic events which people call modern warfare.

The problem to be considered in this chapter is why people should wilfully engage in activities, which, even if they do not cause total destruction of life or property, mutilation or bereavement, bodily or mental wounds, at least occasion so many petty annoyances as to make life extremely drab. Let us ask:

(*a*) what is there in the psychological make-up of people which allows or forces them to acquiesce in their own destruction?

(*b*) how do people make the adjustments of personality which enable them to cope with the changed social relationships of war conditions?

To attempt even tentatively to answer these questions it is necessary to discuss the nature of personality, and its relation to the socio-economic imperatives of a particular culture-pattern.

Until recently, it was customary to regard personality in one of two ways, either as an entity which must be dealt with as a whole, and could be interpreted only as a unit; or as something made up of traits which could be individually measured, and then summed.

There have been various suggestions that neither of these methods is entirely satisfactory. One of the first came from H. G. Wells, who in "The Illusion of Personality" (1) asserted that a current concept of personality as a unit which persisted in space and time was not based upon fact. He suggested that every man has many personalities, each a function of the situation which evokes it.

Moreno (2) has formulated a valuable concept of roles. According to him, the relation between the individual and his culture is achieved when the individual assimilates various roles offered him by his culture-pattern. "The tangible aspects of what is known as 'ego' are the roles in which he operates. . . ." He considers the role the most important single factor determining the 'cultural atmosphere' of personality.

85

He postulates that the child, unable to understand what is going on around him, acts out the roles which the adult plays, ". . . for it is in the earliest stage of role assimilation (matrix of identity) that the child is experiencing a form of living, pre-unconscious as well as pre-conscious; it is strictly act-living. . . . The later way of assimilating a role is through conditioning, perception, objectification."

Forerunners of these ideas can be found in C. G. Jung's theory of fragmentary personalities in the collective unconscious, (3) and K. Koffka's concept of the ego. (4) Jung tries to explain why the individual may suddenly be 'possessed' by another personality; Koffka to show that when the geographical environment is identical for participating individuals, the 'behavioural environment' of each will differ.

T. H. Pear (5), when he defines Personality as "The effect upon others of a living being's appearance, behaviour, etc., so far as they are interpreted as distinctive signs of that being (a person may be aware or unaware of these signs)" breaks away from the idea of personality as a unity, preferring to attach the idea of relative unity to the term 'self', or perhaps 'ego'. He would replace the term 'dissociation of personality' by 'dissociation of self'.

So far then, there are these possibilities: (a) Personality is not a unit; (b) It is a product of the behavioural environment and is largely composed of 'projections' (i) about ourselves (ii) about others.

To hold this view leads to the first major problem: is personality a momentary illusion, or does it contain a constant, persisting factor? A non-psychologist might say that Mr. X at 15, 25, and 50 respectively is a recognizably constant entity, but that some of his views may have altered. Any attempt to theorize about personality is certain to be unsuccessful if made only from the aspect of the individual; but to consider the cultural aspect alone will probably result only in description and will fail to explain the dynamics of personality.

Any individual behaviour-pattern appears to be derived from two sources (a) the culture-pattern, (b) the individual's own mental variations; probably arising from specific differences in his upbringing.

Gregory Bateson (7) postulates that each culture-pattern produces an *eidos*; a cognitive 'picture'[1] of what the individual in such a culture should be like, and how he should think, and an *ethos*: an affective 'picture' of the feelings which should accompany the cognitive events.

Many other writers have suggested that the individual 'pictures' himself and his relations, and tends to try to mould his life according

[1]This is presumably not merely a visual image, but may be an awareness.

to this concept. Freud and Moreno (2) discussed this under the terms of 'ego-ideal' and 'matrix of identity' respectively.

According to Freud, the culture-pattern would be grafted on to the individual, first *via* the super-ego, and secondly *via* the ego. Atypical elements in the family-situation would be reflected in the individual by the culturally determined super-ego. According to Moreno, the individual builds up his matrix of identity by participation in the roles of the people who look after him. According to both writers his ideals will not agree entirely with those of his culture-pattern; consequently the 'average man' is a mythological creature.

To use different terms, the individual chooses certain roles because of the stresses of his 'social field'. Everyone knows that his life is made considerably easier if he accepts the culturally approved way of living: strains and tensions reduced if his behaviour-pattern coincides to a great extent with the culture-pattern.

A main assumption both in the culture-pattern theory and Freud's is that ideational and affective processes are formed by the early interaction of the young child with its environment, especially the parents. Consequently, in much of its behaviour the child thinks and feels in a culturally approved manner. In other words, he is taught, implicitly and explicitly, certain roles which, on appropriate occasions, he 'ought' to play. In any culture certain roles will become 'over-learned' and these patterns of responses will be most frequently used. Some of these will be stereotypes (9). I have suggested that these may be mentally 'carried' in the form of visual images. People's minds seem to be organized ideationally around certain patterns of thought. These remain consistent so long as the culture-pattern does so. All the same, each individual would differ in some way or other from his fellows.

If this theory holds and is supported by evidence, an individual's 'specific' pattern might conflict with his own 'introjected' share of the culture-pattern. Inside the individual there might be more than one field with conflicting forces, analogous to those exerted by opposing magnetic poles.

We now add to the possibility that part of the individual may conflict with the culture-pattern, the fact that culture-patterns themselves contain conflicting elements; e.g. the professed pacificism of Christian ideology and the belligerent thinking and action of many Christian clergymen. Even in peacetime, within the culture-pattern itself such conflicts are often relieved by the allowance of exceptional situations in which aggression is permitted.

Yet for the individual the conflict often remains unrelieved. Not only may some specific constituents of his own ideational system conflict with his introjected, culturally approved system, but idiosyncratic conflicts may arise when his own 'untidy' sentiment-system clashes with the conflict-charged cultural systems. So this overlapping of conflict-charged situations may force the individual into difficulties, because it reinforces urges for which the culture itself has made a certain amount of compromise.

Let us next inquire how far this concept of conflicting culture-patterns or 'configurations', as Clyde Kluckhohn calls them (6) might be elucidated by using the concept of roles. To think of conflict as due to mutually exclusive roles, rather than to mere clashes of conflicting energies, might clarify certain theoretical issues.

The make-up of personality may perhaps be compared to a handful of sand thrown on a moving surface. Any variation in type or rate of movement of the surface produces an instant change in the configuration of the grains. So changes in the 'valences' from the environment may alter materially the configuration of roles in personality.

Does this concept of personality illuminate questions raised at the beginning of this chapter? Consider first a personality acquiescing in his own destruction, though he belongs to a culture in which death through warfare is considered to bring neither overwhelming prestige nor entry to Valhalla. If only a limited number of elements can constitute the 'life-space' and can be in focus at any one point of time, and if external circumstances prevent a large number of potential response-patterns from fulfilment, room is left for others to enter (when certain grains or combinations of them are lost, others automatically take their place). The new patterns creep in, supplanting the previous ones.

The external impetus to change comes from variations of valence in the culture-pattern. When war breaks out, the valences change, e.g. international strife is lessened. People who would otherwise never have mixed socially will work or even play together, owing to the change in prestige roles. Mr. Jones, whose social position normally precludes him from knowing Mr. Brown, is not unwilling to know him as his equal or superior in the Services, or as a fellow-fire-warden. The re-evaluation of roles happens first in the culture-pattern, and then is gradually 'absorbed' by the individual.

The rate of acceptance of new roles by a person will be hastened or retarded by the 'material' already in him. The fussy little man longing for power, will readily accept the role of guardian to one of the multiple regulations and restrictions which wartime produces. And it will probably be easier for people whose prestige-roles in peace-time are secure, than for those whose position is precarious, to accept on equal or superior terms, someone from a much lower social stratum.

Reasons for the individual's acquiescence in his own possible destruction are less simply stated, or perhaps possible explanations lie within a 'field' obscured by concepts with high prestige value among certain psychologists and philosophers. Examples are Freud's example of the 'death instinct'[1] and Trotter's of gregariousness. These terms are classificatory, not explanatory. They do not help us to understand the nature of such behaviour and are useless for prognostication.

If we regard the personality as an ever-changing configuration, many difficulties of the instinct-theories disappear. The individual may not acquiesce in war because of a death-instinct, but because when war threatens he is frightened of death. His 'mental security systems' which in a peacetime society shelter him from dying from unnatural causes are abolished, and with them go many role possibilities. The security of the home, the awareness of being one who contributes to that security, simple faith in the policeman, and the doctor, the belief that to get food you have merely to buy it; these and many related concepts are swept away. The consequent decrease in security causes impoverishment of the personality through the loss of many potential roles.

The individual therefore searches for new feelings of security and for new roles to fill the gaps caused by those torn from him. When his society is in a state of war it offers the individual a new security; that of not having to solve many personal problems. He is offered ready-made solutions: to accept them not only saves him emotional struggle, but brings him prestige. He will be given new roles to play, offered weapons, effectual or ineffectual, to fight the hostility he feels around him, and he often knows or suspects that further military restrictions on his personality may be balanced by greater sexual freedom.

Has this view of the relation of personality-structure to society's apparent ability to keep out of war, practical applications? To answer this the first necessity is to study intensively societies in which prestige is important; the second, to conduct many researches into the relation between economic factors and psychological 'events', e.g. Ralph Linton's study of the Tanala, which shows how changing the economics of production in a society can seriously disintegrate

[1]Footnote criticized by W. McDougall in *Psychoanalysis and Social Psychology*.

personality-organization. If similar work could be extended to many different types of culture-pattern, then in time we might ascertain which roles, or role-configurations, in different cultures will be upset by different types of economic change.

BIBLIOGRAPHY

1. Wells, H. G. "The Illusion of Personality." Thesis in University of London Library.
2. Moreno. *Group Therapy*.
3. Jung, C. G. *The Integration of the Personality*. Kegan Paul.
4. Koffka, K. *Principles of Gestalt Psychology*. Kegan Paul.
5. Pear, T. H. "Personality in its Cultural Context"; *Bulletin of John Rylands Library*, Vol. XXX, 1946.
6. Kluckhohn. C, "Patterning as Exemplified in Navaho Culture," *Language, Culture and Personality*, U.S.A. 1941, pp. 109–30 (quoted T. H. Pear "Psychological Implications of the Culture-Pattern Theory," *Bulletin of John Rylands Library*, Vol. XXIX, 1945.
7. Bateson, G. *Naven*. Cambridge University Press.
8. Freud, S. *New Introductory Lectures in Psychoanalysis*. Allen and Unwin.
9. Kerr, M. "An Experimental Investigation of National Stereotypes," *Sociological Review*, 1944.
10. Trotter, W. *Instincts of the Herd in Peace and War*. Fisher Unwin.
11. Linton, R., quoted in A. Kardiner. *The Individual and His Society*. Columbia University Press.

CHAPTER V

WOMEN IN PEACE AND WAR

by J. Cohen

UNLESS we are prepared to behave like ostriches in a sandstorm we must admit that the world today is passing through the most critical phase in its history, a phase which threatens an end to what we usually call civilization. The great nations of the world fresh from the burial of their war dead are busily piling up, in feverish haste, menacing stores of new weapons. Political indignation, more righteous than ever, masks a less reputable motivation working beneath the surface. The belief is spread, as if it were self-evident, that the best way to ensure peace is by forming regional units as a step towards world unity. The formation of regional units is certainly a 'step', but whether it is a step *towards* or *away from* world unity remains to be seen. It may be that the very process of forming regional groups is likely to exacerbate inter-group tensions. On psychological grounds it may be suspected that the formation of regional units reduces the fluidity of the situation in the sense that more powerful influences will be needed to change the character of regional blocs than are needed to change the relationships between individual unit states. It is perhaps likely that the formation of regional structures generates barriers and counter-barriers which will be more rigid, hostile, and difficult to break down than the barriers separating rival nations in the present state of affairs. Possibly any step taken in this direction is not irreversible, since there are forces in the situation which may lead to reshaping on a world rather than a regional pattern. But there is grave risk of the formation of regional blocs being 'a crossing of the Rubicon' for the modern world. In this situation we may well wonder whether any discussion of this or that aspect of war which does not restrict itself to short-term issues can be of more than academic interest. The subject chosen for consideration in this chapter is no doubt open to criticism on this score. It may seem a far cry from the issues of war and peace to the place of woman in society. But is it? Is it not remotely possible that the causes of war intrinsic in a system of sovereign States are the result of the male as against the female 'element' in these societies? Is it not conceivable that wars occur because of the overwhelming influence of men in government, administration, and international affairs?

Might not a full emancipation of women promote a more peaceful order?

The number of males and females in any given society is approximately equal. More males than female infants are born, but the males have a higher mortality so that from about the age of fifty there is a 'surplus' of females. In hardly any society, however, is there an equal sharing of power. There are still many countries where women have no right to a political vote; in many places men have also not yet attained this right. In some areas of the world today women are denied even the most elementary freedom; they are "not much better than beasts of burden, the hewers of wood and drawers of water"(1). The central problem of democracy and, indeed, of peace may be formulated in terms of the distribution of power and it is a question whether there would be a greater likelihood of ensuring a peaceful order if women were everywhere to be placed on an equal footing with men in this respect.

DIFFERENCES BETWEEN THE SEXES

Like the sex function itself, the divergence between the sexes is part of the process of evolution. Nevertheless, the elaborate effeminacy of women in some classes of modern society may largely be a product of civilized life, since it is not found among most savage and barbarian tribes or even among the peasant women of continental Europe and Asia whose toil at home and in the field is at least as exacting as that of their male partners. Among many agricultural communities women appear to be the chief toilers upon whom falls the main burden of husbandry. Only in certain societies and social groups has woman been cultivated solely for sexual and decorative purposes to the exclusion of almost all others. There is no good reason to suppose that such a practice has anything to do with the biological functions of the female or that it satisfies any inborn dispositions of her sex. In physical characters as well, differences between the sexes appear to have been much less striking among primitive peoples in Africa, Asia and Australia than they are among the more civilized people of Europe. Determination of sex in a prehistoric skeleton is regarded by some anthropologists as a very doubtful exercise, because the bones appear to have been almost equally massive in both sexes and because differences in the shape and size of the pelvis were, apparently, not nearly so pronounced as they are among modern Europeans (2, p. 660).

It is not surprising therefore to find that equality of the sexes is much more marked among the most primitive than among civilized peoples. Primitive culture and industries were closely associated with the activities of the household and it is natural that women should have played an equal part with men or sometimes even a leading role. Among savages medicine has always been to a great extent the monopoly of women, who practised the arts of healing, midwifery, and surgery and possessed the available knowledge of herbal remedies. The technique of making pottery has generally been a woman's craft. Even today among some primitive peoples, for example, the Manus of New Guinea, women are responsible for dealing with the economic matters of the home and young or else stupid men are guided in all their affairs by the shrewdness and social knowledge of their wives (3).

On the average, women are about ten centimetres shorter than men of the same stock, though there is a good deal of variation between different ethnic groups. Their cranial capacity is less, but in proportion to their body bulk, they have as large, if not larger, brains. Their bones tend to be smaller and lighter than those of men. About 36 per cent of their body mass is muscle and about 28 per cent fat; in men the corresponding proportions are about 42 per cent and 18 per cent. Women tend to accumulate in their systems incompletely oxidized material ready for pregnancy or lactation and when not thus used it forms adipose tissue (4, p. 145). The development in the human female of local deposits of fatty tissue not found in the apes led, in the course of evolution, to marked changes in the general form of the body and to more marked sex differences than existed among other primates (5, p. 52). One of the characteristics of women is greater trunk-length relative to stature. This feature appears to place her a step nearer the ape, but it is probably a sex character associated with maternal functions and due to greater length of the pelvis. Relative to stature, men have longer arms and legs than the women; in this respect men are nearer the ape. Pulse rate is higher in women, but lung or 'vital' capacity is lower and so is basal metabolic rate except during pregnancy and lactation.

In sensitivity to touch and hearing and possibly pain, women seem to be superior; in smell, taste, and cold, on the other hand, men appear to have better discrimination. There are no marked sex differences in visual acuity; slight defects of eyesight seem to be more common in women and serious ones commoner in men. Colour-blindness and neuro-muscular defects such as stuttering are commoner among men than among women. Men are also more frequent sufferers from albinism and deafmutism.

Sex differences in educability and specific aptitudes are not very appreciable. The average female is blessed with about as much intelligence as the average male, but there is evidence of greater variation in male than in female intelligence. The fact that there are fewer females than males in institutions for mental defectives is probably in part due to the smaller proportion of mentally defective females in the population and possibly also to the fact that low-grade females more frequently escape detection and adjust themselves in domestic surroundings. The experience of industrialized communities during the past twenty or thirty years has shown that, apart from some of the heavier kinds of work, women are capable of participating equally with men in almost all commercial, industrial and professional vocations. The menstrual rhythm does not handicap them unduly, provided allowance is made for it by welfare and recreational facilities and by avoiding excessive hours of work.

Sex differences in temperament are much more difficult to measure. Endocrine secretions, particularly the male or androgenic and female or oestrogenic hormones respectively, doubtless influence personality but their relative importance is still undetermined. One instance is worth noting, namely prolactin, a hormone secreted by the pituitary gland in the brain which seems to be the main biochemical 'cause' of maternal behaviour. Extracts from prolactin injected into virgin animals stimulate the mammary glands and induce maternal responses such as nest-building and retrieving the young otherwise observed only in late pregnancy and after delivery.

Protective behaviour is probably part of the parental function of the female and is certainly exhibited in most vertebrates. McDougall has asserted that the maternal impulse of the female may be the foundation of all forms of altruistic behaviour in human society, and that altruism in the male is acquired by him through association with females and with young children. That the erotic impulse is distinct from the parental one is widely accepted. The two impulses are probably antithetical in that sex inclines to cruelty and parenthood to kindness. A greater readiness to jealousy, quarrelsomeness, and irritability has also been attributed to women. These traits may have favoured survival in early times when conditions led to competition among women in securing food for their children. Monogamy, to which, as a *de facto* institution, women have always been bound more than men, may also have encouraged jealousy in the former. It may well have been reinforced by woman's close dependence on the stability of marriage and the home, in which her interests have been almost exclusively centred.

Evidence has been adduced to show that woman is far more emotional and more responsive to stimuli than man both in a normal way and in abnormal manifestations such as hypnagogic phenomena, ecstasy, trance, catalepsy and hysteria. It is admitted, however, that this greater responsiveness or affectability can be reduced by appropriate training.

The study of Terman and Miles (6) throws a good deal of light on sex differences and is worth considering in the present context. The results of this study showed that in the particular samples observed there is no clear dividing line between the sexes mentally. A considerable degree of overlap between the sexes was noted in respect of many traits of personality. Some males are mentally more 'feminine', as judged by the tests, than some females, and *vice versa*. Many traits that had long been regarded as inborn characteristics of the female or male appear to be due to differing social and environmental influences in the early years. Women reveal more partialities and antipathies whilst men are more generally neutral in their attitudes. Timidity is marked in women; courage in men. Kindly and sympathetic activities occur more frequently in the mental associations of women than in those of men, who are much better informed on subjects of an aggressive nature. Unsympathetic treatment of human beings evokes more anger in females than in males; the weak, the helpless and the visibly distressed are more apt to stir the hearts of women, who are also more concerned at female than male distress. Condemnation of offences is more often forthcoming from females, especially in offences common among males. There is little sex difference in attitude towards serious offences. The differences most marked are in respect of disgust, less in those of fear and least in anger and moral censure. There is no evidence that any of these differences were innate. On the contrary, the fact that they vary with age, marriage, size and composition of the family, occupation, education and other factors indicates that environment is the decisive influence. Take, for example, age. Increase in years tends to make women more masculine and men more feminine, and in extreme old age differences appear at their minimum. Boys and girls between fourteen and eighteen years differ about twice as much as men and women between seventy and eighty years.

The difficulties in attributing differences in social behaviour of men and women respectively to differences in sex are well illustrated in the sphere of crime. Statistics of crime in England and Wales show that far more males than females are found guilty of offences.

G

In 1945, for example, 99,000 males were found guilty of indictable offences as compared with 17,000 females. But we should be unjustified in concluding that girls and women are proportionately devoid of 'criminal tendencies'. Men are much more exposed to temptation than women and they have greater opportunity to commit crime. A bank-clerk is more likely to embezzle his bank than is his wife, occupied in household duties. Men also have freer access to firearms and other weapons. Crimes like rape can only be committed by males, and there are only very few crimes like concealment of birth and procuring abortion to which women are more tempted.

ATTITUDES OF WOMEN TOWARDS WAR

It would be illuminating if we could discover what women in different countries actually think about war; whether, for example, they are more hostile to war than men are. Unfortunately little is known on this subject. There is some evidence that in the United States men are more favourable to war than women (7, pp. 1023–4). Moreover, patriotism, which appears to be positively correlated with warlike attitudes, is said to be weakest among housewives as compared with other vocational groups.

In 1945 after the first atom bomb had been used, a peace-wave swept over large sections of American women (8, p. 3). Undue confidence in the stability of the peaceful attitudes of American womanhood is, however, likely to be rudely shaken. An opinion poll carried out in the United States in 1947 showed no sex difference in views on the question whether young women should enlist in units of the armed forces in peacetime (9), though it would be unsafe to infer from this that there is no divergence between the sexes in respect of a general attitude towards war. Further studies in this direction are needed.

SUBORDINATION OF WOMAN IN WESTERN SOCIETY

The lack of capacity in vocations followed by males which has traditionally been ascribed to females in European societies is to be traced to the low status assigned to woman by the early Christians. Not, however, by the earliest Christians by whom woman seems to have been accepted as man's equal, and at the very beginning of the era many vocational possibilities were open to both sexes without distinction. Women, mostly unmarried, accompanied the Apostles on their journeyings. An outstanding example was Thekla who followed Paul in healing the sick. There were women visionaries and martyrs, and others who gathered in devotional settlements for giving help and advice to the needy and for cultivating simple handicrafts (10, pp. 148–55). This broad outlook soon narrowed, and to the early leaders of the Church woman became the fount of evil and responsible for the Fall of Man. Accordingly the Church Fathers decreed that man should be woman's lord and master so that she should never again be in a position to entice him to sin.

Early Christian asceticism scorned erotic pleasure in any form and this inevitably meant the degradation of woman. The patristic writings are replete with abuse and denunciation of women. "Converse with women," wrote St. Jerome, "is the road to the Devil," and St. John Chrysostom declared:

"O Evil! A wicked woman is worse than any evil! Deadly are dragons and poisonous snakes, but the deadliness of a woman is deadlier than the poison of serpents. The wicked woman is never chastened: treat her sternly and she rageth, mildly and she runneth wild. Easier is it to melt iron than to tame a woman. He who hath a bad wife may know that he hath received the reward of his sins. There is on earth no wild beast to be compared to a bad wife. What quadruped is fiercer than a lion? None, save a bad wife! What serpent is deadlier than the dragon? None save a bad wife". (11, p. 842).

A prolonged assignment of woman to a low social status in time produced a conviction that she was by nature incapable of anything better. Vocational opportunities open to the male in law, the Church, and in the arts and crafts, were consequently denied to the female. St. Thomas Aquinas even held that woman suffered from a congenital deficiency of the mind, a view reminiscent of that of Plato who believed that woman represented a stage of transition between wild beasts and man. In the year A.D. 585 an assembly of bishops at the Synod of Macon debated whether women were human beings. After long and earnest deliberation they reached a positive conclusion.

These disabilities were removed in the medieval convents and monasteries, where women were free to cultivate a variety of devotional, intellectual, artistic, medical and other interests. Sometimes their culture reached a very high level as, for example, in the case of Hilda of Whitby, Hrotswitha (or Roswitha) of Saxony and St. Hildegard. The last named was a medical writer of influence, though swayed by astrology and pharmacological superstitions; she believed, for instance, that Eve's first menstrual period was the direct consequence of her moral lapse. But the monastic life was a secluded one and removed from social intercourse. Whatever talents women displayed had to find an outlet within the walls of the convent. With the dissolution of the monasteries at the time of the Reformation, women lost almost all the cultural opportunities afforded them under monasticism.

There must have been a great deal of misogyny in the Middle Ages, at any rate in the fifteenth, sixteenth and seventeenth centuries. A symbol of the spirit of the times was a book—*The Witches' Hammer* (*Malleus Maleficarum*—c. 1488)—by two German professors of theology —Sprenger and Kraemer. The work has been described as the "most horrible document of the age" (12). It was the text-book of the Inquisition. Directly or indirectly it brought death or torture to untold thousands of innocent people, above all women, on the grounds of sorcery and witchcraft. It propagated the belief that witches were fifty times as common as sorcerers; hence the work is essentially an attack on woman. The book's popularity may be judged by the fact that it exhausted nineteen editions before 1670.

"As a final impression one may carry away from the perusal of the *Malleus* the anti-erotic, misogynous nature of the book. The rule of sex in the whole history of our civilization and man's attitude towards woman's part in social life as one of the factors of social problems are thrown into painful relief in this piece of legalistic and theological literature of the early Renaissance. The Old World seems to have risen against woman and written their gruesome testimony to its own madness. Even after she had been tortured and broken in body and spirit, woman was not granted the privilege of facing the world in a direct way. . . . Never in the history of humanity was woman more systematically degraded. She paid for the fall of Eve sevenfold, and the law bore a countenance of pride and self-satisfaction, and the delusional certainty that the will of the Lord has been done" (12, pp. 161–2).

There were, however, a few outstanding defenders of women among whom should be mentioned Juan Luis Vives (1492–1540), and Cornelius Agrippa (1486–1535) the author of a book entitled *On the Nobility and Pre-eminence of the Feminine Sex*.

As a result of these medieval influences, a number of features have gradually become associated in Western tradition with the female sex. Some of the most 'characteristic' female traits may, however, have a still earlier origin. Thus the notion of chastity appears to derive, according to one theory, from the man's insistence on his partner's fidelity, a requirement made in early patriarchal communities and designed to safeguard the transmission of property to true heirs. At a later stage, this became a demand for virginity in the pre-nuptial state, a precaution presumably taken to reassure the father in cases of doubt as to the paternity of the first child. According to another theory retrospective claims to bridal virginity grew out of the savage custom of infant betrothal. But the counter-demand for chastity in the male would have been considered wholly irrelevant among the ancients and, indeed, up to the present day has never been made with anything like the same seriousness as in the case of woman. In Rome the freeborn woman was required by law to avoid all sexual intercourse before marriage and to be faithful to her husband after marriage. The man, however, was subject to the same code only to the extent of not impairing the chastity of a virgin or the wife of another man in collusion with her.

During the Middle Ages, the character of the medieval marriage arrangement confirmed the subordination of women. Throughout this period, "marriage was an arrangement of convenience, an enforced legal contract, designed to secure certain political, military, or economic advantages" (13, p. 17).

The desire that women should be chaste grew in time into the belief that they were so in fact because of natural disposition. And so much have women themselves come to believe the superiority of their supposedly pure nature as compared with the grosser male that they now strongly resent any suggestion to the contrary. As Briffault remarks, "from being forcibly compelled to be chaste, women came first to be regarded as naturally chaste, and by the insistent pressure of that opinion came at last to regard an imputation of unchastity or impurity as a slander against their natural disposition" (14, pp. 125–6).

Apart from chastity, women are also widely believed to be more sympathetic, tender, protective and fearful. There is a certain physiological basis for some of these beliefs. Thus tenderness may be associated with the greater number of pulsations of the heart on awaking from sleep observed in women as compared with men (4, p. 332). Woman has also been credited with other special qualities as, for example, by Lavater, the eighteenth-century physiognomist, and by numerous other writers.

The lower status of woman is well illustrated in the controversies over the rights of women to enter medical schools on equal terms and in equal numbers with men. It has been pointed out that "brute force is not needed in the practice of medicine", yet, apart from brute force is there any quality to which men may lay exclusive claim? Objection has even been raised to the title 'female physician' which, it is suggested, should be replaced by the title doctress'.

"The title 'female physician'," wrote a feminist, "is expressed by two words, one meaning an animal, the other a man, making a compound idea repulsive to almost every ear and injuring the popularity of women's medical education and practice. The word 'doctress' is a pleasant soft word, explaining the rank and sex, and mingling in an idea of the woman and her vocation, tenderness with respect" (15, p. 122).

ARE MALES MORE AGGRESSIVE?

It should, perhaps, be possible to obtain some hint of the relative aggressiveness of the sexes from a consideration of the way mating operates. In nature, according to Darwin (16, p. 64) sexual congress is a form of selection and involves a struggle between individuals of one sex for the possession of members of the other. In the human species it has nearly always been the males who have struggled for the possession of the females. Those who fail in the struggle will tend to leave few or no offspring. Among animals, success in sexual conflict is generally dependent on the possession of special organs like horns or spurs. On the other hand, among human beings in a civilized state success of the male will as often as not depend upon social and economic advantages as upon sheer physical strength or vitality, though doubtless native vigour will frequently be an important factor and hence tend to be perpetuated in the offspring. There seems to be a resemblance between the methods of some savages in securing their mates and the methods of certain animal species. Darwin (ibid.) observes that male alligators behave rather like savages in a war dance, fighting, bellowing and whirling around for possession of the females. Similar observations have been made of male salmon, stag-beetles and some hymenopterous insects. In the last-mentioned species the female behave in a manner reminiscent of ladies in the Age of Chivalry, watching the conflict unconcernedly in nearby security and finally retiring with the victor. The struggle seems to be most intense among polygamous species.

If sexual selection takes place, as Darwin believed it does, there will be a tendency for survival to favour the more attractive women. Now if attractiveness to the male were correlated with non-aggressive traits like amiability and submissiveness or a conciliatory disposition, this might be taken to support the view of war as essentially a male phenomenon. But no one has yet taken the trouble to ascertain whether this correlation describes the facts. The problem is a profitable one for research.

In general, organized fighting has been the prerogative of the male. This custom may be regarded as part of a wider rule by which division of labour by sex seems to have been guided. In the view of Havelock Ellis, tasks involving sudden bursts of energy, such as fighting or hunting, were the lot of men, whilst to women were assigned tasks such as caring for the young and supervising the domestic economy, which called upon a continuous output of energy at a lower level of intensity. Nevertheless, there have been instances of warrior women among savages. The negro Amazons of Dahomey in West Africa are perhaps the most notable example. These women have been described as 'brave fighters' who have 'time and again surpassed the male corps in daring and ferocity'. Women have fought, when the need has arisen, in Australia and Africa as well as among the Celts, Teutons and Slav peoples. The Australian native women, in particular, are said to have fought as bravely as, and even more ferociously than, the men.

In other instances where women have not participated in battle they have actively assisted their men in all sorts of secondary ways such as mutilating or emasculating the enemy when wounded or overpowered and subjecting prisoners of war to refined torture. In North Mexico, for instance, it was the custom for those captured in war to be given over to the womenfolk to be dealt with by them. These prisoners are said to have suffered the most inhuman tortures and every conceivable insult and humiliation at the tender hands of their warders who seared the victims' flesh with flaming brands before burning them at the stake or disposing of them in some equally cruel manner. Captives were often cooked and eaten, the bones being retained as trophies (17, p. 298). Among the Pondon tribes, women spectators, observing the course of battle from a convenient point of vantage, encouraged their men by erotic songs and gestures and by exposing themselves (7, p. 76).

Boadicea and Joan of Arc are among the most well-known examples of women providing leadership in battle. There are other instances on record including the Countess of Montfort at the siege of Henne-bont, Queen Phillipa at the battle of Newcastle-on-Tyne, Blanche of Champagne, and Blanche of Castile. The last mentioned organized two fleets, broke up the barons' league and, in 1230, succeeded in repelling an attack by the King of England (13, p. 146). According to the *Chronicles* of Froissart, Margaret, Countess of Flanders wrote in these words to her enemy! "your brothers, my sons, are in your hands; I will not be turned from my purpose on their account; they are exposed to your will and pleasure. Put them to death, cruel villain, and eat them, one boiled with pepper, and the other roasted with garlic" (*loc. cit.*).

Generally speaking, however, with the growth of patriarchal society and the spread of Christian influence women tended to be excluded from war-like functions. During the Middle Ages fragmentary historical records show that women, far from inspiring great military exploits, took only a passive part in war (13, p. 195). The more war-like the group, the greater was the tendency to relegate women to an inferior social status and to impose heavy restrictions on their powers, rights and activities. But the strength of this established tradition did not prevent women taking part in fighting in the First World War in those countries where the civilian population was involved. It is reported that the women could show themselves to be as heartless as the men. With the emergence of 'total' warfare in the Second World War there was an increasing use of women in auxiliary military duties, even in the combatant roles of gunner and aviator, especially in Soviet Russia, and they were prominent among the partisan fighters of Yugoslavia. In the United Kingdom some half a million women were serving in the Women's Auxiliary Services in 1944, the year when mobilization reached its peak, as compared with about 4·5 million men. Since the war, women's auxiliary units have been embodied as regular components of the armed forces of the United Kingdom.

EFFECTS OF INCREASING THE SOCIAL PARTICIPATION OF WOMEN

The most interesting question to consider is whether an increased participation by women in industry, commerce, the professions and public affairs, including local and central government, would bring about a marked change for the better in social institutions, law, and above all in state policy. According to Freud, the interests of women would appear to be incompatible with culture in the sense of an expanding civilization, because woman tends to be emotionally bound to the home by children and domestic ties and therefore hostile to any change which might endanger these ties. Her freedom of movement and choice of occupation are hampered by pregnancy and child-rearing. Hence her influence tends to lead to conservatism and cultural stagnation. Man, on the other hand, is not so bound to the domestic hearth; his interests are wider and freer and his mobility less hampered by the claims of child care, and so he is more likely to seek change and novelty and cultivate social activities outside the scope of the home.

This view of Freud would seem to apply to the ordinary man hardly less than to the ordinary woman. It would be extremely hazardous to suppose that women are constitutionally less capable than men of creative work in science, art or public life. Until we equalize the social opportunities of the sexes as much as possible we are unlikely to ascertain true sex differences in social behaviour. In view of the heavy disabilities under which women have lived in the past we have no reason to assume that they have no capacity for improving their relatively undistinguished record even in those spheres of activity which men jealously guard as their own. The fact that some women in spite of every obstacle have achieved great intellectual distinction suggests that others, given the opportunity, might also do so. We may have something to learn from many primitive peoples among whom diplomacy is in the hands of women, who have to make decisions for peace or war. The relatively small number of women prominent in contemporary politics is doubtless due to the fact that they are economically at a disadvantage as compared with men. It is also true that a political career for a woman is a handicap to marriage and the care of a family, and would be opposed by many husbands. Since the Second World War, however, distinguished women have come to the fore politically in many countries where the status of woman outside (or even inside) the home was previously low. In Japan, women now have the suffrage and there are some forty women members of the Diet. In China, Madame Chiang Kai-shek and Madame Sun Yat-sen have played leading political roles. In Poland, Madame Wassilewska, in Rumania, Madame Anna Pauker, the Foreign Secretary, and in India, Madame Pandit, the Minister of Public Health, have achieved eminence in spheres from which women were formerly excluded entirely. In Yugoslavia, the newly introduced sex equality has transformed the relationships between the sexes and opened the way for the participation of women in all walks of life on equal terms with men. In France, too, women have been granted the suffrage since the end of the recent war.

Experiments in female suffrage before the First World War were regarded by sceptics as 'a stratagem in order to win the masses'. Treitschke, the German social philosopher, described the attempts as 'flippancy'.

"In the exercise of this right by women," he wrote, "there are only two alternatives possible. Either the wife, or it may be, the daughter, votes as the husband and father does, and thereby an unwarranted privilege is granted to married men, or wife and daughter are good for nothings, then they vote against the man, and thus the State carries its dispute in frivolous fashion right into the peace of the home, the very place where we should rest from the noise of political life" (18).[1]

A recent anthropological survey (19) of post-war Germans is worth considering in this connection. Contrary to the opinion that the status of women in the German household is relatively low, the investigator reports that the role of the mother, at any rate in Protestant families, is 'actually a dominant one'. Apart from submissiveness in sexual matters, the German Protestant mother controls the behaviour of her children and expects unquestioned obedience. She is 'mistress in the home'. The effect of the war must have given many women a new place as head of the family and forced them to make decisions and assume all the care and support of their children. "The outcome of the war has done much to destroy whatever traditional illusions German women may have had about the supposed innate superiority of men" and the "dispirited condition of most German men makes the women appear all the more self-confident by comparison" (ibid.). On the whole there seems to be a narrowing of the behaviour differences between German men and women.

To appreciate this point of view, it must be borne in mind that in German tradition, far more so than in England or the United States, a woman's importance is determined not so much by her own worth as by her husband's status, rank or professional standing, which she retains after her husband's death.

At present, it would seem that German Protestant women do not aspire to political influence. They prefer the 'importance of being a woman'. Marriage and motherhood are the objects of their aspiration rather than political participation.

It would be instructive, and at the same time serve to check Treitschke's prediction, if we could ascertain the extent to which wives vote as their husbands do, and daughters as their fathers. An

[1]One may wonder whether the 'peace of the home' for which Treitschke yearned has not something of a deceptive character. Balzac once remarked that "a woman is never so much a gossip as when she is silent, and never acts with so much energy as when she is in repose". Is this perhaps indicative of a cultural difference between the women of Germany and France?

inquiry of this kind is now practicable in view of the available techniques of opinion measurement, and might throw light on family integration, social mobility and class differences.

Unfortunately the great hopes that were placed at the beginning of the century in granting the franchise to women have not been fulfilled. The barely perceptible effects of female suffrage on social and international stability is an indication that the factors making for economic and political unrest are not such as to vanish in the presence of a woman's vote. This is, of course, no argument against female suffrage but simply a pointer to the need for more radical treatment of the situation. As Miss Louise M. Young has said, "the winning of the franchise did not carry with it the tacit acknowledgment that women were expected to assume responsibility for governing proportionate to their numbers. Nor did the fact that millions of women were compelled to enter the labour market re-define the status of woman as wife and mother" (20).

The most impressive instance of women directing their efforts towards an anti-war measure is the part women in the United States played in bringing into being the Kellogg-Briand Pact. This pact made war illegal. It thus had an important impact upon international law, and provided a legal basis for the Nuremberg Trials of war criminals. It is hardly an exaggeration to say that this pact would not have existed had it not been for the tremendous efforts made by organized women in the United States. Ten national women's organizations uniting to form a Conference on the Causes and Cures of War arranged 14,000 meetings at which resolutions were passed demanding that the pact be enacted (21).

EFFECTS OF DEMOGRAPHIC TRENDS

A new factor of increasing importance may be introduced into the world situation as a result of demographic trends. The prospect of a considerable fall in the size of the population of certain countries as a result of a decline in fertility rate suggests possible surprising effects on the balance of power between the sexes and, indirectly, on world affairs. A woman biologist speculating on such an outcome envisages a time when all children will be born either as a result of an accident or through the mother's initiative with the more or less reluctant consent of the father. Mothers will then fully realize the power they hold over the future of the state. They may so exploit the new circumstances as to monopolize important spheres of government and take over the property rights of men whom they would restrict to routine domestic tasks such as the care of the children and the home (22). Such an arrangement would not be very unlike that found among termites, ants, bees and other social insects where reproduction is restricted to queens and those males necessary for the purpose. The rest of the females have no reproductive functions and become workers devoted to the care of the young. Many such insect communities are run by females; when the males have performed their single function of impregnation they either die or are killed and eaten. But we cannot assume without further evidence that this is likely to happen in *homo sapiens*.

CONCLUDING REMARKS

The most urgent task in the world today is to bring about great social changes without war or violence. The changes include gradual adjustments towards equalizing the standard of living among the different peoples of the world. This is perhaps the basic ground for disharmony out of which grow psychological and social tensions. Human behaviour is characterized by a polarity which shows itself in fundamental plasticity, on the one hand, and refractoriness or resistance to change, on the other. The problem of overcoming this resistance so that the forces making for necessary change can work freely and peacefully, is one of finding the 'sensitive zones' of society which are most responsive to the need for peaceful change on the required scale. Social therapy, like individual therapy, depends on the presence in the patient of something to which an appeal can be made. Therapy consists in detecting and utilizing the healthy 'organ' or processes in the interests of the individual patient or community as a whole.[1] It is in this perspective that we have to consider whether the emancipation of women might not so alter the character of man-made society as to reduce the chances of war as a method of solving human differences.

The part of women in instigating and organizing aggression has been altogether subsidiary to that of men if only because of their subordinate social role since the beginning of civilization. Men and not women have been the administrators and legislators since the emergence of urban culture, a fact which is attributable to the need for male leadership in defence. It is perhaps reasonable to assume that a complete emancipation of women leading to their full par-

[1]"Give me a solid joint in the universe," said Archimedes, "and I shall move the earth out its joints"; *see* R. Waelder, "The Scientific Approach to Case-work," *The Family*, October 1941, Family Welfare Association of America.

ticipation in communal and world affairs would entail radical changes in the structure and functions of man-made societies. Such changes are perhaps more likely to work towards peace than towards war. Child-bearing, the rearing and protection of children during their period of growth, the provision of a secure environment and adequate nourishment for mother and child, are incompatible with the perils of war. It may be said that the functions of womanhood, physically and mentally, are essentially creative, protective and preservative. Woman's interests are naturally invested in life-giving and life-prolonging activities. Hence a diversion of human energies to the waging of war means a frustration of woman's natural needs and tasks. It is fitting to conclude with the words of Dorothy Thompson: "Gentlemen of the United Nations Security Council, you must come into the room of your mother unarmed".

REFERENCES

1. Kenyon, D. "Victories on the International Front," *Ann. of the Amer. Acad. of Pol. and Soc. Sc.*, Vol. CCLI. 1947.
2. Briffault, R. *The Mothers: The Matriarchal Theory of Social Origins*. London: Allen and Unwin. 1927.
3. Mead, M. *Growing Up in New Guinea*. London: The Bodley Head. 1931.
4. Ellis, H. *Man and Woman*. London: Heinemann. 1934.
5. Smith, G. Elliot. *The Evolution of Man*. London: Oxford University Press. 1924.
6. Terman, L. M., and Miles, C. C. *Sex and Personality*. New York: McGraw Hill. 1936.
7. Wright, Q. *A Study of War*. Chicago: University of Chicago Press. 1942.
8. Beard, Mary. "Woman's Role in Society," *Ann. of the Amer. Acad. of Pol. and Soc. Sc.* Vol. CCLI. 1947.
9. *The Public Opinion Quarterly*. Princeton: Princeton University Press, p. 682. 1947–8.
10. Eckenstein, L. *The Women of Early Christianity*. The Faith Press. 1935.
11. Pareto, V. *The Mind and Society*. London: Jonathan Cape, Vol. II. 1935.
12. Zilboorg, S., and Henry, S. W. *A History of Medical Psychology*. New York: W. W. Norton. 1941.
13. Gist, M. A. *Love and War in the Middle English Romances*. Philadelphia: University of Pennsylvania Press. 1947.
14. Briffault, R. *Sin and Sex*. London: Allen and Unwin. 1931.
15. E. W. Thompson. *Education for Ladies: 1830–60*. New York: King's Crown Press. 1947.
16. Darwin, C. *The Origin of Species*. London: John Murray. 1901.

17. Davie, M. R. *The Evolution of War*. New York: Yale University Press. 1929.
18. Treitschke, H. *Lectures on Politics*. London: Gowans and Gray, transl. A. L. Gowans. 1914.
19. Rodnick, D. *Post-war Germans*. New York: Yale University Press. 1948.
20. Young, Louise M. Foreword to *Ann. of the Amer. Acad. of Pol. and Soc. Sc.*, Vol. CCLI. 1947.
21. Allen, Florence E. "Participation of Women in Government," *Ann. of the Amer. Acad. of Pol. and Soc. Sc.*, Vol. CCLI. 1947.
22. Charles, E. *The Menace of Under-Population*. London: Watts. 1936.

CHAPTER VI

SOME NEGLECTED ASPECTS OF WORLD INTEGRATION

by J. C. Flugel

THE PREVENTION OF WAR: THREE COMPLEMENTARY APPROACHES

AMONG the sparse blessings of the present time we may count as one the general conviction that war is undesirable. With the collapse of the Nazi and Fascist systems there are no longer any vocal representatives of the long line of thinkers who have looked upon war as in itself a good and noble undertaking. But most men, though they consider war an evil, are yet impelled to think it may be unavoidable, or if not unavoidable at least preferable to the alternatives of domination by an alien race or the imposition of what seems to them an intolerable political regime. Distasteful and horrifying as is the prospect of war to almost every human being, the problem of the prevention of war has still to be faced. Hence this book and many others dealing with the same all too familiar theme. Hence also lectures, speeches, pamphlets, debates, articles and sermons in a thousand different places and many different tongues, all devoted to a problem the solution of which seems no less difficult than it is vital. It is humiliating and perplexing that with general agreement as to the danger and undesirability of war, humanity should yet have discovered no means whereby it can avoid being dragged into it against its will. No wonder that the more thoughtful members of our race should everywhere be addressing themselves to this problem, at once so intriguing in its psychological and moral implications and so urgent in its practical appeal.

The suggestions for the prevention of war that have so far been put forward can be variously classified. Most conveniently perhaps they can be considered as falling into three main groups, the moral, the political and the psychological. The first of these, which is the oldest, we might almost say the classical, method of approach, is based upon the obvious consideration that war with its resort to force, violence, murder and destruction is utterly opposed to that kind of conduct which nearly all the great religious and moral teachers have thought to be desirable; it is essentially an appeal to our moral and religious sentiments. The second, which also goes back to antiquity, though it has vastly increased in importance in recent centuries (and

H

especially in the last few decades), seeks a remedy not in moral improvement but rather in political and legal organization; it represents the line along which most of our active contemporary endeavours are being concentrated. The third approach is more essentially modern. It recognizes the importance of the urges that impel to war and of the very real satisfactions which (alongside of its evils) war can provide. It seeks to determine the nature of these urges and satisfactions and in the light of the knowledge thus obtained to modify or deflect the urges and to provide possible alternative sources of satisfaction. It is the method which was perhaps first clearly suggested in William James's famous essay on "The Moral Equivalent of War", and which has in still more recent times been followed by those who seek to unravel the connection between war and human aggression generally as manifested from nursery days onwards.

While all of these approaches clearly have their place, it would seem fairly certain that, correctly regarded, they are complementary rather than alternative. Moral appeal, here as in so many other directions, is often helpless when opposed to powerful psychological or social forces. Political and legal organization is of little avail without the will or force to implement it, while studies of individual aggressiveness or of the individual satisfactions found in war and combat generally have to be supplemented by the study of war as essentially a conflict between large adult human groups. Morals and psychology have to take account of the fact that war is a group phenomenon, but the fact that war is an affair of groups does not mean that the findings of morals and psychology are inapplicable to it.

All three approaches should thus be co-ordinated and the essential task consists in discovering where and how the necessary connection between them can and should be made. Nevertheless, in order that we may avail ourselves of paths already trodden, it is perhaps permissible to review these approaches in the order named, considering them, however, from the point of view of the psychology of groups, especially of national groups, which are those between which in our present age wars are chiefly waged.

THE MORAL AND RELIGIOUS APPROACH

Few if any religious or ethical systems have successfully forbidden war, though some have enjoined non-violence in strong terms. Christianity which, judging by the teachings of its Founder, should have been a religion of non-violence, has lamentably failed in this respect, the God of Love having all too often become the God of

Battles. Since the fall of the Roman Empire and before, Christians have been continually fighting one another and the ministers of Christ have been often willing to bless the arms that were to butcher and enslave their fellow-Christians. Theological belief and moral precept have proved impotent in the face of military ardour, patriotic appeal or political expediency. We can only speculate as to what would have happened had the leaders of the Church at the zenith of its powers made a resolute attempt to live up to (and to make their followers live up to) the precepts of their Teacher. Today when political sentiments have so largely taken the place of those formerly centred round religion, their powers are obviously far more limited, but there seems little doubt that, even now, were the great religious organizations to proclaim with a united voice that war is utterly incompatible with the dictates of religion, they would be a potent source of good in this direction and would incidentally add immensely to their own prestige. The respect which has been felt for the Quakers and sundry others who have consistently practised non-violence (including Mr. Gandhi as an outstanding individual) testifies to this. But on the whole, religious bodies, like the secular moralists, have been unable to understand or to cope with the problems of morals in the mass. Their appeal has been primarily to the conscience of the individual, and though the saying *vox populi vox Dei* has been current for many generations, its full implication, i.e. that group emotion drowns—or, more strictly speaking, replaces—both the voice of individual conscience and the voice of God seems hardly to have been realized, so that the necessary precautions against the swamping of individual morality by group emotion have not been taken.

The Christian religion, with its early converts chiefly from among the poor and relatively powerless and with the absorption of much of its energies in theological and other-worldish problems, had always been weak in the application of its moral doctrines to mundane and political affairs, except in so far as they linked up with religious dogma or ecclesiastical power. But in any case the moralization of group behaviour is a hard task, the full difficulties of which we have, thanks to the labours of modern social psychologists from Le Bon onwards, only recently begun to appreciate. Alike in its psychological mechanisms and in its recognized sphere of application, morality is primarily an affair of individuals, and certain special efforts both of thought and of social organization are required before it begins to manifest itself in the relations between groups. Hence these relations are often on a lower moral plane than those between individuals.

Some writers indeed, such as Reinhold Niebuhr in his *Moral Man and Immoral Society*, have pessimistically assumed that they must necessarily be so. Here is a colossal problem for the moralist and social psychologist which is still awaiting detailed study. Pending the results of such investigation we need not perhaps be blankly pessimistic. It seems fairly clear that groups which are integrated into a greater whole are capable of behaving decently to one another and can indeed perhaps exercise a morally uplifting influence one upon the other, sometimes in the form of moral rivalry. But we must probably agree that intra-group behaviour is on the whole far more moral than inter-group behaviour; and in so far as the latter is moral it is often because the groups in question are for certain purposes themselves members of a larger group, so that it can at bottom be reduced to behaviour of the intra-group variety.

This would seem to be a matter of great import, some of the wider implications of which we will deal with presently. For the moment we may notice that the groups whose behaviour is most conspicuously and disastrously lacking in morality are national sovereign states. In virtue of their sovereignty they tend to recognize no legal or moral obligations except to themselves and (temporarily and so long as it may prove convenient) to their allies. These are the groups which provide the menace to peace, and which it was sought to control by international law and to integrate into a larger whole by means of the United Nations and formerly by the League of Nations. All three of these endeavours afford evidence, of course, of a realization for the need for control of our 'immoral' national societies. The small measure of their success when in opposition to real or assumed national interests reveals the true difficulty of the task. It is our dawning realization of this difficulty that is belatedly and still on all too small a scale beginning to direct the interests of social psychologists and large social organizations (we may mention particularly the United Nations Educational, Scientific, and Cultural Organization's Project for Research on International Tensions) to the urgent necessity for research in this direction. In our next two sections I shall deal with certain aspects of the manifold problems with which they will find themselves concerned. Before passing on to these, however, we may well note that a fuller realization of the immorality of nations clarifies the goal for what we have called the moral or religious approach to the problem of the prevention of war. This approach needs to concern itself not with the general preaching of morality, which has been heard *ad nauseam*, but with its particular application to the behaviour of nation states. There is an urgent need for such states to realize that the precepts of morality apply to them in their relations with other human groups as much as to individuals in their relations with their fellow-men. As regards the latter it is considered virtuous for a man to forgo some personal advantage if this involves injustice, hardship or unkindness to another. We are only beginning dimly to realize that the same holds true of states, that modesty, humility, charity, self-sacrifice and neighbourliness may be as becoming to states as they are to individuals, and that boastfulness, bullying, aggressiveness and breach of faith are as morally contemptible in a nation as they would be in an individual.

States as such, however, have no minds: only the individuals who compose them are capable of feeling shame or moral obligation. In the last resort it is therefore still to individuals that the appeal must be made, not, however, on behalf of their own purely personal behaviour but as citizens who are ultimately responsible for the behaviour of their states. They must be made to feel that they are their nation's keepers and that when their nation behaves disgracefully they are themselves disgraced. The chief difficulty in achieving such an attitude lies in the fact that it involves resistance to the very natural tendency for the individual to hand over his conscience to the group and to feel relieved of all personal responsibility in the face of group power and group emotion. Collective responsibility is nevertheless far from impossible. A man feels to some extent responsible for the behaviour of his family, his school, his ship, his regiment and sundry other collectivities with which from time to time he may identify himself. It is only a further extension to the state that is required, and if the moral approach is to be at all effective, its aim must be to produce just this extension.

There are, of course, a number of methods by which the task can be made a little easier, and these themselves deserve careful exploration. One would consist in endeavouring to produce a more general appreciation of our human liability to hand over our conscience wholesale to a group ('Twenty thousand little monkeys can't be wrong' as a popular song once put it) or a dictator ('Mussolini is always right' as the Italian youth was taught). Perhaps indeed a judicious use of irony, as indicated for instance by the two phrases we have put in brackets, might help in this direction. In the second place the appeal can be linked up with the emotional value of democracy (in the western sense), for democracy involves both the right to a say in the conduct of a nation and a corresponding responsibility for that conduct. In a democracy each citizen can say with a certain element of truth 'L'État, c'est moi', meaning alike that he possesses to some extent power of direction, pride in achievement and trusteeship in a moral sense. In the third place, if with Ranyard West[1] we could adopt the view that law is the embodiment of the collective conscience and that international law is therefore the conscience of mankind, we might go an appreciable way towards investing the somewhat arid and intellectual concept of international law with the emotional energy which alone will give it some real effective power. Fourthly, and perhaps of most importance, it will be well as often as possible to supplement the cold abstract notion of the state with the warm concrete images of individuals, not, of course, the 'stereotyped' individuals corresponding to the traditional notion of the Englishman, German, Frenchman, Russian, Japanese, etc., but real men and women in all their rich humanity and variety. John Hersey's account of the atom-bombing of Hiroshima owed its shattering effect very largely to the circumstance that it was written entirely in terms of individual experience and thus aroused a sympathy and fellow-feeling which no description of impersonal horrors, however eloquent, could have evoked. The more we are made to think of what war means to individuals, the blasting of their bodies, the racking of their minds, the blighting of their hopes and the utter disorganization of their plans, the pathetic destruction of the little things they loved and used—all of them matters which we ourselves can understand from our own personal experience—the more will the monstrous moral iniquity of war be made manifest to us.

This leads us naturally to a fifth step. Sympathy with others helps us to see things from their point of view, so that we can adopt not a crudely condemnatory attitude but an enlightened understanding one. Just as in dealing with a 'naughty' child or with a young delinquent it is, we are beginning to realize, usually more profitable to try to understand the culprit's psychological motives and mechanisms than blindly to punish or to blame, so also with the delinquencies of nations. Nations are indeed extraordinarily like naughty children in much of their behaviour. As I[2] have put it in more detail elsewhere, they are apt to display a painful resemblance to schoolboys in their least engaging moments, and this in itself suggests that methods appropriate to the one form of trouble may be appropriate also to the

[1]*Conscience and Society*, 1942.
[2]"The Moral Paradox of Peace and War," *Conway Memorial Lecture*, 1941.

other; and as Susan Isaacs[1] representing much recently acquired psychological wisdom has said, children need a "good strict" parental figure to save them (and others) from the consequences of their own aggression. It is the same kind of understanding but helpfully controlling influence that is needed by the nations, and in so far as we rely on moral or religious persuasion in attempting to prevent war, it must be of this sort—of the same sort ultimately as any successful reformer of youth, be it parent, priest, physician, magistrate or social worker, would bring to bear in his dealings with an asocial boy or girl. How to institute such an authority and to integrate it with our other efforts towards peace is itself a problem which we have hardly yet begun clearly to envisage. One thing, however, is already fairly certain. As is the case with individual delinquents, we must find outlets for the activities of nations that do not run counter to, but are in harmony with, the general good; and this we can best do by enlisting their services, and indeed their friendly rivalry, in some worth-while co-operative undertaking—a most important point to which we shall return.

All that we have said so far with reference to nations and their individual citizens applies of course specially to the leaders of nations and those who exercise authority in one nation's dealings with another. Indeed we must refrain from exaggerating the power and importance of the ordinary citizen, real and significant though his influence and responsibility may be. All democracies, especially the vast ones of the modern world, depend for their successful working on the delegation of authority, and the most that the ordinary citizen can do is to ensure within the measure of his powers that his elected representatives live up to the standards which he himself upholds. If it is true that a country gets the government that it deserves (and in a democratic country it is surely the case to a considerable extent) this should present no insuperable difficulty. A good statesman, moreover, is one who really leads his country, does not merely follow it. In so far as statesmen are slightly in advance of the general run of citizens as regards their attitude to international morality, there will be a good prospect of the age of pre-adolescent anarchy among the nations soon coming to an end. But in turn there is need of a special study of the peculiar temptations to which statesmen themselves are subjected. Just as the driver of a high-powered car needs to beware of the sense of omnipotence with which the control of such mighty machinery may endow him, so also must those who control the terrific power

[1] *The Social Development of Young Children*, 1934.

of a modern industrial nation be on their guard against the reactivation of infantile or schizophrenic fantasies of world destruction, of the kind against which Glover in particular has warned us.[1] We can hardly feel safe in this respect until we have ensured the proper moral and psychological education of our statesmen.

Thus the moral approach to the prevention of war reveals itself on inspection to be considerably wider than it might at first appear. It is a necessary and legitimate approach, but one which must be used in a variety of directions, some of which have hardly yet been tried or even contemplated; furthermore it must be adroitly blended with sympathetic insight and psychological understanding. Only then will it develop its full usefulness.

THE POLITICAL APPROACH

The difficulties of the present age are largely due to the existence of a mighty struggle between two apparently incompatible principles. On one side is the tendency towards the creation of 'One World', to use Wendell Willkie's terse, expressive phrase; a tendency fostered by all those developments of science which have, to use another phrase, 'annihilated space,' which have brought peoples on different portions of the earth's surface into closer contact and inter-dependence. On the other is the recrudescence of a vigorous sense of nationhood which divides the world into regions with frontiers more jealously watched and guarded than perhaps at any previous period; regions, too, which are often distinguished from one another by differences of language and of political or economic systems or ideals. We cannot here enter further into the origin, nature and relative desirability of these two great conflicting tendencies. We must accept them as facts (as most contemporary thought and practical endeavour have accepted them) and consider only whether it is possible to prevent the conflict between them leading humanity to chaos and disaster, perhaps even to destruction.

The League of Nations was a noble experiment towards finding a solution. On the purely political side at least it has proved an utter failure. The United Nations Organization is a new attempt, which has not yet failed but is already meeting with considerable difficulty. Both schemes have endeavoured to impose a system of wider integration upon existing national states, a system which inevitably would restrict their 'sovereign powers' but which does not seek to destroy them as existing centres of loyalty and integration. It is clear that in both cases

[1]Edward Glover. *War, Sadism and Pacifism*, 2nd ed. 1947.

the chief difficulty has lain in the imposition of the wider integration. The older and for the most part well-established national units vigorously resist any infringement of their sovereignty and in any serious conflict of interests the strong loyalties they evoke almost always prevail against the claims of the new and relatively upstart organization which seeks to represent the interests of humanity as a whole. Clearly then one of the essential tasks is the creation of a strong emotional appeal in favour of the wider organization. Its importance and the beneficence of its functions must be brought home to the populations of the world in such a way that a new loyalty to it will be created. In the second place this new loyalty must as far as possible be made to harmonize with, rather than conflict with, the older, national loyalties.

Neither of these steps would seem to present any really insuperable difficulty. There are quite a number of examples—on a large scale and a small—of federation or integration of smaller units with a larger whole. The amalgamation of business and administrative concerns has been a constant feature of twentieth-century history. On the academic side the relations of the Colleges to the Universities of Oxford and Cambridge are suggestive, while on the vaster political scale we have the various examples presented by Switzerland, the United States, the British Commonwealth and Empire, and the Soviet Union. From all of these no doubt something can be learnt, both positively as providing happy, relatively frictionless examples of integration, and negatively as revealing sources of discord to be avoided. The chief points to be studied, however, for the purpose here in view, are not concerned with legal or administrative forms but with the creation of loyalty and goodwill on the part of all who are involved. No doubt all these examples differ significantly from the particular problem of integration of nations into the world-wide organization of UNO, but so far as they go, they are encouraging as showing that loyalty to a whole that embraces them all can be achieved by units that were (and in some respects may still be) in mutual competition. There is thus every indication that the task is not impossible. On the other hand the requisite measures on a sufficient scale have hardly yet been undertaken. UNO, like the League of Nations before it, has relied far too much upon a purely intellectual appreciation of its necessity, and the propaganda in its favour has been sadly lacking in emotional punch, tending to create 'principles' rather than 'sentiments' in McDougall's sense.[1] In other words it

[1] *Character and the Conduct of Life*, 1927, pp. 76ff.

has given rise to a feeling that UNO *ought* to be supported rather than an intense and urgent need on our own part to the effect that we *must* support it. And yet what fine opportunities for emotional appeal are ready to our hand! UNO itself is a name pregnant with the suggestion of a United Mankind inhabiting One World; with its centre at Lake Success, a word of potent augury, and its various subsidiary meetings held at pleasant and interesting places throughout the earth, as though to give each constituent country a sense of participation in its deliberations and achievements. It is this sense of participation which is the most important step for healing the apparent conflict between national and international interests. The nations should be made to feel that their own well-being is inseparably bound up with the success of UNO—as indeed it is, in any sense of true prosperity and safety, as distinct from that of a largely meaningless but dangerous 'sovereignty'. One obvious step towards this is to devise for UNO the symbols to which we are accustomed in our patriotic loyalties and then to employ them on all suitable occasions in association with the corresponding national symbols, so that the two loyalties may, so to speak, fuse together. A flag was devised for the League of Nations, but seldom if ever used officially. UNO also has a flag, but at the moment of writing the mere fact of its existence, let alone the nature of its design, seems to be known to very few. This deficiency should be make good and the display of the UNO colours together with a national flag would symbolize most eloquently the harmony between patriotic and international aspirations, so that we should feel that in honouring the one we were also paying our respects to the world organization to which as a nation and as individual citizens we are proud and happy to belong. An anthem also is required, as regards the choice of which a competition open to all composers of the world, the tunes to be judged by an international jury of musicians, if adequately publicized, might arouse an interest worthy of the great issue at stake; and again the playing of the anthem in conjunction with the familiar national one would help to consolidate the two loyalties in the way required.

These matters of flag and anthem will be particularly important in connection with the armed forces which it is proposed that UNO shall have at its disposal. Here, even more than elsewhere, the problem of creating an integration rather than a conflict of loyalties will become acute, and here too, even more than elsewhere, the most hopeful means would seem to consist in resorting to symbols of the old familiar kind.

In more general matters too UNO can hardly afford to dispense with the arts of the propagandist and the advertiser, and in turn it is difficult to imagine that these arts can ever be put in the service of a better or more vital cause. In view of the fact that our lives and all that we hold dear may well depend on their success, the nature and activities of UNO and its satellite organizations ought to be of deep and daily concern to us. Its leading personalities and the places where they meet should evoke images no less warm and intimate than those of our own sovereign, our chief statesman of the moment and our Houses of Parliament. Yet it is almost certain that only a tiny fraction of the world's educated people could call up a recognizable image of Mr. Trygve Lie or Lake Success or could pick them out from half a dozen pictures of other people and places. UNO clearly needs a publicity department that will put it and keep it on the map of our daily thoughts and aspirations and that will produce in us some real thrill at the possibilities it opens up. Attractive pamphlets with pictures and diagrams that 'jump to the eye' should figure prominently on our bookstalls. There should be broadcasts, similar perhaps to "The Week in Westminster" or "Today in Parliament" which should present short and pithy reports of the chief speeches and the principal subjects of discussion or brief accounts of leading personalities. Our cinemas should drive home the appeal (perhaps under some such general heading as "The World in Council") with short documentaries illustrating the problems with which UNO and UNESCO have to deal. In schools the activities of UNO should be brought into intimate relation with the teaching of geography, while a central publicity office should be in intimate touch with United Nation Societies or bodies with a similar function in all member nations, feeding them with up-to-date information and encouraging its dissemination by means of lectures, debates, discussions or travelling exhibitions which could visit the remoter towns and villages.

If UNO means anything at all, it is an experiment of vast and stirring significance, which in its colourful variety of personalities, places, and problems, should well repay a little showmanship. Nor need it lose in dignity or efficiency thereby. In recent years large and powerful nations have themselves become advertisers on a considerable scale, for it has been realized that the successful working of a complex modern state requires the understanding and co-operation of all individual citizens. How much greater is the need of UNO, itself a new and all too little-understood organization, with few or no traditions behind it, and dealing, as it must, with problems which often concern primarily certain remote and only dimly realized (but none the less important) regions of the world! And as to efficiency, adequate propaganda, besides increasing the general popular interest and drive behind UNO, would surely also afford encouragement to those actively participating in its deliberations and decisions, while their sense of responsibility would be increased by the knowledge that 'the eyes and ears of the world' were focused on their doings. National governments in their turn would have an increased respect for UNO, aware that their own citizens were well informed concerning it, were ready to play their part in implementing its decisions and were looking towards the advantages that increased world co-operation would bring in its train. Finally, as to the cost of propaganda such as we have indicated, it would, of course, be considerable, especially perhaps in the early stages. Nevertheless, it would be trifling compared with the cost of armaments and the increased economic difficulties that would be unavoidable in the event of UNO's failure, and after a little while when the proceedings of UNO had acquired recognized news value, a good deal of the expense might well be borne by existing agencies connected with the Press, broadcasting, the cinema, etc.

In referring above to the question of an anthem, no suggestion was made of the words or the language to be used. In an anthem the tune is more important than the words, for it is likely to be far more often played than sung. Nevertheless, for active participation by the general public singing is necessary, and for singing there must be words. The choice of a text should hardly be a matter of great difficulty; there must be quite a number of suitable verses in a variety of languages, or alternatively there are plenty of writers who would be prepared to produce new ones. But when we come to a choice of language we are obviously on more difficult ground. Shall there be versions in many different languages, so that each world-citizen may sing it in his own tongue? This would seem the obvious solution for immediate purposes. But it is evident that we are here touching the fringe of a vast problem. Like any other international organizations, UNO and its satellites must inevitably be handicapped by the diversity of language among those concerned. True, it has been amply shown that important legislative and administrative bodies can carry on their work, even though the proceedings have to be bilingual or trilingual. True also, that, with the help of highly skilled interpreters and a somewhat costly equipment, the modern technique of 'simultaneous translation' is capable of overcoming many of the disadvantages inherent in a polyglot assembly. UNO as a world assembly is worthy of the finest skill and equipment that the world can produce, and its own proceedings may thus suffer comparatively little from the barriers of language. But as the embodiment and creative centre of a united world, it (or its important satellite UNESCO) ought surely to concern itself with the choice of a second language to be taught in the schools of all member nations, so that educated men may be able to communicate freely with one another, whatever part of the earth they may inhabit and whatever mother-language they may speak. 'One world' can only be a world the different parts of which are intelligible to one another through the peculiarly human medium of speech, and the overcoming of the curse of Babel is surely a necessary step in the creation of such a world. It is a step that would fulfil the dreams of many thinkers from Descartes and Leibniz onwards, and the taking of that step would be an incomparable gesture signifying the active will to greater world-wide understanding. It is a step too which can perhaps only be officially taken by a body with the powers and prestige of UNESCO but which by it could be taken most appropriately, as one that is in fullest harmony with its great and noble function.

Practically and linguistically the adoption of a second tongue for all would be a relatively easy matter, though it would naturally take a few years before a sufficient supply of teachers could be gathered to implement the decision on a world-wide scale. It is where the choice of the language in question is concerned that difficulties are likely to arise—and these difficulties are almost entirely of an emotional kind. Some of them have been already dealt with by the present writer[1] and there is no call to enter into detail here. Suffice it to say that the first matter for decision is whether choice shall be made of an existing 'natural' language or of an artificial language. The advantages and disadvantages of the former are fairly obvious. A natural language is a 'going concern', spoken by many people; there is no question that it works and in some cases (e.g. especially with English in India and elsewhere) it is already used as a means of communication by those whose native language it is not but who have no other tongue in common. On the other hand, natural languages are mostly difficult to learn, with their queer spellings, strange pronunciations, peculiar idiomatic expressions, complex and eccentric grammars, while the proposed choice of any one of them is apt to arouse fierce rivalries,

[1]"Some Psychological Aspects of the International Language Movement with Special Reference to Esperanto" in *Men and Their Motives*, 1934.

partly on matters of prestige, partly because whatever choice is made it would confer some real advantage on those who speak it as their native tongue. The choice of an artificial language would largely obviate these difficulties. It is far easier to acquire (according to experiments conducted under the supervision of Thorndike[1] the time spent in learning is from five to fifteen times as profitable—as measured by linguistic progress—as time spent on a natural language) and it is 'neutral', inasmuch as being a learnt language for all, it confers no special prestige or practical advantage on any particular linguistic group. The difficulties here might seem to lie: (1) in the question of whether an artificial language really works, (2) in the selection of any one artificial language from among the numerous schemes propounded, (3) in the conflicting emotions, loyalties and jealousies that tend to be aroused both by the general idea of an artificial language and by the choice of any one of them. Here again it is the third or emotional category that is important; the first two difficulties dwindle on inspection. Of the hundred or more linguistic schemes put forward only some half-dozen have actually been put to use at all, and only one of them—Esperanto—has been consistently used in a practically unaltered form for a long period. The sixty years' test of this last-named language, including its exclusive official use in more than thirty international congresses and the creation of a not inconsiderable literature, puts it in a class apart and in itself gives a satisfactory answer to the question whether an artificial language really works. It is clear from the history of the subject that what has more than anything else prevented the spread of an artificial auxiliary language has been the constant flow of fresh projects and the desire to modify existing ones, rather than any inherent social or linguistic difficulty. It is the somewhat dogmatic loyalty (if we like, we can call it fanaticism) of Esperantists which has kept their language alive throughout the chaotic changes in world history since its inception and in spite of the counter-attractions provided by the numerous competing schemes. The experiment they have provided demonstrates clearly enough that an artificial language is a practical proposition, while the general spirit of Esperantism, which it took over from its founder, Dr. Zamenhof, is one that is entirely in harmony with the present need for a united world; linguistically it stands in the same relation to natural languages as UNO stands politically to the nations which it 'organizes'. It

[1] E. L. Thorndike. *Human Learning*, 1931; *Language Learning*: Summary of a Report to the International Auxiliary Language Association in the United States, 1933.

would seem only appropriate that UNO should avail itself of this instrument which is so admirably suited to its purpose and which lies ready to its hand. The present writer, however, cannot claim to be himself free from the emotional bias that affects this subject. All that he would urge is that the subject is important, highly germane to the activities and ideals of UNO, and that it merits full unprejudiced investigation. By officially sponsoring an international language UNO would take a big step towards the implementation of its aims.

In all that we have said so far we have been dealing with form rather than with matter—with the measures that UNO or any comparable international organization should take to make itself effective and to foster the spirit of world unity in which alone it can fulfil its function. It cannot be our business here to consider all the detailed steps that UNO will have to take in promoting the smooth working and integration, of world society as a super-national unity—which steps may be regarded as the 'matter' of its deliberations and decisions. As a transition, however, from problems of 'form' or machinery to problems of 'matter', we might raise the question whether there are not certain general principles that might be adopted, in the light of which more detailed and specific problems should be considered as and when they arise and with the help of which they might find a more consistent and satisfactory solution. The prior acceptance of certain general principles might save much subsequent dispute, not to speak of inconsistent and unjust decisions, in much the same way as the existence of certain laws or legal principles reduces injustice and facilitates legal decisions by enabling each case to be subsumed under a particular relevant law or principle.

At least one such set of principles is already being prepared. I refer to the Universal Declaration of Human Rights—a sequel to the attempt at an up-to-date version of the 'rights of man' made by the distinguished committee that sat under the chairmanship of Lord Sankey. After preliminary consideration over more than two years this Declaration was finally passed and proclaimed by the General Assembly of UNO on December 10th, 1948. It represents the first part of an International Bill of Human Rights, the other two parts being a Convention on Human Rights and measures for implementation respectively. At the very least this represents a real effort on the part of the collective conscience of mankind to face difficult, delicate and controversial moral questions. It will establish an ideal which we may not always be able to live up to, but which will at least help to guide us in the right direction. It may also help to clear the air between the great competing social systems of communism and western democracy. The Soviet has made it clear that it is even more keen than the western nations on the economic and social rights, the right to regular work and leisure, to social security and so on, as also concerning the absence of racial discrimination (a matter on which it has perhaps made one of its greatest contributions to human culture). It cannot, on the other hand, see its way to agree that the individual has rights of appeal against the state, a very essential matter to the western mind. During discussion of the draft Declaration the Soviet delegation reserved its right to present later 'a Soviet draft declaration of human rights'. If this materializes, the subsequent discussion may succeed in focusing the clear light of thought upon one of the sharpest points of difference between the assumptions underlying the two great systems which at the moment threaten to divide the world, and clear thought is a very valuable means of dispelling dangerous and turbulent emotions. If in this relatively limited but important sphere the commission can succeed in substituting for the notion of competing and utterly conflicting ideologies the spirit of co-operation in which each partner brings his own values and experience to bear upon the common task, this particular venture of UNO will have more than justified itself, even apart from the ultimate consequences of the Declaration of Human Rights itself.

There are, of course, many other matters in which the preliminary formulation of general principles may be a useful task. There is the great field of racial, cultural and religious differences, which are already vexing the world in many quarters and which are likely to cause still greater difficulties in the near future (e.g. the colour question in the United States and in South Africa). The Declaration of Rights itself goes some way to meet the great problems that arise within this field, but further guidance is clearly called for in certain directions, and here the world of the western democracies may surely draw upon the experience of the Soviet Union in its apparently successful experiments in dealing with the amalgamation within its system of a great variety of social cultures and races.

Closely connected with questions of race and culture is the problem of the varying density and pressure of population in the different countries of the world. Here, in the opinion of the present writer, is a supreme example of a 'neglected aspect of world integration', but as he has dealt with this at some length elsewhere[1] there is no need

[1] *Population, Psychology and Peace*, 1947.

for further detailed elaboration in the present chapter. As with the cases of international language and of racial and cultural differences within a given border, we are here face to face with problems which are made difficult by the deep emotions that they frequently arouse. But that is only an additional reason why they should be considered as matters of principle, to be discussed in the relative calm of the council chamber before they are actually forced on us in an acute form by the outbreak of some bitter conflict. If it is to fulfil its functions smoothly, the United Nations must display foresight into the problems of the near future as well as tact and insight in dealing with those which actually confront us and demand immediate treatment. Nowhere perhaps are the future problems more menacing and difficult than in the matter of population, and nowhere is it more important that matters of principle should be faced and settled while there is yet time. Just as the individual human organism can more easily deal with a potentially traumatic situation if it is prepared for it, so also no doubt the vastly more complex organism of human society as a whole. The necessary work of preparation is one of the most essential and beneficent tasks that falls within the purview of UNO as the embodiment of the world in council.

The Psychological Approach

The psychological approach to the problem of war prevention is concerned with the mental conditions that conduce to war, the impulses that find satisfaction in it and the possibility of reducing their intensity or of so modifying their expression that they can find another and less harmful outlet. It is a vast field about which we still really know very little.

Since war itself consists of aggressive social action, it is presumed that the aggressive impulses or the 'fighting instinct' of the individual play an important part in it; hence, it has been suggested, the development of aggression from the earliest days of life onwards is not irrelevant to the problem. Furthermore, since, by almost general consent among psychologists, aggression is (whatever else it may be) a natural reaction to the frustration of desire, it would seem to follow that, if we wish to keep aggression within manageable bounds, we must seek to abolish unnecessary frustration. A country where essential needs are reasonably satisfied would, it is presumed, be less liable to go to war than one whose inhabitants are suffering from serious discontent or irritation, whether openly manifested or suppressed. In the latter case the people feel that they have little or nothing to lose by going to war, and will welcome the relief afforded by the opportunity of expressing their aggression against a foe who can be made the scapegoat responsible for all their ills, while in the former case they will have much to lose and relatively little to gain.

As to how far the liability to war is connected with the arousal and treatment of aggression in early years, we can still do little more than guess, though there is perhaps some evidence that unnecessary harshness of upbringing may help to foster an attitude in later life which may be conducive to war and other forms of violence. The general question of the possibility of reducing aggression by diminishing frustration is suggestively treated by Dolland *et al.* in their *Frustration and Aggression* and by Money Kyrle in his *Aspasia*, who stresses particularly the importance of frustration of the sexual impulses both in earlier and later life. The immensely strong prohibitions and consequent inhibitions in the sexual sphere are certainly a great source of frustration which may well merit far more consideration in this connection than it usually receives. The whole problem, however, is greatly complicated by guilt and super-ego reactions, which may result, among other things, in a turning of the aggressive impulses against the self—the nemesistic process as, following Rosenzweig, I have elsewhere ventured to call it. The risk of war could conceivably be much reduced, either by a great relaxation of sexual constraints, which would reduce frustration, or by a great increase in ascetic practices, which would help to substitute an inward for an outward direction of aggression.

We are also largely ignorant as to how far war tends to be fostered or prevented by the expression of aggression in other social spheres, e.g. by aggressive play, competition in business or sport, duelling or personal quarrels. On the one hand these latter may increase the risk of war by encouraging aggression generally (in virtue of what some psychologists have called the 'law of development by stimulation'). On the other hand it may reduce it by affording other outlets (where, therefore, the 'law of the displacement of impulse' would be operative). Connected with this are such questions as the following, the full answers to which are still to a large extent unknown:

What is the relation of free speech to the likelihood of war and other forms of violence? (It is often held that free speech, with the opportunity it affords for abreactive denunciation, is on the whole a valuable safety valve, preventing the accumulation of suppressed aggression; on the other hand it must also have some inflammatory influence.)

Is playing at soldiers in youth—either with leaden toys or in mock fighting between gangs—conducive or not to a warlike attitude in later life? (Experiments in 'transfer of training' may have some bearing here. If so, we might perhaps expect that there would be little transfer unless the 'common elements' were stressed.)

Is sport, especially international sport, a substitute for war by draining off aggressive energies into a harmless but exciting field, or does it at bottom foster war by promoting the idea of competition between nations, aggravating questions of national prestige, etc.? (Here again perhaps much depends on 'transfer', though the super-ego element involved in sport, both in adherence to rules and to certain unwritten laws of 'sportsmanship' are important as contrasting strongly with the 'all in' nature of 'total' war.)

In view of the general belief—for which there seems considerable justification—that women are on the whole swayed relatively less by the group loyalties that are involved in war and relatively more by the individual and family loyalties that are antagonistic to it, would it be advisable to confine to women (or failing this to men with a similar distribution of loyalties) all posts which involve the making of decisions between peace and war? (We may well get the impression that in a thorough-going gynaecocracy there would be more petty squabbling than in a world governed by men, but in view of the horrific possibilities of modern war, the alternative of increased 'cattiness' might on the whole be a distinctly preferable one.)

In addition there is the question of 'patterns of culture'. According to the culture-pattern school, a 'pattern' selects from among the vast possibilities of human nature and encourages those impulses and those channels of expression which fit in with it, while neglecting or discouraging others which do not harmonize with it. The evidence which this school has produced so far is of a striking character, and the general views that they have based upon it are far more optimistic than the opinions of those who lay more stress upon the fundamental similarity of human instinctive equipment. These are views which deserve the fullest investigation and appraisal from our present stand-point; it would seem indeed that an intensive study of the kinds of culture-patterns that are associated with peaceful, as distinct from warlike, inter-group activities would constitute one of the most urgent and promising directions for immediate research. If we understood more thoroughly the nature of such patterns, it does not, of course, follow that we could at once produce them in a world the parts of which, though more interdependent than ever before, are still distinguished by wide differences in existing culture. But we could set about the task with greater insight than we seem likely to derive in a comparable time from any other branch of study.

Here at least is a bright ray of hope, though it may still prove an illusory one. Elsewhere, however, the outlook seems black, so far as concerns the acquisition of reasonably sure knowledge in a reasonable time. The variables are so many and the problems so complex that Glover's suggestion[1] of a research body required to make interim reports every fifty years and major reports at intervals of a hundred years seems far less fantastic than it might at first appear. But if our ability to prevent war should depend upon the fruits of such research alone, it would seem only too likely that, with the continued rapid progress of physical science, our civilization will be in ruins long before the research body in question will have had an opportunity of completing even the preliminary stages of its inquiries.

Faced by our urgent present difficulties, we may, therefore, feel ourselves compelled to fall back on such 'hunches' or incomplete knowledge as we have, hoping that they will enable us to escape our more immediate dangers and that progress in social science will eventually allow humanity to steer its course in such a way as to avoid the self-inflicted catastrophes that threaten it.

Our most promising hunches so far concern on the one hand the avoidance of excessive frustration, and on the other the direction of aggression into harmless (or even profitable) channels. These might be called respectively the negative and positive psychological approaches, and both may be linked up with the questions of loyalty and social integration that we dealt with in the last section.

On the negative side (leaving out of account the doubtful but possibly very important frustrations of early life) we must clearly seek to reduce the obvious discontents of adults which may lead them to seek or accept war as an outlet for their aggression and as a not unwelcome change from a painful or monotonous existence. These frustrations may themselves be primarily material or directly psychological (though, of course, at bottom they are all psychological, since material conditions only exercise the effects that here concern us in virtue of the fact that they frustrate deep and essential psychological needs). Among the former are actual physical hardships caused by lack of food, housing, clothing, etc., together with the threats of hardship connected with economic insecurity and unemployment. An alarmingly large proportion of the world's population is suffering such hardship

[1] Edward Glover, op. cit.

(and has perhaps always done so), and to this extent there is always a large number of persons whose discontent may under suitable circumstances be canalized in war. So far as these causes of frustration are concerned, we may hand the problem over to the economists for their solution (perhaps, in so doing, asking them not to lose sight of the factor of population pressure, which, as indicated in our last section, may be particularly important in the present connection).

Turning to the more directly psychological causes, we are faced, by way of transition from these economic factors, with the question of satisfaction in work and the conditions under which work is carried out. Here the industrial psychologist comes into the picture. Adequate vocational guidance and selection, for instance, can clearly reduce much unnecessary discontent by ensuring as far as possible that each individual is doing work that is suited to his capacities and temperament. But from a wider point of view even this will hardly be sufficient. Work is seldom so absorbing that it constitutes an obvious end in itself; almost by definition it is an activity that is carried on for some ulterior object. This ulterior object must therefore in turn be satisfying and the relation between it and the work must be clearly realized. This applies not only to the economic reward of work but also to its wider social and ethical implications. At a relatively simple level it has, for instance, been found that repetitive industrial work becomes more satisfying and interesting if the worker can see exactly where his job fits into the total process of constructing some useful object (e.g. an aeroplane). Better still if he can be shown how important his particular job is for the efficient use of the object in question (as when, during the war, flyers came to an aircraft factory to explain from their own experiences the importance of good welding or riveting in enabling an aircraft to stand up to the strains to which it is exposed in war). At a still higher level it is highly conducive to a sense of satisfaction and personal worth if a worker is made to understand clearly that his work is of value to the community, that it plays an essential part in the welfare of the nation (and therefore ultimately of the world) as a whole. This is a point of view which (as research has shown) has been all too little appreciated, especially perhaps in time of peace—though the present shortage of labour and commodities is fortunately producing a much more vivid realization of the importance to the community of many forms of work which were formerly regarded with far less respect than was their due. It is a matter in which we can perhaps profitably learn something from the totalitarian regimes, and especially from Russia. It is a matter, too, which, in its bearing upon active group co-operation, leads us naturally to what we have called the positive psychological approach, the provision of sublimated outlets for 'aggressive' impulses.

One of the great advantages of war is that it provides an obvious and immediate purpose for social co-operation on the largest scale, so that each individual in 'doing his bit' feels that he is contributing to a great cause. It may not be possible or even desirable to have so much concentration and integration of effort in peacetime; life would lack that variety of values and outlook which is a characteristic of true civilization. Nevertheless some considerable sense of common value and endeavour there must be. We need to attain some condition intermediate between the quasi-fanaticism of war and the apathy, depression, and sense of loss of direction which afflicts humanity in so many parts of the earth today. In seeking the means for this we may learn something both from the condition of war itself and from the totalitarian regimes which, with all their evils of regimentation and suppression of individual freedom, have yet revealed very clearly the advantages to be derived from a sense of co-operative endeavour. Can we in some reasonable measure achieve the advantages without the attendant evils?

It is towards some such solution that the world seems to be groping, and in view of the precarious economic situation, of the vast shortage of necessaries of many kinds in many countries, the general nature of the immediate steps to be taken seem fairly clear. We must embark on a great co-ordinated work of 'reconstruction' in which the peoples of the world can join together in an effort that is at once for their own good and for the advantage of humanity in general. Since the cessation of hostilities, the Marshall Plan would seem to be by far the most hopeful and constructive step in this direction. It is indeed a magnificent gesture, the possible significance of which it is difficult to overrate. The richest and most powerful nation in the world, a nation, moreover, whose historical traditions had hitherto impelled it to remain as far as possible aloof from the political and economic difficulties of the rest of the world, has come forward with an offer of help to all those who are willing to co-operate in a great scheme of rehabilitation. It has said in effect that it is willing to share its great resources with all countries which are willing to help themselves within the framework of this great co-operative effort. Unfortunately the suspicions that divide the USSR from the western world have prevented this combined endeavour from embracing as large a portion of the earth as it might have done. Still, enough remains to achieve a very striking success, and the great enthusiasm that has greeted the idea of Western Union has shown that many people are ready to co-operate on a scale larger than any that seemed likely a little while ago. Had a great constructive proposal of a similar kind been in readiness some two years earlier, had it embraced all our allies and (what is no less important) our late enemies, we might now have been much farther advanced along the lines of united achievement. But the necessary preparation could hardly have been made while the efforts of so many nations were still engaged in the mere struggle for survival. And it may still not be too late. The door, though not yet fully opened, as it should be, to our late enemies, is still open to our great eastern ally, should she and her satellite countries see fit now or a little later to join in the constructive effort. Failing this, the next best course would seem to consist in inviting her to join in a sort of friendly rivalry. We might say to her in effect: "You believe in one system, we in another. Let us see which system can achieve most towards the building of a world good in all those aspects which we agree in considering to be desirable—and our systems, which seem to us so different, have yet many common values. Towards the attainment of some of these values we have (as we believe) made the greater contribution. We can regard our systems as great social experiments. Mankind as a whole will eventually judge which has been the more successful. Meanwhile, let us carry on with our experiments without putting difficulties in each other's way, confident that, in so far as our results are better, our methods and point of view will in the long run be approved and adopted by humanity".

The notion of friendly co-operative rivalry, comparable in some respects to the rivalry of scientists who hold different theories but are willing to put them to the test, is, of course, capable of application to national differences generally. Every nation and every culture has probably some form of excellence in which it has outstripped others, and to some extent (though perhaps not in its entirety, since it may depend upon a particular pattern which we cannot or may not wish to reproduce) its achievement may be adaptable for general use. If we regard our different national cultures as so many experiments, we may profit from them all—by way of acceptance and doubtless also by rejection. And if we can introduce something of the spirit of teamwork as it manifests itself in science, each nation can be proud of its experimental contribution. A pride in its achievements in the fields of art, literature, science, economic development, hygiene and social service may, we can hope, take the place of pride in mere size, numbers or power of arms. It will be the pride of the civilized man rather than that of the barbarian and bully. At the same time it is a pride which can be integrated with loyalty to the greater human whole of which the nation is a part.

Diversity of culture and some considerable difference in political and administrative systems can thus perhaps be made to harmonize with that degree of integration which alone can bring peace to the world. Nevertheless, at the present moment it is cohesion and co-opera-tion, rather than diversity, that we need to stress. Our strong or over-strong nationalistic sentiments and national traditions can be relied upon to preserve us from the dangers of a drab monotony. What is now required above all else is a strong co-operative drive for common ends, and for many administrative purposes it may be desirable to direct this effort along functional rather than along nationalistic lines. It is a striking fact that, while organizations on a federal basis and for rather general purposes (however admirable these purposes may be) have encountered all sorts of difficulties and obstructions con-nected with the real or supposed clash of national or ideological interests, organizations on a functional basis for relatively narrow and specific ends have often run with quite surprising smoothness. The International Postal Union has performed its work so quietly and efficiently even in this troubled twentieth century that we seldom have to think of its existence, while in more recent years the Inter-national Labour Office and sundry other functional organizations connected with the League of Nations achieved far greater success than did the League itself in the political sphere. It would seem advisable therefore that those aspects of the co-operative work of reconstruction which are specific, yet world-wide rather than regional in character, should be entrusted to organizations of a functional rather than an 'international' kind, i.e. the stress should be laid on the nature of the job rather than on the nationality of those under-taking it or on the way in which it may affect any given country. (And incidentally this suggests that in the main organization of UNO itself less stress should be laid on the nationality and more on the individuality of representatives, who should be no more closely associated with their country than say, members of Parliament, with their constituencies.)

Here too, however, there is still need for a sense of overall unity and integration. Functional, international and national organizations must alike feel that they are working as so many teams engaged upon various aspects of a common task and inspired by common ideals and purposes. And it is here that we come up against one last problem which we have not yet squarely faced. A nation, as we have already said, achieves its highest degree of co-operative integration in war, when it has to preserve and assert itself against an outer enemy. How is any organization of mankind to obtain a similar incentive to integrated effort, in view of the fact that it will have no outside human enemy to face? The only plausible answer that has, I think, so far been suggested is that the human race as a whole should regard itself as opposed to an outside non-human enemy, an enemy who is to be found in all those forces of the universe which oppose human progress and which tend to shorten, embitter and destroy human life. Here, perhaps, as William James suggested nearly half a century ago, is to be found the real moral equivalent of war. The battle of Mankind versus Nature is an unending one, one that can absorb our finest energies, one, moreover, that, as I have said elsewhere, has to be fought on many fronts, so that there is room for the services of every nation, every organization, every individual. It is the kind of war in which the human victories take the form of triumph over some dread disease, of the overcoming of some threat of famine or natural calamity, of success in harnessing the forces of Nature to serve the human will, and (last, not least) in the development of the human spirit to its highest levels. Such an attitude, if it were general and consciously realized as such, might well unite mankind in much the same way as would invasion from another planet.

Unfortunately it is also an attitude which tends to arouse super-stitious fears and to which religious influences have also often been opposed, for it seems to involve arrogance or what the ancient Greeks called Hubris, a temerity on the part of man to set himself up against the forces of Nature, before which it would perhaps be wiser and more befitting to bow down in humble reverence. Against this view, it may be pointed out that all life is in a sense a revolt against inanimate nature, since it seeks to preserve itself in the face of threats and obstacles. Man is merely the most hubristic of living creatures, since his adaptability and intellect enable him to assert himself more effectually than others. And furthermore, since life, including human life, is itself a product of Nature in the widest sense, man is but fulfilling the purposes of nature in moulding her to his own will. This at any rate is the synthesis which modern thinkers like Julian Huxley[1] are proposing for the older antithesis between Man and Nature, and if we are willing to adopt it, the quasi-moral objections

[1]*Evolutionary Ethics*, 1947.

to the attitude fall to the ground. If we like, we can say that man in fighting nature is still fulfilling the will of God. Finally, we can point out that the same battle has to be carried on in a more intimate field, viz. in the soul of man himself, in the understanding and control of those forces which man carries in himself and which make for his own degradation or destruction. (To this extent, therefore, our statement that the enemy should be non-human requires some qualification, though for simplicity's sake it may be allowable, if we except the particular field of psychology.) Here we can point back to what was said earlier with reference to what we called the moral approach to the problem of the prevention of war; and with regard to the importance of this moral approach religion and science are agreed, though the modern science of the mind has made us realize that the psychological aspects of morality are more complex and therefore require more subtle handling than had previously been realized. But it would be inappropriate now to go further into this deep question. We have only mentioned it to show that here is a philosophy that harmonizes well with the integration of mankind in a common effort against a common enemy. And it may well be that only such a philosophy will endow us with the vision and incentive necessary to escape the unparalleled destruction that would result from a world war fought in the atomic age.

CHAPTER VII

GUIDE LINES FOR
RESEARCH IN INTERNATIONAL CO-OPERATION

by Gordon W. Allport

CONFRONTED with the cheerless spectacle of the modern world, an increasing number of today's prophets are saying that our international troubles are wholly *moral*. Technical progress, they point out, brought in its wake a perilous secularization of life. Among its macabre consequences we reckon technological unemployment, technological warfare, and now the black portent of atomic destruction. The present century, in spite of its unexampled inventiveness, has been the bloodiest century on record in terms of international, civil, and criminal violence.

Secularization, these prophets continue, led mankind to forget the Commandments of Moses, the ethics of Confucius, the self-discipline of Krishna, and the vision of Christian Brotherhood. It were better now, they say, for each man to look to his own salvation. Let religion revive. Let character be restored. Only then may we expect human relations to improve.

Can one doubt that these advocates of moral reformation are right in arguing that the great moral creeds of the world, *if taken in their purity*, would help control the ravages of technology? Were men to backtrack from the present gulf of secularization, were they to start practising their creeds, peace on earth would be more readily achieved.

But the manifest difficulty in accepting this seemingly simple counsel lies not in the falseness or inapplicability of our creeds, but in their sheer antiquity. Many, perhaps most, inhabitants of the earth would recognize "Love thy neighbour as thyself" as a worthy imperative. But this commandment tells twentieth-century man very little about how he may translate his affectionate purposes into action. How, in an age of giant industries, bureaucracy, instant communication, and atomic energy, shall one effectively love one's neighbour?

Suppose a factory owner, a man of goodwill, wishes to practise the Golden Rule. What does the rule tell him about fair and just wages? Without research into living costs, the needs and aspirations of his employees, the standards for safety and health, he cannot intelligently be a Christian. The age of shepherds and Sadducees

141

bequeathed him a sound moral orientation but none of the skills or knowledge needed to implement his ideals.

Suppose that I am persuaded that I should love my neighbour as myself (or, at least, that I should live at peace with him). My neighbours, I know, are two and a half billion in number. What concretely shall I do in my capacity as a world citizen? Shall I press for the Quota Force Control amendment to the United Nations Charter? Shall I work for birth control in India or for a gigantic loan for industrial upbuilding in that country? Shall I approve or disapprove Scheme X for the international control of crime? Only social research, focused upon overlapping problems of nations, will tell the answers.

Perhaps my ethical views are in the modern vein. I may prefer to be guided by the insights of Kropotkin, Lenin, or Dewey. But so long as my moral standards are meliorative and not pejorative, I am confronted always with the need for knowledge in order to implement my belief.

Sound moral purpose is by no means lacking in the world. It still flows from the great creedal literature of past ages, even while it is being reinterpreted in the light of modern conditions. The present chasm between technology and morals, as reflected by the bloody twentieth century, has formed chiefly because physical engineering has outstripped social engineering, because physical science has been allowed to outdistance social science. The worship of technological efficiency, for its own sake, is an almost universally recognized evil; but its control through moral efficiency awaits knowledge and instrument.

POLICY, RESEARCH AND OPERATIONS

Perhaps the most heartening event of our times is the establishment of the Economic and Social Council of the United Nations, its dependent specialized agencies, particularly UNESCO. The last of these in the Preamble to its Charter, strikes the keynote of a new era. "Since wars begin in the minds of men it is in the minds of men that the defences of peace must be constructed." The implications are crystal clear: man's moral sense condemns war; let us therefore study scientifically the sources of this evil in men's minds and scientifically remove them.

But it is here that an initial misgiving arises. Can research into the causes of war be translated effectively into operation? During the past five years a certain pessimism has descended upon many of the world's most active social scientists. Aiming to improve morale in wartime, industrial relations in peacetime, amity between races, they have pressed ahead with research and have proffered solutions. For the most part their findings have been disregarded, and their zeal correspondingly dampened. Political expediency, power politics, selfish national purposes, have conspired to overlook, to 'place on file', their counsel. Atomic scientists, we know, were listened to respectfully in their capacity as technological producers, but when they spoke earnestly regarding the moral and economic implications of their discovery, a chorus of special interests tried to drown them out. Today unmoral technology is in the saddle; the socially minded engineer is a pedestrian left far behind.

The situation can be remedied in three ways: (1) Boldness in taking risks is called for. Everyone knows there are serious inherent limitations in social research. It is likely that social investigation can never attain an exactness equivalent to that of physical technology whose ravages it aims to control. Unlike physical and chemical research, social studies are infrequently additive, and their powers of generalization are limited. But just what the inherent limitations of social science may be we cannot tell until an opportunity of adequate scope is given it. The possible imperfectibility of social engineering is no excuse for failing to encourage its growth, or to employ its aid wherever practicable.

The United States alone spent two billion dollars on the invention of the atomic bomb. What is there absurd in spending an equivalent sum, if necessary, on the discovery of means for its control? And, as the Preamble to the UNESCO Charter states, it is undoubtedly in the minds of men that the defences of peace must be sought. Success cannot be guaranteed; it is entirely possible that social engineering may fail to implement the moral sense of mankind and that mankind may go under. But we shall never know the potential value of social science unless the risk is taken.

(2) Policy makers (I speak of the Department of State as well as of the highest policy authorities in the United Nations) can and should open their minds continually to the documented advice of social scientists. When it is good, they should follow it. Publicity given to relevant research, to the recommendations of social scientists, and to the policies finally adopted, will reveal the extent to which international practices are determined by selfishness and momentary expediency, and to what extent they conform to the best social knowledge available.

(3) Let social scientists continually strive to attain a standard in research that merits respect. Too often in the past their findings have been trivial or incompetent. Equally often they have failed to make even the soundest of their principles intelligible, or their applicability clear. Psychologists, sociologists, anthropologists, economists have *much* to learn about practical orientation of their studies, and about effective means for communicating their results to policy makers.[1]

If developments move in the direction of the three suggestions just offered the integration between policy bodies and social scientists will be greatly improved. Much encouragement comes from the knowledge that during recent years beneficial co-ordination has already been achieved. In numerous instances social science gave indispensable aid to the war effort. In spite of resistance and some hostility social science scored triumphs, notably in the areas of psychological warfare, personnel selection, morale building, effective communication between the government and the public.[2] The scope of these successes is sufficiently great to raise our hopes high for the potential results of team-work between social scientists and administrators in the area of international co-operation.

Social research must be international. While the natural scientist or the medical scientist operating alone in his individual laboratory may do significant research, of importance to the entire world, it is safe to say that almost no social research of international significance can be successfully carried forward in this manner. Even if a whole nation should concentrate its energy upon social investigations it is unlikely that it could accomplish much of *world* significance. A single nation's culture-bound outlook is restrictive. True, in the past social scientists of one nation occasionally travelled abroad in their quest for data, but their reports have seldom been broad-gauged enough and free enough from provincialism to serve as a guide to international policy of any type whatsoever.

At the present time barriers of language, of inadequate facilities

[1]Suggestions for bridging the chasm in communication and for improving the relevance of social research are made by A. H. Leighton, *The Governing of Men* (Princeton University Press, 1945), esp. pp. 390-7; and G. W. Allport, "The Psychology of Participation," *Psychological Review*, 1945, 53, esp. pp. 128-30.

[2]Although a record of the successful wartime applications of social science to administrative policy has not yet been completely compiled, some indication of their variety and nature can be obtained from D. Cartwright, "American Social Psychology and the War," *Journal of Consulting Psychology*, 1946, 10, 67-72.

(especially in smaller and poorer countries), meagreness of intercommunication, and lack of incentive to focus upon common problems, conspire to separate and segregate the social scientists of the world. As yet the resources of their knowledge and skill, as well as their eagerness to aid, have not been tapped in the interests of world peace.

To obtain the concerted effort of the world's social scientists, even in regard to limited and special topics, we now need international stimulation, facilities, and co-ordination. Thousands of highly skilled physical scientists worked in collaboration on a *national* scale for the production of the destructive atom bomb. The control of its destructive potential, and the realization of its latent benefits, will require equally many, and equally able, minds co-operating on an *international* scale.

WHAT IS KNOWN AND WHAT IS NEEDED

International social research need not start at scratch. Already much initial work has been done. Even now a sufficient number of general principles are known, and widely enough agreed upon, to set the guide lines for urgently needed investigations. What is more important, these principles might *immediately* be applied with immense profit to the conduct of international relations if the proper officials were so disposed.

In examining these principles and their usefulness as guides to concrete research and policy, two limitations should be held in mind. First, they are offered as illustrations rather than as a final system. An adequate survey should, of course, have the benefit of wide discussion and concerted approval by a large number of social scientists assembled from many nations.[1]

Secondly, the discussion is limited largely to psychological principles, with some borrowing from social anthropology and sociology. The potential contributions of economics, geography, political science, and history are unquestionably large. But these disciplines fall outside the range of the present survey.

Trends toward Collective Security. Perhaps the first principle to which the social scientist would call attention is the unidirectional historical

[1]The list of principles here offered is not, however, quite as individual and arbitrary as may appear. Several of them are contained in "Human Nature and the Peace," a statement subscribed to by 2,058 American psychologists, all members of the American Psychological Association. The "Psychologists' Statement" is published in full in the *Psychological Bulletin*, 1945, 42, 376–8; likewise in *Human Nature and Enduring Peace* (ed. Gardner Murphy), Year Book of the Society for the Psychological Study of Social Issues (Boston: Houghton Mifflin, 1945).

trend towards the formation of a world government. From the cave-man to the twentieth century human beings have formed larger and larger working and living groups. At some time in the dim past families became clans, clans turned into tribes and states. Federations followed. Empires had their day. Commonwealth and regional unions have flourished. During the past century non-political international organizations have sprung up in bewildering numbers, especially among scientific, professional, and recreational groups. The League of Nations, followed by Hitler's sinister and abortive New Order, were chapters in the same saga. The United Nations is the latest and best hope mankind has devised, though it is not necessarily the final effort. Even now it is unclear whether one world is the next step in the series, or whether mankind is doomed first to live through a divided period, a pro- and anti-Russian world.

The social scientist also warns that, though bound to come about, the form of the future world government is as yet undetermined. A tyrannical global system is a distinct danger. And it is precisely for this reason that maximum effort in study and research is needed to insure that future developments shall be such as to implement the moral sense of mankind. Unless social engineering hastens to the support of democratic ideals, a tyrannical form of world government, or an additional period of divisiveness and war, may be expected to occur. Almost as bad would be the creation of a benevolent bureaucracy from which individual initiative and participation are excluded. No social structure is solid unless the citizens themselves feel that they themselves have a part to play in shaping their mortal destinies.

Participation in Own Destiny. Various lines of research in recent years have demonstrated the inescapable importance of personal participation in matters affecting one's own welfare. People almost always want to solve their problems for themselves, or at least feel that they play an important part in the process of achieving a solution. International relief organizations have learned that charitable hand-outs seldom strengthen the recipient or win his gratitude. Apathy, boot-licking, or resentment may accompany 'benevolence' of any sort, whether it be alms or an imposed political system. On the other hand, personal efforts at upbuilding and rehabilitation are usually undertaken with joy by a person who feels that the product he achieves will be his own and not suffer destruction or expropriation.

Thus, human progress and human happiness seem to depend not upon what one has in hand, but upon one's freedom to grow and to build. The inhabitants of certain villages in Poland and in Czechoslovakia have recently rebuilt their destroyed communities through co-operative efforts, declaring themselves to be supremely happy in the process. But in many localities of the world freedom to build is denied. And people who are denied such freedom become reactive, bitter, resentful and destructive.

Though the guide line here is clear, and fortified by much research in group dynamics and industrial relations, we still know far too little about the process of eliciting participation and encouraging co-operative enterprise. We know too little about the techniques of linking the basic motives of self-interest to the best of all means for attaining it, namely, mutual aid. There are also cultural differences to be taken into account, even though all peoples seem potentially capable of co-operation. How best to engage this ability, and how best to extend the circle of co-operative endeavour, until the international orbit is achieved—all are subjects for instant research.

Economic and Social Insecurity. Persons who feel that their livelihood or safety is threatened generally make poor citizens—of a town, a nation, or of the world. They tend to be defensive, restless, suspicious. Now, since poverty is well-nigh universal, and social insecurity widely prevalent, it becomes imperative to determine the types of provisions, guarantees, and reassurances that are most needed to allay fear and unrest. What are the standards of security and well-being below which no people can fall without social disaster ensuing? Up to now these standards have been guessed at through intuition and in terms of expediency, but only the results of an objective investigation will serve.

While certain minimum guarantees against starvation and disease may be a legitimate objective for all nations acting in concert we repeat that human interests are best served when people themselves are consulted and permitted to play an active part in providing for their own security. Just what sorts of self-help can be encouraged, and in what order of priority, are subjects for research not speculation.

We know that criminality, especially among children, can often be traced directly to feelings of psychological insecurity. National unrest likewise is often derived from apprehensiveness. War springs in part from conditions of chronic suspicion and deprivation. All these social ills cry for sustained research into the conditions of, and remedies for, intolerable insecurity. Some available studies suggest that a certain amount of social and economic uncertainty is conducive to personal growth; but that privations that bring morbid anxiety lead to anti-social conduct.

One form of insecurity especially injurious to the cause of peace, arises from the frequent inconsistency of national and international policy. An important factor in the downfall of democratic Germany and in the rise of Hitler was the German people's dismay at the shifting policies of the Allies. To the Germans, Versailles meant one thing, the Dawes Plan another; reparations indicated one attitude, non-enforcement of reparations another. Punitive treatment was inconsistently mixed with friendship. By such an inconsistent administering of rewards and punishments even a rat can be made neurotic. Under similar circumstances the child, the adult, or the social group grows restless and embittered. It is always necessary for each nation to know precisely where she stands in the international family.

Psychological security, on an international scale, therefore requires a policy of clear commitment, frequently reiterated, and carried forward with unvarying consistency. To arouse hopes, and let them fall; to start one ill-considered policy and switch it in midstream; to invite co-operation and then reject it—are fatal errors. Although research seems scarcely needed to prove this point, the phenomenon in question should be clearly recorded and prominently advertised in order to influence continually the operations of policy and deliberative bodies.

International Conference Procedure. At the root of much of the vagueness and inconsistency of international decisions lie the human failings that come to light in the work of committees and assemblies. Men, even trained statesmen, do not know how to deliberate efficiently. Up to now in social science only a bare beginning has been made in the study of the processes of discussion, group criticism, and decision. We may expect much basic work to be done in the future even without international support. But so essential is it for international groups to learn how to employ the most effective conference procedures, that money and time would be well invested in additional investigations.

The parliamentary problems of international bodies are unique, for when individuals come together from contrasting cultural backgrounds, employing different languages, and reflecting diverse traditions, the ordinary difficulties of efficient mental co-ordination are found to be exaggerated. How shall representatives of different nations learn most effectively to deliberate together unless international support and encouragement are given to this vital line of research?

Focusing on Children. Social scientists know that in a single generation it is theoretically possible to have a world language, to build universal loyalty to a world state, and to eliminate most racial and national prejudices. They know equally well that the goal cannot be achieved in practice, for it is from their parents that children chiefly learn their social attitudes. The older generation unfortunately inclines to be firmly set in its bitterness and in its blindness. Although children, with their almost limitless plasticity, will acquire much of this burden, they still constitute the best possible focus for our internationalizing efforts. Children can readily identify with symbols of world unity, even while holding inviolate their loyalty to family, neighbourhood or nation. Multiple loyalties are not necessarily incompatible. Wendel Willkie was no less a Hoosier or an American because he acclaimed One World.

To overlook children is to be stupidly inefficient from the standpoint of social engineering. Twenty-five years is not too long to await results in the perspective of social evolution. Social scientists might reasonably advise that adults be largely disregarded in favour of children. The establishment of health centres, nutritional standards, curricular standards, welfare stations, model schools, a children's village, research in social attitudes, social training, and symbols, might well hold the centre of the stage. The children of today are the custodians of the United Nations of tomorrow. The problems we cannot solve they will inherit, and their ability to cope with these problems will exceed ours only if their loyalties are stronger and their initial training sounder.

There is a simple psychological reason why international bodies tend to overlook children. Delegates assemble in an atmosphere of cameras, microphones, and bald heads. Where are the children? While in an adult world adults tend to forget them. Would it not be well to arrange the entrance to the General Assembly, to the Security Council, and to UNESCO Headquarters so that it would lead the delegates twice a day through a nursery-school play yard—just as a reminder?

To focus upon child welfare, education, health, and juvenile research would have an extra advantage. What every parent wants (with few exceptions), the wide world over, is a better opportunity for his child than he himself had. A United Nations devoted to providing such an opportunity would win the allegiance of adults far faster than through a direct appeal to their adult-centred interests.

One dare not minimize the political obstacles in the way. To take a single example, the task of teaching the children of the world scientific facts about race will turn out to be a vexatious problem. Sovereign rights will seem to be threatened. The Senator from

Mississippi will scarcely welcome scientific facts about race in Mississippi's public schools—especially if the curriculum is devised in consultation with Russian and Negro scholars. The children are plastic and willing; adults are the bigots. Yet even here research and patience may discover not only a scientifically sound curriculum for international use, but also, in time, the effective means for introducing this curriculum into backward areas.

The Common Ground of Human Nature. To teach children the ways of peace requires, among other things, a factual knowledge of the peoples of the world. What, up to now, have anthropologists given us? And what have the schools been teaching? Broadly speaking, both have accented the *differences* that divide the families of mankind. Even though there has been little malice in the practice, the results have often been harmful. The American child, for example, learns with horror about headhunters, about infanticide; and he learns to laugh at the Dutch who clop in wooden shoes, and at the quaint observances of Easter among adherents to the Orthodox faith. The implication of inferiority is a usual by-product of our present method of teaching cultural and national differences. Less dramatic, but far sounder, would be the teaching of the common considerations of justice and morality that are identical over vast areas of the earth. Practices that may *seem* to differ dramatically often indicate common aspirations and common values. The prayer wheels of Tibet and the silent Quaker meeting have virtually identical functional significance; so too the initiation rites of the Pawnee and the American high school commencement.

Except for the work of some anthropologists, notably the Cross Cultural Survey developed under the direction of George P. Murdoch of Yale University, little effort has been spent in the search for the common ground of mankind. Up to now research has usually emphasized differences. A vast project of investigation, absolutely basic to the interests of peace and to the success of the United Nations, is the preparation of an *encyclopedia of the uniformities and similarities* in respect to the aspirations, beliefs and practices of all peoples. The successful execution of this project would call for the co-operation of many kinds of social scientists in many countries. Such a set of volumes, sure to be epoch making, would serve as a reference guide for innumerable aspects of world policy for years to come.

One large aspect of this research will inevitably deal with the problem of *national character.* Here lies much virgin territory to be explored. What is common ground for mankind cannot be fully understood, or intelligently employed, unless the perturbations of national and ethnic variants are objectively known for what they are.

The desires and opinions of the common man. It is not merely the enduring uniformities and equivalences in culture that need to be known, but likewise the *current* state of world needs and world opinion at successive periods of time. Here too internationally sponsored social research is indispensable.

In the modern day it is unnecessary to remain in ignorance of the aspirations, hopes, wishes or judgment of the common man. Particularly when statesmen find themselves deadlocked through their demand for incompatible solutions to international problems, it would be salutary to know what the people of the world think. In many cases a knowledge of public opinion would aid in re-defining the issues and in devising peaceful solutions.

One cannot deny that adults in every nation are frequently as belligerent and uncompromising as their statesmen in matters pertaining to boundaries and sovereignty. But at the same time a study of the view of the majority of the common people would probably reveal that more important to them than boundaries are matters of self-respect, pride, food, shelter, marriage, the welfare of their children, and the opportunity to identify with some successful group (not necessarily with their own belligerent nation). To focus on matters that are of *prior* importance to the citizenry would often bring a re-definition of the issues and disclose unexpected solutions. For the root desires of two people are seldom incompatible with one another. When they confront each other with the basic *desires,* co-operation can usually satisfy both sets of interests. But when they confront each other with rigid *demands,* there is often no solution short of war.

In brief the time has come for a continuing international service in public opinion. Polling now exists in more than a dozen countries. Facilities and talent are both available. They await international co-ordination and utilization.

Communications. A reciprocal research service is required in order to achieve effective communication to the public of all lands. How may radio, motion pictures, television, books, news services, periodicals, lecturers be best employed in order that people everywhere may be informed in affairs of international import? Purely local research, such as that done in America, is inadequate. It overlooks entirely the difficulties of polylingualism, or varying habits, tastes and practices in other lands. The task of communicating effectively with a world audience requires internationally sponsored research.

A special phase of the communication problem deals with the strategies of propaganda. It is recognized today that propaganda has its uses in the service of good causes, but that at the same time it may be a device of doubtful ethical justification. To what extent propaganda techniques may legitimately be employed in the interests of international co-operation is a subject for searching discussion. But such discussion cannot profitably take place unless the essential features, the strategies and tactics of propaganda, are first scientifically analysed.

Condescension and its Perils. A principle upon which social scientists almost unanimously agree is that human relations founded upon an attitude of condescension are perilous. So far as is known no group of people is content to think of itself as inferior to any other group, nor is any single individual normally willing to regard himself as of less worth or merit than another. In spite of periods of history when slavery or feudalism seemed to lead a temporarily peaceful existence, it may be safely asserted that policies based on condescension will sooner or later lead to violence. In the world today the unrest of citizens formerly regarded as second-class is manifest. Dark-skinned people are moving ahead towards independence. The white-skinned third of the world's population cannot prevent the movement. The English-speaking tenth certainly cannot do so. It is for this reason that an attempt to preserve the older imperial and colonial systems is doomed to breed violence and war.

Although a fully integrated security system will unquestionably require the abandonment of the colonial mentality and the adoption of dignified trusteeships, yet it will not be possible to devise the optimum arrangement for these trusteeships without consulting the desires of the populations most directly affected. Even the military demand for uninhabited volcanic island bases cannot be evaluated apart from the effect of this demand on world opinion. Careful research on human sentiments in many countries is in order before the question of bases and trusteeships can be settled in a manner that will make for eventual peace rather than war.[1]

[1]Professor Arthur N. Holcombe has written wisely on "The International Trusteeship System" (*Annals of the American Academy of Political and Social Science*, 1946, 244, 101–9). But Professor Holcombe, like most political scientists, gives an *a priori* interpretation of the probable effect of this or that policy upon public opinion in Russia, Britain, or America. The time has come when guesses are no longer an acceptable basis for policy. Pre-testing is practicable, and prediction of opinion can be based on science rather than on hunch.

Perhaps the basic principle of the science of human relations is that in order to deal effectively with any other mortal, it is necessary to find out how he feels. Xenophobia and condescension give way in the face of psychological knowledge. Mutual understanding grows. Projects of investigation in this area range from the analysis of the genesis and nature of race prejudice, to the assembling of a world-wide collection of self-told narratives, graphically illustrated, to serve as material for broadening our appreciation of people who represent other colours, other creeds, other nationalities. Research in the fields of ethnic differences, ethnic similarities, and inter-racial understanding is almost limitless in scope. And it is upon social engineering derived from this type of research that we shall have to rely in order to offset the ravages of hostility and condescension which in the past have poisoned our ethnic attitudes.

Need of Symbols. For most people the concept of a single, demo-cratically oriented world is difficult to hold in mind. As a rule, personal loyalty can adhere to an abstraction only when the abstraction is richly symbolized. Christianity rivets attention upon the cross, nations focus upon their respective flags. Greece has its Acropolis, America its Statue of Liberty. The Moslem faces Mecca. International mercy is represented by the Red Cross. On his lapel the veteran bears insignia of his military history and his status.

Up to now the great majority of symbols are nationalistic. Artists and musicians, architects and designers, are to a large extent culture-bound. Inevitably their productions favour single nations rather than the concert of nations. As yet there is no world flag, no world music. World parks, gardens, universities, and symbolic documents are lack-ing. There is no world capitol. A few fine words have been spoken: The Atlantic Charter, the United Nations Charter, the Preamble to UNESCO. But these symbols are undramatized and insufficiently known.

Does it not follow that an early and urgent task is to stimulate by commission or competition the devising of adequate UN symbols? It should be done on an international scale.

To carry out this task successfully research is indispensable. With modern techniques world opinion can be consulted. Proposed symbols can be pre-tested before adoption. Market research determines the effectiveness of trade marks. Why should not the United Nations do the same? Tastes in music can be ascertained. So too inclinations respecting a common language. If schools were to teach the vernacular and, in addition, one universal tongue, what should the latter be?

It would be fanciful, of course, to assume that symbols can be arbitrarily or synthetically created. They grow out of deep feeling and are accepted only on the basis of conviction. At the same time millions of people already have both the requisite feeling and conviction. In their search for symbols, stimulus and incentive, guidance and research are now in order and needed. In time, of course, more and better symbols will emerge, but they will have a fairer' chance of success if deliberate attention is paid to the course of their development.

It is in this connection that international parks and universities should be considered. For quite apart from their utilitarian significance they have profound symbolic meaning as well.

SUMMARY

Our plea is for an accelerated development of social engineering based on social research, to the end that we may overtake and control the ravages of a rampant and amoral technology.

The argument assumes that the basic moral sense of mankind is sufficiently established in direction and in motive power to employ with profit the principles and instruments that the nascent science of human relations has already developed and will continue to develop at a rapid rate if adequate support is given.

The principles stated in this paper derive from psychology, sociology, and anthropology. In all probability they would be endorsed by most specialists in these disciplines. Yet a completer list of principles and fuller account of the applications would result if many social scientists were to work in concert upon the problems here treated. Such concerted action should be instigated on an international scale.

Should any 'hard-headed' statesman scorn the guide lines here offered as an expression of futile idealism, he himself would stand revealed as the most impractical of men. For scientific facts in the social field, as in any field, can be disregarded only with peril. The Einsteinian equation, $E = MC^2$, was once dismissed as pedantry. The formula led to the release of atomic energy. The 'pedantry' of social science might even now contribute enormously to the establishment of peace and international co-operation were its applications understood and employed by policy makers.

Yet it is true that social science has as yet by no means realized its potential power as a welder of international relations. Nor will it do so until adequate support is given on both a national and international scale. Since its most needed discoveries pertain to worldwide problems, it is international support that is most acutely needed. The co-operation of social scientists all over the world, as yet nonexistent, would not be difficult to achieve.

Though some of the research required for international policy is of an *ad hoc* and momentary character, often statistical in nature, the pivotal investigations that are needed for long-range planning fall for the most part in the areas this paper has surveyed.

In all cases the research here recommended is intimately related to basic principles of social science. These principles, so far as they are now known, and as rapidly as new ones are formulated inductively with the aid of research, should be allowed to direct policy.

There follows a brief re-listing of the essential areas of research mentioned in this paper. Though manifestly incomplete, the topics are both accessible and important. They are intended to serve as a starting point for discussion among interested groups of social scientists and policy makers.

1. Prepare an historical survey of the trend towards larger and larger units of collective security.
2. Determine the conditions for democratic mass participation.
   (a) The conditions required for a sense of freedom to build.
   (b) The conditions for linking self-interest to the techniques of mutual aid.
   (c) The conditions for widening the individual's circle of co-operative enterprise.
3. Determine the effects of economic and psychological insecurity.
   (a) Under what circumstances, and in what degree, does insecurity serve as an incentive?
   (b) Under what circumstances, and beyond what point, does insecurity engender morbid and anti-social reactions?
   (c) Study especially the relation between childhood insecurity and the formation of delinquent and hostile attitudes.
   (d) What forms of insecurity lead to national unrest and to warlike sentiments?
   (e) What international policies, if consistently maintained, would lead to an optimum sense of security?
4. Investigate international conference procedures.
   (a) What are the requirements of effective deliberation and group decision in large assemblies? In committees?
   (b) How are these requirements modified when participants are of different cultural and linguistic backgrounds?

5. Direct main efforts upon children.

   (a) How are multiple loyalties created without mental conflict?
   (b) Explore the possibilities of a Children's Village for war orphans or stateless children.
   (c) Prepare international standards for health and nutrition.
   (d) Investigate the conditions for the formation of attitudes.
   (e) Devise model curricula for the elimination of ethnic prejudice and for the explanation of the interdependence of nations.
   (f) Determine on world-wide scale parental aspirations for children.
   (g) Devise methods for keeping policy bodies aware of children and their needs.
   (h) Explore methods for the installation of child training projects in all countries.

6. Determine objectively the common ground of mankind.

   (a) Prepare an encyclopedia of the uniformities and similarities of cultures.
   (b) Interpret cultural difference in terms of functional equivalences.
   (c) Explore in detail the conception of national character.

7. Ascertain current opinion.

   (a) Establish a continuing operation for revealing the state of men's needs, aspirations, opinions; commence in countries where machinery is already available.
   (b) Centre attention upon common needs rather than upon divisive demands.
   (c) Translate findings into implications for policy.

8. Investigate channels of communication.

   (a) Study the merits of all media in respect to their value for international co-operation.
   (b) Experiment with programmes and determine their effectiveness.
   (c) Determine the strategy and tactics of propaganda, and methods for building immunity.
   (d) Trace the dissemination of ideas through rumour, through illicit and authoritative channels.
   (e) Explore continually the problems of polylingualism and the conditions for a world language.

9. Clarify the problem of race.

   (a) Solve the problem of identities and differences in racial abilities and temperament.
   (b) Prepare authoritative ethnographic maps.
   (c) Examine the psychological effects of policies of condescension.

(d) Estimate in advance the probable effects of proposed policies respecting bases, trusteeships.

(e) Determine the causes of xenophobia.

(f) Determine the conditions for mutual understanding between individuals of diverse backgrounds.

10. Develop symbols of international co-operation.

(a) What symbols appeal to diverse groups?

(b) Pre-test plans for world centres, flag, music, parks, universities, and other symbols of unity.

(c) Determine means for encouraging the development of effective symbols.

PART II

CHAPTER VIII

FRUSTRATION AND AGGRESSION
A REVIEW OF RECENT EXPERIMENTAL WORK

by Hilde Himmelweit

ONE of the strange aspects of human behaviour is the relative readiness of man to accept the belief that war is inevitable and to become, in times of war, an active member of a belligerent force. War entails sacrifices; separation from family, interruption of work, physical hardships and danger to life. It involves the overthrow of many values and standards considered important in peace, and with it the acceptance of new standards.

Psychologists have tried to account for man's acceptance of war by pointing out that war activates the most basic of all human drives, that of self-preservation. Once this is aroused, all others become subordinated to it. The drive for self-preservation is aroused by some real or imagined threat to the group to which the individual belongs. Many psychologists, however, have felt dissatisfied with this explanation because it does not account for man's readiness, if not eagerness, to believe in and to search for the existence of such external threat.

Psycho-analysts (11, 13) have postulated some positive unconscious force within the individual, welcoming the occurrence of war and with it the removal of inhibitions that exist in times of peace. This positive force is thought to be pent-up aggression seeking an outlet that is socially approved, thus becoming acceptable to the ego. According to Freud, such pent-up aggression is due to frustration.

Greatly oversimplified, there appear to be three main conditions producing frustration: (a) external obstacles set up by an unfavourable environment, which prevent the individual from reaching his goal; (b) internal obstacles, set up by man's super-ego which prevents free expression of drives unacceptable to it; (c) the simultaneous activation of two mutually exclusive drives where satisfaction of one precludes immediate gratification of the other: (b) and (c) are the more important in so far as they are the result of strong primitive impulses in discord with one another.

Memory of such conflict becomes repressed, as a result of frustration, external or internal; the tension produced by the activity of the drives is unabated and seeks some indirect outlet, some lightning conductor for its discharge. As Glover (13) points out "a situation of

161

L

war brings the external world into internal conflict". War, or any other aggressive activity of the group, because of its group character, becomes acceptable to the ego and super-ego forces of the individual. Moreover, since it implies close identification with the group it gives an outlet for the simultaneous discharge of two apparently paradoxical impulses—those of love and those of hate. The love impulses are directed towards the group of which the individual is a member and the hate impulses against the 'enemy', who may be real or conjured up to allay the conflict within the individual himself.

Later, Freud altered his view that aggression is the result of frustration, and postulated the existence of Thanatos, an aggressive instinct *per se*. This is an independent impulse to destroy which stands in direct opposition to Eros, the impulse of love and of life. Imbalance between these impulses may lead to an over-activity of Thanatos. This expresses itself either as aggression turned inwards, the most extreme form being suicide, or aggression turned outwards. The particular character which the discharge of hate will take depends upon the particular strength and nature of the super-ego or repressing agency, upon the ego-ideal which the individual has built up, and upon external reality.

Freud's first assumption, that aggression is the result of frustration formed the basis of a book *Frustration and Aggression*, by Dollard, Doob and their colleagues (7), published in 1939. It starts with "the assumption that aggression is always a consequence of frustration. More specifically the proposition is that the occurrence of aggressive behaviour always presupposes the existence of frustration, and contrariwise, that the existence of frustration always leads to some form of aggression." The authors attempt to provide evidence for this hypothesis from experimental, clinical and social psychology.

They define frustration as "that condition which exists when a goal response suffers interference". This interference may be due either to the inaccessibility of the goal or to punishment that would follow the attainment of the goal. The man who misses the country bus, the only means of transport to bring him to town for an important engagement, experiences the first kind of frustration. An example of the second type is the punishment that a mother may deal out to her child for taking a forbidden sweet.

Aggression is defined by the authors as "an act whose goal response is injury to an organism or organism surrogate", and (rather prejudging the issue) as "that response which follows frustration". The function of aggression, unlike that of a substitute activity, does not consist in reducing the instigation to the goal response itself, but only the secondary tension set up by the frustration.

Two hypotheses concerning the relationship between frustration and aggression are postulated: (1) the strength of the instigation to aggression varies directly with the amount of frustration experienced; and (2) the strength of inhibition of any direct overt act of aggression varies positively with the amount of punishment anticipated as a consequence of that act. Thus overt aggression directed against the frustrating agent itself will be inhibited or displaced on to some 'neutral' agent whenever experience teaches the individual that overt aggression will lead only to further frustration.

Dollard (7), while stressing the need for caution in applying psychological theories to sociological events, tries to account for the alleged increased aggressiveness and war-readiness of a totalitarian people by means of these two hypotheses. People living under a totalitarian regime suffer additional frustrations due to excessive regimentation and restriction of their personal liberty. At the same time, while the inducement to an aggressive response to these frustrations is great, its direct expression against the frustrating agent, the state, is repressed by that agent even to the extent of prohibiting discharge of aggression in the form of verbal criticism. The stage is thus set for pent-up aggression to become diverted and to seek discharge along channels approved by the state. This would explain the readiness of such people to direct their aggression against groups of which they are not members, e.g. Jews, capitalists, foreigners. This focusing of aggression on to some such group, which is then made the scapegoat for all the frustrations experienced, may lead eventually to overt attack in the form of war.

One may comment that while such obvious examples can be quoted which appear to lend support to the frustration-aggression hypothesis, they do not in themselves constitute evidence that aggression is *invariably* the consequence of frustration.

Dollard and his colleagues stress the deliberate bias of their book, stating that "various consequences of frustration other than aggression will be largely ignored". In a symposium in the *Psychological Review* (1941) on the same topic, N. E. Miller (25), one of the original contributors, states that whilst the frustration-aggression concept is useful as a working hypothesis, it is incomplete and should be modified: "Frustration produces instigation to a number of different types of responses, one of which is an instigation to some form of aggression". Whether aggression will become the overt response in any particular case will depend on a number of factors, one of which is the past success of different responses in reducing tension produced by frustration. (35, 36).

It will be shown here that this modification of the frustration-aggression hypothesis is more in line with experimental evidence than is the original theory.

Since 1939, much interesting work on the effect of frustration on behaviour has been carried out, and it seems pertinent, after nearly a decade, to review this work to ascertain the light it may throw on the following problems:

1. The range and depth of the frustration experiences which can be experimentally induced.
2. The range of reactions other than aggression, to such frustrations.
3. The nature of the aggressive responses reported in the researches.
4. Situational factors which influence reactions (and in particular, aggressive reactions) to the frustrating experience.
5. Individual differences found in frustration tolerance and in responses to frustration.

The following review of the experimental work will be confined to laboratory and field experiments with human subjects, both adults and children. Summaries of the many interesting researches on animals will be found in N. R. Maier's (21) reports. Anthropological material has been omitted as it is descriptive and comparative, not strictly experimental. Clinical studies too are quoted only in so far as they are experimental.

Before discussing the reported reactions to frustraiton it is essential to specify the nature of the frustrating experiences produced. As Gardner Murphy (26) remarks "the investigation of the relation of frustration to aggression becomes in large measure, an investigation of the locus, the degree, the quality and the form of the frustration. ﹍ ."

Investigators who worked with children induced frustration experiences of the following types:

1. *Physical obstruction:* e.g. withdrawal of bottle from the infant's mouth during his feeding period (22), and sudden arbitrary withholding of attractive toys which nursery-school children had first been encouraged to handle (4). The physical obstruction here consisted of a wire mesh curtain which was lowered so that the goal was still in sight, but no longer attainable.

2. *Frustration due to satiation:* Burton (6) gave the child the task of filling a very large board with coloured pegs; the initial interest

turned into boredom, and the task became frustrating. Seashore (37) invited children into his room singly and faced them with a large stack of blank paper instructing them to draw a man. When one drawing was completed, the child was handed another sheet from the stack with the remarks that he should try and make a better drawing. The frustration here was in part satiation and in part withholding of approval by the adult.

3. *Frustration due to a discrepancy between desire and ability to solve a task:* two examples illustrate this kind of experiment. Sherman and Jost (39) asked children to complete puzzles which looked simple but were in fact too difficult. Zander (42), who had carefully studied the different kinds of frustration experiences, emphasized the importance of inducing frustration after initial success. He made it appear that the task at which the subjects now failed was no more difficult than the one at which they had previously succeeded, i.e. the problem, from past experience, was felt to be within the individual's level of achievement. On three consecutive days, he taught children number series by flashing the numbers on a screen and teaching the children how to predict which numbers would appear next. During these trial periods the children met with success. On the fourth day, whenever they predicted the number which was to come next, they found that they had guessed wrong. The deception (flashing the wrong number on the screen) was carried out in such a manner that the children were unaware of it. They experienced the situation as an inability on their part to deal with a task which looked identical with that of previous days: i.e. the failure was of their own making.

Experiments with adults have been usually of this third type. Various ingenious devices have been used by different investigators to make the failure situation one which had real meaning to the individual and which could not readily be dismissed as being a laboratory situation too remote from the subject to involve his pride and desire for achievement. The subjects were thus made 'ego-involved' (38). This was usually achieved by suggesting that it was a test of special skill or of intelligence and that failure to perform it correctly reflected on the individual's general level of ability.

Rosenzweig (32) analysed the difference in reactions produced when he confronted two groups of adults with the same frustrating experience, which, however, he invested with different meaning for the two groups. The first group was told that their assistance was needed in a test, that their performance would not reflect on their ability as this was an untried test of some theories of the experimenter. The second group was invited with some formality to take an intelligence test, i.e. implying that failure in their case would reflect upon their own ability. Rosenzweig showed that the two groups differed in their reactions to the frustrating experience, which although outwardly identical, had a different meaning to each. He suggests that a frustrating experience should be analysed in terms of the reactions it produces. These can be of three kinds: 'need persistive' or 'ego-defensive', or a combination of these. In the first group of subjects, need persistive reactions only were called into play, i.e. frustration was induced because the puzzle had not been completed and the drive to completion was as yet unsatisfied. In the second group, ego-defensive reactions were also caused, i.e. there was a need to defend the self against the experience of failure since the situation was one of challenge to the ego. This method of analysing the frustrating situation in terms of its meaning to the individual is valuable, and, as will be seen later, helps to throw light on the different types of reactions called forth by frustrating experiences.

4. Frustration of a rather different type, namely, that induced by *unsatisfactory leadership*, was studied by Lewin, Lippit and White (20). Their experiment is outstanding, not only for the ingenuity of the experimental set-up, but also for the thoroughness with which all variables were controlled and the observations made. Reactions of ten-year-old boys to different types of adult leadership were studied. Four voluntary clubs of five members each were formed to meet weekly in order to engage in extra-curricular activities of their own choosing. Each group was run for a period of six weeks by an autocratic, a democratic, and a *laissez-faire* adult leader in turn. The characteristics of the democratic leader were that he would support group discussions and decisions arrived at by the group. He was ready to be consulted if the need arose. His comments on the work were fair-minded and objective. In contrast, the autocratic leader imposed activities on the group, giving them commands covering brief periods only, so that planning was rendered difficult. His comments on the boys' work were personal and subjective. The *laissez-faire* leader took no part in the discussions, gave no guidance, nor made any comments, merely supplying information when asked for it. Steps were taken to ensure that the only experimental variable was the role played by the adult and not his personality. Thus the person who had acted the part of the autocratic leader in one group would take that of the democratic leader in another. The groups had previously been matched

for physical status, age, I.Q., socio-economic background, and social behaviour ratings obtained by the Moreno technique.

The effect of these different 'social climates' on the behaviour of the members to one another during the sessions, to other groups in the general meetings, and to outside individuals were studied. The hypothesis underlying the experiment was that the *laissez-faire* and autocratic leadership imposed frustrations which were absent when the groups were run on a democratic basis. This hypothesis seemed plausible for when, at the close of the experiment extending over many weeks, the children were asked individually which leader they had liked best, they all preferred the teacher who had assumed the democratic role in their particular group. (It will be remembered that different teachers in turn assumed the democratic role.)

This is an excellent example of a field experiment analogous to a real life situation. The observations made were both intensive and extensive, consisting of minute by minute group structure analyses, impressionistic-written records by the different leaders, cinematographic records, the introduction of psychology students, in the guise of cleaners, to study the delayed effect of the frustration experience at the end of each period, an interview with each child at the close of the experiment, and at each transition from one type of leadership to another, interviews with parents about home discipline, talks with teachers about the children's behaviour for the rest of the week, and Rorschach records.

A possible weakness of the experiment lies in the artificiality of the conditions. Teachers were asked to act roles of autocratic and *laissez-faire* leaders which were foreign to their personality and training. These two types of leadership were felt as especially frustrating by the American boys since they run counter to those with which they are familiar in their schools. Reactions of children brought up in less progressive, more authoritarian schools would probably be less pronounced. There is need for caution in generalizing from a single experiment carried out in a given cultural milieu.

A few years later Frederiksen (8) studied the effect upon the negativism of young children of interference by the nursery-school teacher. The situation was similar to that arranged by Lewin and his collaborators. The nursery-school children were divided into two groups, and for a period during the day one group was arbitrarily directed and its spontaneous activities interfered with. The two groups of nursery-school children had previously been matched for the number of social contacts made (studied by the time-sample technique) and for the degree of acquiescent or negativistic behaviour they had shown to a variety of standard tests. An indication of the effect of the frustration was obtained from a shift in their score of acquiescence on re-test at the close of the experiment, and from observations of the children's behaviour towards one another and towards their teacher.

This survey of the different types of frustration experiments shows that, to use Rosenzweig's terminology, both need-persistive and ego-defensive reactions have been called into play. Frustration experiences have been produced: (a) by arbitrary withdrawal of desirable objects; (b) by preventing subjects from completing a task; (c) by inducing in the subjects a sense of failure and a distrust of their own abilities, and finally (d) by curbing an individual's drive for self-expression and self-assertion through interference from outside.

In spite of their apparent variety, these experiments are limited in the kind of frustration experience they induce. The limitations are: (a) the frustrating experience is of a temporary character only, usually in a friendly setting which minimizes its effect; (b) the experiments involve the conscious rather than the unconscious needs of an individual by inducing intellectual failure, temporary hampering of movements, etc. They touch the fringe only of the frustration experiences considered important by Freud and upon which his frustration-aggression hypothesis is based. They are all experiences in which the environment sets up obstacles: they do not reproduce the more important unconscious frustrations that result from internal conflict—conflict aroused by the simultaneous activation of two mutually exclusive drives or by the repression of drives unacceptable to the super-ego.

The experimental set-up thus imposes severe limitations upon the quality of the frustration experience induced. However, within these limitations, the investigators displayed much ingenuity in creating laboratory situations that were analogous to real life situations. Lewin and his collaborators (20) came nearest to the achievement of this aim. In their experiment the obstacle set up by the environment was less obvious; it was cumulative and indirect; striking at the more unconscious needs of the individual for self-expression and self-assertion. It is hoped that further experiments of this kind will be carried out with larger numbers of groups.

Freudian psychologists rightly emphasize the need for evaluating the frustration experience 'historically'. The individual does not react to the frustration in the experiment as an isolated experience, but interprets it in the light of previous conscious and unconscious frustrations and in particular in the light of his infantile frustrations. The analysts suggest that the effect of frustrations that occur in infancy and especially in the child's relationship to his mother where both love and hate impulses are active, are particularly important in influencing the individual's reactions to later frustrations. To one individual, the experimentally induced frustration may be an isolated, rather unusual event, and therefore have for him a different psychological meaning and produce reactions different from those of another individual, for whom this experience is but the culmination of a continuous series of frustrations that he has encountered throughout his life.

Without a detailed developmental history of each subject, it is difficult to take into account this difference in susceptibility to the frustration experiment. Thus, as Murphy (26) remarks, "we should speak of temporary or of permanent frustration, of local or of general frustration, but not of 'frustration in general' ". The practical difficulty of assessing previous frustration experiences has led investigators to assume, for the purposes of the inquiry, that the subjects under investigation do not differ significantly from one another in the extent, quality and quantity of past frustration experiences. This neglected dissimilarity of the subjects is probably the most serious weakness of all the studies reported to date. There is great need for the intensive psychiatric study of the subjects. The experiments are thus limited in the type and intensity of frustration experiences they evoke, and fail to create situations that have the same inner psychological meaning for different subjects. These limitations must be borne in mind in evaluating the findings.

Moreover, we are considering here frustration 'without hope', i.e. obstacles are put into the way of the individual in such a manner that he can see no way of overcoming them. As Alexander (2) points out, frustration with hope differs essentially in the reactions it produces from frustration without hope. An example of frustration with hope is the situation a farmer faces who finds his crop endangered by an oncoming storm. He will react by increased activity because he can see a way of minimizing, if not preventing, the harm produced by the obstacle.

How does the individual react to these frustrations without hope which are induced in the experiments? The first and immediate reaction is an *increase of tension* throughout his organism. Evidence of tension is obtained from introspective reports, from observations of the subject's level of motor activity which increases during frustration, and from somatic measurements carried out before and after the frustrating experience.

Haggard and Freeman (15) noted increased palmar secretory activity after frustration. The most thorough physiological investigation was carried out by Jost (16). The frustration-situation consisted in inducing failure to recall a previously learned number series. The groups tested were twenty normal children, and eighteen children who suffered from various forms of maladjustment. He recorded a number of reactions such as galvanic skin resistance, respiration, pulse rate, heart rate, blood pressure, hand tremors, etc. It was found that both groups showed significant changes in the psychogalvanic skin resistance level, in hand tremor, and heart rate before and after the frustrating experience. The groups differed significantly from one another in the extent of the changes and in the length of time needed to return to the pre-frustration level of physiological activity. The neurotic group showed more extensive changes and took longer to return to the pre-frustration level. The interesting individual differences found will be discussed later. Jost shows conclusively that both well-adjusted and maladjusted children respond to frustration by an increase of activity at the physiological level. He suggests that frustration produces in a subject both covert and overt activity, the latter depending on the individual's past experience, the momentary situation and the general culture pattern. A measure of the covert activity, at the more physiological level, would serve as an index of the strength of the frustrating experience itself.

This physiological approach to the problem of frustration is useful, particularly when coupled with a psychological evaluation of the different overt reactions displayed by the subjects. It should be possible to determine the intensity of the frustration in terms of these physiological indices and in terms of the physiological 'Recovery Quotient' referred to by Haggard and Freeman (15). Subsequent correlation of these indices with different types of frustration reactions should prove illuminating.

The counterpart of the tension produced at the physiological level, is the *emotion* aroused at the psychological level. The immediate reaction to a frustrating experience is an emotional one. In fact, the amount of emotion produced might indicate the amount of frustration aroused. This need not tally, however, with the individual's conscious evaluation of the situation.

We thus know that frustration produces an emotional reaction and an increase of tension in the individual. How is this tension discharged? Leaving the study of the aggressive responses to frustration to the last, we find evidence of a variety of other responses. For the purpose of clarity, these will now be listed separately, although in most experiments subjects displayed more than one kind of reaction.

1. *Regression* or lowering of the level of performance. This reaction comes out clearly in the interesting experiment of Barker, Dembo and Lewin (4) who induced frustration in thirty nursery-school children by lowering a wire-mesh curtain between them and some attractive toys with which they had previously been encouraged to play. They assessed on a four-point scale the constructiveness of the children's play prior to the frustrating situation. The lowest level of constructiveness of play consisted in using toys simply as objects, disregarding their specific character, e.g. shaking toy telephones, spilling pegs. At the highest level of constructiveness, the toys were used with due regard for their special characteristics and elaborate pretence games were played, e.g. a truck was driven to Chicago where cattle which had been put on the truck were sold. After the frustrating experience, the children still had the old toys, on which the original estimate of constructiveness had been made, to play with. It was found that the frustration led to a decrease in the level of constructiveness of play. The average decrease was seventeen months mental age from an average pre-frustration level of fifty-five months.

Under frustration, behaviour became disorganized and less mature. The children displayed exaggerated motor activity and aggression. The decrease in the level of constructiveness has been ascribed in part to a heightening of the emotional tension and in part to a feeling of insecurity about the future. Planning a more elaborate game requires calm and a feeling that such activity is approved, or at least will not be interfered with, by the adult in charge. Barker, Dembo, and Lewin (4) noted wide individual differences in the extent of 'regression' shown, e.g. eight children remained as mature in their play as before. In part this difference depended on the amount of frustration experienced as measured by the time a child spent hitting against the barrier or trying to lift it. (The correlation was found to be ·5.)

A similar decline in planning activity was observed in Lewin and Lippit and White's experiment on 'social climates' (20). The boys worked less well when under autocratic or *laissez-faire* leadership, than under democratic leadership.

Seashore and Bavelas (37), who asked the children to make a series of drawings of a man, found that the drawings when analysed in terms of mental age, showed a lowering of the mental age level as the child became frustrated.

Frustration thus appears to lead to a lowering of performance in the intellectual field—we can all quote examples from our own experience to show that frustration is not conducive to calm thought and planning. Nevertheless, one cannot assume that frustration leads to a lowering of all kinds of performance. As Murphy (26) points out, acts such as hammering nails into a piece of wood or kicking a football would probably be carried out with more strength and zest after than before the frustrating experience, since such activities provide an outlet for the accumulated tension. However, if one evaluated these performances in terms of their accuracy, one might find that it had decreased.

2. In their frustration experiments Barker, Dembo and Lewin (4) noted that some subjects displayed primarily anger directed both against the task and the experimenter. Others reacted to frustration (inability to perform an allotted task) by 'going out of the field' to use Lewin's (19) phrase. They ceased to try to overcome the sense of failure by increased effort but instead evaded the entire situation and left the room. Such act was frequently accompanied by deprecatory remarks about the experimental set-up. This response to frustration is important, and it would be interesting to know what kind of personality or what type of previous frustration experiences cause a subject to select this particular mode of reaction. It may possibly be related to the impunitive type of response that Rosenzweig (32) noted when he gave his subjects a picture frustration test. In this test, different frustrating experiences are portrayed and the subject is asked to furnish the response that the frustrated individual in the picture would give.

3. Somewhat similar to the 'going out of the field', is the *apathy and resignation* which Marie Lazarsfeld and Zeisl (18) reported as a common response of Austrian villagers to a continuous period of unemployment during an economic depression. The reason for this reaction lies probably in the prolonged character of the frustrating experience and may well have succeeded reactions of protest. Continuous frustration must lead to a decline of tension requiring immediate relief. We have no evidence to judge whether such reaction of apathy is a general one, with which given individuals react to all kinds of frustrating experiences, or whether it is specific to *any* frustration of long duration.

Apathy and resignation were also noted by Allport, Bruner and

Jandorf (3) when they analysed the accounts by ninety German refugees, of their reactions to the Nazi persecution. They found that the kind of reaction shown by the different persons appeared consistent with their personality make-up. "Besides aggressive responses, direct or displaced, we find defeat and resignation, regression, conformity, adoption of temporary frames of security. . . ."

4. On the other hand, Allport and his colleagues (3) point out that many individuals reacted to this experience by *increased effort*. A similar reaction was also noted by Zander (42) in his experiment with school children, where they experienced failure in recalling a given number series which they had previously been able to repeat successfully. Comparing the reactions before and during the frustrating situation, he found a wide diversity of reactions. Under this challenge, some of the best adjusted children displayed heightened attention and increased effort. Since frustration here was induced for one experimental period only, it is difficult to know how long such increased effort would have lasted. It is possible that, when the frustration experience continues over a longer period and is unaffected by increased activity, this reaction would be superseded by one of a different kind, possibly by its antithesis, apathy.

5. Rosenzweig (31) noted *repression* as a response to frustration. He asked his subjects to recall all the puzzles they had attempted in the previous session. The need-persistive group recalled a higher percentage of unfinished puzzles, while the ego-defensive group recalled a higher percentage of finished puzzles. Rosenzweig carried out these experiments with children of different age levels, with problem children, and with normal and neurotic adults. He found amongst normal children a decreasing tendency with age to repress the memory of the unfinished puzzles. Neurotic children and neurotic adults behaved like young normal children in repressing the memory. This is an interesting study, as it shows that the kind of reaction displayed to frustration is related to the individual's general adjustment and maturity level (29).

The reactions just described, and those of *aggression*, are those reactions most commonly encountered in the different frustration experiments. They are all behavioural in character. In addition a great diversity of verbal reactions other than aggressive ones have been reported. These have been listed by McClelland (24). He induced failure in undergraduates, most of whom he knew personally, by arranging that their scores on a card sorting test were always less than their prediction of what they would be able to score. He reinforced the impression of failure by derogatory remarks. His criticism of the subjects was personal, couched in unacademic language. This not only enhanced the frustrating situation, but also created for the subjects an atmosphere of informality in which they could give vent to their feelings. A microphone had been installed, and verbatim records of the session were taken in an adjoining room. McClelland stresses the great variety of verbal responses given. Apart from aggressive outbursts, the subject made excuses; headaches and absence of sleep were reported to explain the failure (rationalization). Or the experience of failure was played down by 'I was never good at this sort of thing', suggesting that the subject would not fail in other situations. Comments stressing the poor quality of the material and derogatory remarks about the investigator's personality were made.

These reactions were similar to those found by Rosenzweig with the picture frustration test (33). Rosenzweig grouped the responses into three broad categories: extrapunitive, impunitive, and intropunitive responses and showed that these are linked with different personality types. An extrapunitive reaction is one in which the responsibility for the frustration is attributed to others, impunitive one in which responsibility is attributed to fate or some neutral agent outside both the subject's and the experimenter's control, and intropunitive one where the subject admits, even exaggerates his responsibility for the situation. In the field of neurosis, Rosenzweig found that impunitive responses were given more frequently by hysterics, and intropunitive ones by depressives and patients suffering from anxiety states.

This enumeration of reactions to frustration shows that both on the behavioural and on the verbal plane reactions to frustration are not confined to the aggressive type.

Before dealing with the *aggressive reactions* noted in response to frustration, it seems pertinent to discuss the term 'aggression' itself. Its indiscriminate use has led to much confusion in psychological literature. 'Aggressive behaviour' is used, for example, to denote verbal criticism, swearing, absence of friendliness, forced withdrawal of an object from another person, slamming of doors, as well as overt bodily attack. This list of aggressive reactions is obviously far from complete. In addition, one speaks of overt and covert, displaced and delayed aggression, and of aggression turned inwards. Researches like those of Murphy (27) show that aggressive acts such as snatching a toy from another child or attacking it, are signs of healthy development and exuberance in a pre-school child and that they are positively correlated with their apparent antithesis—sympathetic and co-operative behaviour. Murphy (27) and Bender (5) stress the constructive element in childhood aggression. Anna Freud (12) and Melanie Klein (17), on the other hand, stress the destructive element, taking aggression to be a sign of insecurity and maladjustment, evidence of psychic conflict. Common parlance often uses 'aggressive' as synonymous with 'self-assertive', while in psychiatric literature the frequent linking of the term with 'psychopath' indicates that it is used to describe unprovoked verbal or physical outbursts, and denotes instability of character. In view of all these divergencies, the lack of agreement between psychologists as to the role of aggression in the functioning of the individual and of the group is not surprising.

In the experiments on frustration, aggressive comments were found to be an almost universal reaction. In many studies, this took simply the form of 'letting off steam' and was not the really important reaction shown, e.g. in Barker's and others (4) experiment with nursery-school children, the dominant reaction was a decrease in the level of constructiveness of play, a subsidiary reaction, aggressive comments by the children.

Some investigators do not define clearly the aggressive behaviour they note, but it becomes indirectly apparent that all adult studies, when stating that their subjects behaved aggressively, refer in the main to verbal outbursts of aggression.

With children, physical aggression directed against the obstruction, e.g. the wire-mesh curtain, against other children, and by pre-school children against the adult have been noted. The social taboo on physical violence leads adults to refrain from using it except under extreme provocation which naturally, was not experimentally produced. In its place, tension is released by verbal aggression. Indirect evidence of pent-up aggression was obtained by Rodnick and Klebanoff (30) who gave two groups of twelve students, one well adjusted, the other poorly adjusted, a Thematic Apperception Test before and after a frustrating experience. An analysis of the stories told by the students showed that after frustration, there was an increase of stories with aggressive content.

Since verbal aggression seems generally to accompany reactions to frustrations, it is important to describe the conditions in which it is allowed free rein and is directed against the instigator of the frustration, co-sufferers, or some innocuous outside individual or group. Several interesting investigations give information upon these points.

Wright (41) repeating the experiment of Barker, Dembo and Lewin (4) of lowering the wire-mesh curtain and measuring the decrease in constructiveness of play of children, added a new variable. He studied the effect of the frustration on pairs of nursery-school children described as 'weak' and 'strong' friends respectively. He found that the decrease in constructiveness of play was less for the strong friends, and that these were significantly more aggressive physically and verbally against the adult than the weak friends. It appears that the added security provided by the presence of a friend allows freer outlet of the pent-up aggression. This tendency operated over and above the tendency for stronger aggression to follow a greater degree of frustration. (The correlation between strength of frustration and aggression was found to be ·42.)

Free outlet of aggression thus depends in part on the strength of the frustration and in part on the *field situation*, one element of which may be the presence or absence of friends. Similar observations were made by French (10) who investigated the effect of frustration upon the disruption and cohesion of groups. He used sixteen groups, each consisting of six members. Eight of these groups consisted of members who had not previously met (the unorganized groups) and eight of members who knew each other well, lived in the same house and were members of the same basket-ball and football teams, the captains of which formed part of the group (the organized groups). The task given was to discover how quickly the group could solve problems and they were presented with a choice of three. The frustration lay in the fact that the tasks could not be solved in the time allotted although this was not apparent to the groups. It was found that the organized groups relieved the tension by being far more aggressive to one another (blaming each other for failure) than the unorganized groups. Again it appears that aggression is voiced more freely in an atmosphere of security created by sharing the experience with friends.

In Lewin, Lippit and White's (20) investigation of the experimentally produced social climates, the boys were more aggressive under the *laissez-faire* leader than under the democratic leader. Under the autocratic leader, when the aggressiveness of the group was plotted it was bimodal in character. The members of the group showed extremes of behaviour—very aggressive or very submissive. Those boys who reacted by submissiveness during the club meeting itself, were the ones who inhibited their aggressiveness because of fear of punishment. Confirmation of this view was obtained by noting the behaviour of these 'submissive' boys at the end of the meeting after the leader had left the room. It was found that both types of boys after a session with the autocratic leaders were very much more aggressive, verbally and physically, against each other and against the cleaners. The aggression was thus displaced and given outlet when fear of punishment was removed. Here a psychiatric study of the individual boys would have been of value to indicate why some more than others inhibited aggression in the presence of the leader.

This brings us to the important problem of *displaced aggression*. The above experiment has shown it to operate especially when the setting is such that outlet of aggression against the instigator of the frustration is felt not to be politic. The inhibiting cause may be fear of actual punishment, or great difference in status between the person who experiences the frustration and the one who evokes it. This was confirmed in Burton's (6) investigation of the aggression of young children following satiation. The child in his experiment was bored with the task of having to fill a very large board with coloured pegs; at this point a second highly motivated child was introduced and asked to help complete the task. It was found that the tension the first child had accumulated was discharged in aggressive behaviour against the second child, but not against the adult in charge.

Summarizing these investigations, we find that the degree of aggression shown is in part a function of the strength of the frustration experience, and in part affected by situational factors. Added security given by the presence of friends may enable aggression to be expressed more freely. Aggression tends to be inhibited by a feeling of insecurity and by anticipation of punishment. In these circumstances, it tends to be displaced on to some individual or group of a status more nearly equal to the subject's, and from whom no retaliation is expected. When aggression is displaced, it is often directed to a person in no way responsible for the frustrating situation.

Is the release of aggression as described in these experiments harmful? It is interesting in this connection to note (a) that in Wright's (41) experiment, the children who expressed their aggression freely showed less regression in the maturity of play, and (b) that the organized group of students described by French (10) who railed against each other, finished the experimental session as good friends, while in the unorganized groups a feeling of tension remained. Zander (42) in his experiment showed that the subjects who tended to be more aggressive showed at the same time heightened attention, and concentration. Their behaviour during the frustrating experience

M

was accompanied by fewer neurotic mannerisms and they were the friendliest at the close of the experiment. When the reactions of the children to having to draw what appeared to them an infinite number of men was analysed, Seashore and Bavelas (37) found that the children who showed a high degree of verbal aggression at the same time showed a high degree of compliance in continuing with the task.

These findings suggest that a person who feels secure enough to 'let off steam' by voicing his feelings about the situation is the one who at the same time will deal with it in a constructive manner. It is a method of decreasing the extent of the frustration of the experience and leads to beneficial discharge of tension. The observations of displaced aggression support Dollard's (7) hypothesis and suggest that the danger lies not so much in presenting an individual with a frustrating experience as in placing it in a setting, in which he feels too insecure to seek immediate relief for the accumulated tension. It is interesting to compare these researches with Dollard's (7) description of the readiness of people under a totalitarian regime to seek aggressive outlets by attacking neutral groups.

The evidence points, therefore, very strongly to the need to specify clearly the setting in which the frustrating experience occurred and in particular the interpersonal relationship between the subjects, and between them and the experimenter.

Not only must the situational factors be taken into account, but also the personality make-up of the individuals. Some of the investigations concentrate on the problem of individual differences, usually comparing two groups, one well adjusted, the other poorly adjusted. Other experimenters, while not selecting their subjects to present wide individual differences nevertheless state that one of their most interesting findings is the difference in the intensity and type of reactions. It is found that individuals differ from one another with regard to frustration tolerance and to mechanisms used to relieve tension due to frustration.

A useful definition of *frustration tolerance* is given by Rosenzweig (33). "Frustration tolerance may be defined as an individual's capacity to withstand frustration without resorting to inadequate modes of response." Apathy, resignation, regression, and undischarged aggression would be examples of such inadequate modes of response. This concept is closely tied up with the ability of the individual to delay gratification. It is explained by Rosenzweig (33) in terms of the psycho-analytic concepts of the reality and of the pleasure principle.

The difference in frustration tolerance is particularly marked between neurotic and normal subjects. This has been shown both for the somatic and psychological reactions to frustration. Freeman (9), for instance, found increased palmar skin resistance amongst the less stable of his subjects. Jost (16) found that the neurotic subjects, children and adults, showed more marked somatic changes after frustration. When the maladjusted children were rated for the severity of their emotional disturbance, he found a correlation of ·79 between an additive score of 'physiological instability' and emotional maladjustment. Sherman and Jost (39) in a more detailed investigation of the frustration reactions of normal and neurotic persons, stress the good agreement between the physiological findings and the introspective reports of the subjects concerning the strength of the frustration experience.

Further evidence of the lower frustration tolerance of neurotics has been found at the psychological level. Adams (1) in his study of individual differences in behaviour resulting from experimentally induced frustration, found that while the neurotic students as judged by their score on the Bernreuter test (a rather doubtful indication of neuroticism) were as co-operative as the stable students, they were more tense and agitated.

Rodnick (30) found the changes in the Thematic Apperception material produced before and after frustration to be more marked for the poorly adjusted group.

Zander (42) found that well and poorly adjusted children differed not only in their frustration tolerance but also in the kind of reactions used to relieve the tension.

Finally, Rosenzweig (32) showed that his neurotic subjects used repression as a means of dealing with frustration to a greater extent than well-adjusted subjects.

Petrie (28) gave adult male and female neurotics a variety of brief tasks. At the end of each task, she praised or criticized the subject for his performance. A recall test, a week later, confirmed the findings of Rosenzweig, namely, that the tendency to repress was correlated with severity of maladjustment.

These investigations demonstrate conclusively that an unstable person has a lower frustration tolerance than a stable person. The reason for this difference lies most probably in the psychological meaning of the frustration situation to the individual. The neurotic views the failure experience in a much more personal light; it constitutes a threat to his personality, as Maslow (23) expresses it. The experience is linked consciously or unconsciously with the subject's general feeling of insecurity, of being a failure, for which it provides further confirmation. A stable person accepts the failure or any other temporary frustration more readily. For him it is an isolated experience and he can deal with it in that light—it constitutes a deprivation, but not also a threat to his personality.

That differences in frustration tolerance show themselves very early is shown in Marquis's (22) study of infants. He found the amount of crying, of oral and general bodily activity upon withdrawal of the bottle, varied considerably from infant to infant. Re-examination after three months showed the same individual differences.

Goldman (14) in an inquiry into the hypothesis of Freud that early weaning affects the later personality of the individual, found a positive correlation between early weaning and increased irritability and tension in the adult. Early weaning could be interpreted as a severe frustration experienced in infancy. This experience, analysts believe, subsequently lowers the frustration tolerance of that person. Whilst the finding is important, further research would be needed to establish the causal relationship between the period of weaning and tension in adulthood.

The above account shows that the investigations of the last decade, while failing to create the frustration experiences considered important by Freud, have yet produced many interesting results. They have shown clearly the need for taking into account many more factors than did Dollard and Doob in formulating their original frustration theory.

Any theory of frustration must take account of the following factors:

1. A frustration experience has a different psychological meaning for different individuals; in fact it would not be an exaggeration to say that the psychological meaning of a given situation is unique to the individual. Maslow's (23) classification is useful here. He divides the psychological meaning of frustration situations for different individuals into two principal types, depending upon whether they constitute a deprivation, or in addition a threat to the individual's personality.

2. A frustrating experience that occurs in everyday life or is experimentally induced, cannot be viewed in isolation, but must be placed in the context of the individual's past experiences of frustration. The effect of past frustrating experiences will be to intensify the frustration value of the present situation.

3. Situational factors play a role in determining the intensity

of a frustration experience. An experience, shared with another person, is usually felt to be less frustrating. Not only the interpersonal relationship of co-sufferers but also that between the subject and the person responsible for the frustration, is important. A prohibition made by a teacher, invested with authority, will be felt by the child quite differently from the same prohibition made by the mother. Clinical studies are suggestive in this connection, since they show that the relationship of parent to child greatly affects the child's reaction to any limitation of his freedom by the parent. In a strained relationship, the slightest interference is felt as severely frustrating and produces violent reactions; an improvement of the relationship, as a result of treatment, for example, usually leads to an increase in frustration tolerance.

4. Individuals differ widely with regard to their thresholds of susceptibility to frustration. We have no evidence to indicate to what extent these differences are innate and to what extent they are the result of environmental influences and experiences. They are probably due to a combination of these two factors. The experiments show clearly that they are related to the general adjustment and maturity level of an individual. In fact, a very low frustration tolerance can be taken as an indication of maladjustment; many psychiatrists use it as one of the diagnostic criteria.

In addition, temporary changes in mood may affect the threshold of susceptibility. It is common medical experience that fatigue and ill-health lower a person's frustration tolerance. 'Test-re-test' reliability studies would be of interest.

5. It is probable, as Rosenzweig (33) suggests, that an individual has not one absolute level of frustration tolerance, but rather that he differs in his susceptibility to frustration from situation to situation, depending upon which aspect of his personality the experience touches. This author suggests that "circumscribed areas of low frustration tolerance would correspond to Freudian 'complexes'". Apart from such circumscribed areas which are not frequently found in normal subjects, every individual creates a certain picture of himself. To one individual, failure in a game of tennis may be quite unimportant whilst failure in cricket may be experienced as more frustrating because in that particular sport he has set himself a high standard. Susceptibility to frustration will thus in part depend on the aspirations of the individual.

6. So far we have dealt with the factors which must be taken into account in assessing the strength of the stimulus, the frustration

experience. Turning to the responses evoked, we find a wide diversity such as 'going out of the field', apathy, resignation, repression, lowering of the level of performance, increased effort, and aggression. Frustration experiments have not lent themselves to evoking reactions such as regression and sublimation which Freud describes as methods of dealing with a frustrating situation. Sublimation would lead to a circumvention of the frustrating experience by a shift of the goal. Regression constitutes a return to an earlier, less mature mode of behaviour. In this respect, it is similar to the lowering of the level of performance observed by Barker, Dembo and Lewin (4).

In fitting the wide diversity of responses into the framework of a theory which would enable us to predict which reaction will be evoked under given circumstances, the following aspects have to be taken into account:

(a) The choice of responses will depend on the individual's earlier trial-and-error attempts to deal with increased tension. In accordance with learning theories, those responses which fail to reduce tension, or which even lead to further frustration such as punishment evoked by physical violence, will be inhibited, while the operation of other, more effective ones, will be facilitated.

(b) The situational factors attending the frustration experience, e.g. the presence of friends or strangers influence the overt reactions shown.

(c) The intensity of the frustrating experience. The need for immediate relief of tension may be so great that it leads the individual to adopt a response most likely to achieve this. Under severe provocation, therefore, any individual may react with physical violence even to the point of seriously injuring another person, without stopping to take into account the further frustrations which such conduct will entail. The intensity of the frustrating experience will thus determine in part whether the reaction will be maladjustive or adjustive.

(d) The duration of the frustration experience: The frustration induced in the experiments was of short duration only. It is highly probable that an individual will call into play more than one type of reaction depending, amongst other factors, on the length of the frustration experience. Tension cannot be maintained continuously at a high pitch and the longer the frustration persists, the less urgent becomes the need for its immediate discharge. It is for instance highly probable that the apathy noted in the Austrian unemployed was not the first reaction, but one which was adopted when the frustrating situation persisted.

(e) The extent to which the individual considers the situation remediable. Reactions are fluid, and their choice will depend on whether the individual subjectively or objectively considers the frustrating situation to be within his control, i.e. whether it is frustration with hope or frustration without hope.

The investigations reported so far have clearly demonstrated the complexity of the problem. Before psychologists can predict, with any degree of accuracy, the reactions of the individual and the reactions of the group to given frustrating experiences, more research is needed. The studies of the last decade point the way. The following types of investigations suggest themselves as a means of filling the gaps that exist in our knowledge of this very important topic:

A close study of individual differences with regard to (a) degree of frustration tolerance, and related to this problem, (b) the kind of reaction evoked. Two approaches are needed here. First, the study of clearly defined groups whose main characteristics are known. These groups are then subjected to various frustrating experiences and observations made to see whether the groups differ significantly from one another in their reactions. Groups could be contrasted on the basis of sex, degree of adjustment, personality types (introverts or extraverts), occupational status, intelligence level, age, etc. Secondly, large numbers of subjects should be tested and classified into groups on the basis of similarity of responses. Thus in Lewin, Lippit and White's (20) experiment the children who reacted to autocratic leadership submissively would form one group, those who reacted aggressively a second and those who appeared not to react to the experience at all, a third. Common factors in the personality make-up of the individuals and in their past history could then be sought. These might account for the similarity of reactions of individuals in one group as compared with those in another. Such research would require careful study of the individuals by means of detailed case histories, temperament and personality tests.

Research of this kind would help to prove or disprove theories of various psychological schools regarding the effect of past frustrating experiences upon the individual's reaction to the present situation. Emphasis should be placed on gaining information of the frustrating experiences encountered in infancy, childhood, and adolescence, care being taken to differentiate between frustrations due to objective situations such as poverty, failure to gain a scholarship, etc., and more intangible frustrations due to strained emotional relationships of the individual to his surroundings, his family, teachers and other figures who play a role in his life. It may be that only the psycho-analytic technique can elicit this information. This, however, leads to certain difficulties caused by the inevitable smallness of the sample, the difficulty of adopting relatively objective criteria for evaluating the severity of these experiences, and that of detecting retrospective falsification. It is possible for instance that an individual who reacts poorly to present frustrations, looks back on his past life, over-emphasizing the frustrations he has encountered, as a means of justifying, to himself, his present behaviour. However, in spite of these difficulties, the analytic approach, particularly when coupled with experimental objective measurements of the individual's attitude to the present situation, would be worth attempting and might throw light on some of the factors responsible for individual differences.

Numerous statements about 'the effect of frustration' in the literature treat all frustrating experiences, or even experiences which the experimenter believes to be frustrating, as identical. However, before we can speak of 'frustration' *per se* and of characteristic response-patterns to frustration we must search for proof of their existence. The technique to be used has been employed by various research workers to demonstrate the existence of a general trait, e.g. persistence, fluency. The reactions of subjects to a variety of frustrating experiences would be recorded. By factorial-analysis, one can then ascertain the degree to which it is justifiable to speak of generalized reaction patterns to frustration.

We may find, for instance, a general factor of frustration-toler-ance, by means of which individuals can be differentiated, and in addition group factors. One group factor might relate to experiences that have in common restraint of physical movement, another inability to complete various tasks imposed by others or self-imposed, a third factor might comprise experiences involving discord in the relationship of the individual to his colleagues, and to his superiors. Similarly, there may be generalized response patterns to frustration, e.g. there may be a consistent tendency of some subjects to try to extricate themselves from frustrating situations by 'going out of the field', while others react consistently by aggression, others again by rationaliza-tions, etc.

The value of this type of study would depend entirely on the experimenter's ability to cast his net very wide and to include a far greater diversity of frustrating experiences than have been reported so far. Responses to experiences in the field, in everyday life, and those evoked by the experimenter in the laboratory should be included in such an investigation. This approach to the problem would also help to answer the question whether different areas of susceptibility to frustration exist for given individuals, as mentioned by Rosenzweig (33). These investigations would have to be carried out separately for normal and for neurotic subjects and for different personality types.

More research is needed into the relationship between the strength of the frustrating experience and mechanisms used for the discharge of the accumulated tension. Using the physiological index as an estimate of the strength of frustration aroused by the experience, it may be found, for instance, that an individual adopts one mode of response for frustration-experiences of low intensity and another when the experience is a severely frustrating one. It is likely that the need for the immediate discharge of tension becomes greater, the more intense the experience, and that with such increase of tension, there may be a breakdown of the more socialized modes of reaction, e.g. a shift from verbal to physical aggression. The subject would have to be observed not only during the experiment but also for a period afterwards, to note any signs of delayed discharge of tension.

Not enough attention has been paid to the cumulative effect of frustration. This could be studied experimentally. For instance, children in a holiday camp could be submitted to a series of carefully controlled frustration experiences. Previously, the children would be divided into a number of groups, matched for age, I.Q., sex, and emotional maturity. The frustration experiences would be the same for all groups, the only difference being the time interval between these. Possibly, where the time interval between the experiences is sufficiently long for the effect of the previous frustrations to have died down, the group faced with a new situation would behave differently from another group experiencing frustrations in close succession. The time interval required for a previous experience to cease to affect a subsequent one, will be closely related to the frustration value of each experience; the more intense, the more time will be needed for the individual to return to his or her emotional *status quo*.

Fascinating problems, worthy of further inquiry, relate to the influence of different situational factors on the frustration value of the experience. This could be tested by submitting the subject to similar frustrating experiences varying only the setting in which they occur, e.g. when the subject is alone, is amongst his superiors, friends or strangers.

We have seen from our review of the experimental data, that displaced aggression tends to occur whenever tension is not given a direct outlet. The findings are suggestive rather than conclusive and need to be tested further experimentally. Groups of subjects could be submitted to fairly intense frustrating experiences, and outlet of tension could be prevented by various means such as the presence of authoritative persons, the presence of strangers, etc. The behaviour of subjects during the experience could then be compared with the behaviour when the subject returns to his customary environment, where the need for restraint operates to a lesser degree.

So far, emphasis has been placed upon an individual's reactions to frustration and his level of frustration-tolerance. Few experimental data exist concerning the frustration-tolerance of groups and their mechanisms of discharge of tension. Yet it should not be too difficult to devise experiments involving the frustration of groups. A hint concerning suitable technique has been given by French (10) in his comparative study of the reaction of organized and unorganized groups. A subject that deserves special study in this connection is the shift in the level of frustration-tolerance, and in mechanisms of reaction used, that occurs when the subject operates first as an individual and later as an integrate member of the group. The thesis that the intensity of a frustrating experience for a group will depend on the previous frustrating experiences of its individual members will have to be examined experimentally. This could be done by forming groups and submitting them to similar frustrating experiences, the groups differing only with regard to the amount of frustration to which the individual members had been submitted in the past.

The general problem of the effect of frustration on subsequent behaviour, stands in need of further clarification. This is doubly true of the relationship between frustration and aggression. The difficulty that arises here is due to lack of agreement as to what can be termed aggression, which has been discussed earlier. Hardly any studies touch on the question as to whether there is a general factor of aggression, a notable exception being that of Stagner (40) on social attitudes. He demonstrated the existence of a common factor of aggression, which showed itself in the attitude of individuals to a variety of social problems. Stagner was dealing with verbally expressed attitudes and although by definition, an attitude implies a readiness to act, we yet lack evidence to show that a person who is prone to verbal aggressiveness or holds aggressive views, is equally liable to be physically aggressive in a different situation or to work actively towards war— all these activities being classed under the term 'aggression'. The absence of experimental knowledge of what precisely constitutes aggression makes it well-nigh impossible to draw parallels between the diluted kind of aggression displayed in these experiments, and the aggression exhibited by groups in their attitudes and subsequent behaviour to one another. An example of the difficulty is the finding of several investigators that individuals who displayed aggression freely in the form of aggressive comments, tended at the same time to be less neurotic and to be more amenable and co-operative in their actual behaviour than those who were verbally less aggressive. The aggressive comments served here as an immediate discharge of tension and were followed by compliant behaviour. If this were established as a general truth, nations would vie with each other in asking their neighbours to attack them verbally, to make derogatory remarks about them, since this would lead to peaceful and conciliatory behaviour!

These suggestions regarding future research do no more than outline the contours of the problem. The answer to the question as to the effect of frustration on the individual and on the group can only be achieved by a multiple approach, attacking the problem from all angles until finally the isolated pieces of information form a design. It is indeed a laborious task because of the difficulty of controlling all the variables involved. It is the usual difficulty with which dynamic psychology is faced when it attempts to measure and interpret response patterns which are an end-product, the result of a complex inter-mingling of past and present and of genetic and environmental factors. So far we have stressed primarily the incompleteness of our knowledge. This incompleteness makes it impossible to predict the effect of frustration with any degree of certainty. It also makes the attempt to generalize from the experiments and to draw parallels from their findings to the broader panorama of world affairs a hazardous proposition.

Supposing, however, that some individual, some leader of a group or of a nation, approached the psychologists asking them for guidance how to minimize the ill-effect of certain frustrations which have to be imposed. He would be informed of the uncertain state of our knowledge and be asked to bear this in mind in acting on the suggestions which the psychologists put forward on the basis of the findings to date. No attempt will be made to recall the experimental evidence on which the advice is based since it has already previously been discussed. In trying to minimize the ill-effect of certain frustra-tions which have to be imposed, be it restriction of liberty, of oppor-tunities for self-expression, material deprivations or uprooting from the customary environment due to war, shift of industry, etc., our aim will be two-fold. First, to reduce the intensity of the frustration experience itself, and secondly to provide opportunity for immediate harmless discharge of tension. We have seen that the intensity of the frustrating experience depends on the psychological meaning it has for the individual and on the situational factors in which it occurs. When is the frustration value of an experience intensified? It is intensified when the experience is not shared by the others surrounding the individual, when he feels it to be the result of his own inability, when he feels that no effort on his part can improve the situation, when it is felt to attack his aspirations, to constitute a threat to his personality. Consequently, the frustration value of an experience is lessened when the individual feels that he is not alone in experiencing it, when he can tell himself that he is not responsible for having brought it about, but yet can work towards reducing its effect (frustration with hope, Alexander), and that although the deprivation or restriction interferes with the attainment of some sub goal, it yet aids in the attainment of some greater goal. Frustration-tolerance we have seen to be a function of the general adjustment of the individual. Emphasis should therefore be placed on increasing the mental stamina of the individuals by reducing stress and creating an atmosphere of psychological security.

Harmless discharge of tension is provided in an environment where the individual is not afraid to vent his feelings, where he feels himself surrounded by friends and does not fear the consequences of an outburst. Feelings tend to be repressed not only in a hostile environment, but also in one where the difference in status between the person who imposes the frustration and the one who experiences it is felt to be too great. The well-adjusted individual tends to interpret situations more readily as being of a kind where free expression of feeling does not tend to lead to further frustrations.

We have, from the experiments quoted, sufficient evidence to show that any restriction that has to be imposed has to be rationally explained, that it has to be shared by all the members of the community, and that these members should be given an opportunity for criticizing the restriction and be given an opportunity to work towards its removal. Under such circumstances and provided the individuals are well adjusted, even severe frustrations should have little ill-effect.

When no opportunity for discharge of tension is provided or when the frustrations imposed are too severe for tension to be readily discharged, it will then seek indirect outlet which may well take the form of displaced aggression directed against some individual or group in no way responsible for the situation: it is here that the danger lies.

The researches thus demonstrate experimentally the importance of the lesson which has been applied for centuries by all good educationalists and sound leaders. Whenever a restriction has to be imposed, the psychological ill-effects of such an experience can be reduced by imposing it in a friendly environment, in an atmosphere of psychological security. This lesson applies to the relationships of individuals to one another, but even more strongly to the relationships between nations.

This chapter went to press prior to the publication of *Frustration, the Study of Behavior Without a Goal*, by N. R. Maier (N.Y., McGraw-Hill, 1949). In this book, Maier puts forward the theory that motivated behaviour differs in kind from frustration-instigated behaviour which is essentially "behaviour without a goal," its function being to relieve tension. In consequence such behaviour is stereotyped and mal-adaptive. "Frustration tends to freeze or abnormally fixate a sample of behaviour." Maier shows that this theory will serve to explain case studies and experimental findings both with animal and human subjects. This book should be carefully studied to do justice to this interesting theory with its important implications for therapy and education.

REFERENCES

1. Adams, C. R. "Individual differences in behaviour resulting from experimentally induced frustration." *J. Psychol.* 1940. Vol. X, 157–76.
2. Alexander, F. "A World Without Psychic Frustration," *Amer. J. Sociol.* 1944. Vol. XLIX, 465–9.
3. Allport, G. W., Bruner, J. S., and Jandorf, E. M. "Personality under social catastrophe; ninety life histories of the Nazi revolution." *Char. and Pers.* 1941. Vol. X, 1–22.
4. Barker, R., Dembo, T., and Lewin, K. "Frustration and Regression: An Experiment With Young Children," *Univ. Iowa Stud. Child Welf.* 1941. Vol. XVIII, No. 1.
5. Bender, L. "Aggression in Childhood." L. G. Lowry and others; "The Treatment of Aggression." Round Table, 1943. *Amer. J. Orthopsychiat.* 1943. Vol. XIII, 384–441.
6. Burton, A. "The Aggression of Young Children Following Satiation." *Amer. J. Orthopsychiat.* 1942. Vol. XII, 262–8.
7. Dollard, J., Doob, L., and others. *Frustration and Aggression.* New Haven: Yale University Press, 1939.
8. Frederiksen, N. "The Effects of Frustration on Negativistic Behaviour of Young Children," *J. gen. Psychol.* 1942. Vol. LVI, 203–26.

9. Freeman, G. L. "A Method of Inducing Frustration in Human Subjects and its Influence Upon Palmar Skin Resistance," *Amer. J. Psychol.* 1940. Vol. LIII, 117–20.

10. French, J. R. P., Jr. "The Disruption and Cohesion of Groups," *J. abnorm. soc. Psychology.* 1941. Vol. XXXVI, 36–177.

11. Freud, S. *Collected Papers.* New York. International Psycho-Analytical Library. 1924–5.

12. Freud, A. *The Ego and Mechanisms of Defence.* London: Hogarth Press. 1937.

13. Glover, E. *War, Sadism and Pacifism.* London: Allen and Unwin. 1933.

14. Goldman, F. "Breast Feeding and Character Formation." *J. Pers.* 1948. Vol. XVI, 83–103.

15. Haggard, E. A., and Freeman, G. I. "Reactions of Children to Experimentally Induced Frustration." *Psychol. Bull.* 1941. Vol. XXXVIII, 581.

16. Jost, J. "Some Physiological Changes During Frustration." *Child Develpm.* 1941. Vol. XII, 9–15.

17. Klein, M. Collected Papers. London: Hogarth Press. 1945.

18. Lazarsfeld, M, and Zeisl, H. "Die Arbeitslosen von Marienthal," *Psychol. Monographen.* 1933. Vol. V.

19. Lewin, K. *Dynamic Theory of Personality.* New York: McGraw-Hill. 1935.

20. Lewin, K., Lippit, R., and White, R. K. "Patterns of Aggressive Behaviour in Experimentally Reared Social Climates," *J. soc. Psychol.* 1939. Vol. X, 271–99.

21. Maier, N. R. F., Glaser, N. M., Klee, J. B. "Studies of abnormal behavior in the rat: III". *J. Exp. Psychol.*, 1940. Vol. XXVI. 521–46.

22. Marquis, D. P. "A Study of Frustration in Newborn Infants," *J. exp. Psychol.* 1943. Vol. XXXII, 123–38.

23. Maslow, A. H. "Deprivation, Threat and Frustration," *Psych. Rev.* 1941. Vol. XLVIII, 364–6.

24. McClelland, D. C., and Apicella, F. S. "A Functional Classification of Verbal Reactions to Experimentally Induced Failure," *J. abnorm. soc. Psychol.* 1945. Vol. XL, 376–91.

25. Miller, N. E. "The Frustration Aggression Hypothesis," *Psychol. Rev.* 1941. Vol. XLVIII, 337–42.

26. Murphy, G. *Personality.* New York: Harper and Bros. 1947.

27. Murphy, L. B. *Social Behaviour and Child Personality.* New York: Columbia Univ. Press. 1937.

28. Petrie, A. "Repression and Suggestibility as Related to Temperament," *J. Pers.* 1948. Vol. XVI, 445–8.

29. Rapaport, D. "Freudian Mechanisms and Frustration Experiments," *Psychoanal. Quart.* 1942. Vol. XI, 503–11.

30. Rodnick, E. H., and Klebanoff, S. G. "Projective Reactions to Induced Frustration as Measure of Social Adjustment," *Psychol. Bull.* 1942. Vol. XXXIX, 489.

31. Rosenzweig, S. "Need-Persistive and Ego-Defensive Reaction to Frustration as Demonstrated by an Experiment on Repression," *Psychol. Rev.* 1941. Vol. XLVIII, 347–9.

32. Rosenzweig, S. "An Experimental Study of Repression, With Special Reference to Need-Persistive and Ego-Defensive Reactions to Frustration," *J. exp. Psychol.* 1943. Vol. XXXII, 64–74.

33. Rosenzweig, S. "An Outline of Frustration Theory," *Personality and the Behaviour Disorders.* J. McV. Hunt, New York: Ronald Press Co. 1944. 379–88.

34. Rosenzweig, S. "Further Comparative Data on Repetition-Choice After Success and Failure, as Related to Frustration Tolerance," *J. genet. Psychol.* 1945. Vol. LXVI, 75–81.

35. Sargent, S. S. "Reaction to Frustration. A Critique and Hypothesis." *Psychol. Rev.* 1948. Vol. LV, 108–115.

36. Sears, R. "Non-Aggressive Reactions to Frustration." *Psychol. Rev.* 1941. Vol. XLVIII, 343–6.

37. Seashore, H. G., and Bavelas, A. "A Study of Frustration in Children," *J. genet. Psychol.* 1942. Vol. LVI, 279–314.

38. Sherif, M., and Cantril, H. *The Psychology of Ego-Involvements.* New York: John Wiley and Sons. 1947.

39. Sherman, M., and Jost, H. "Frustration Reactions of Normal and Neurotic Persons," *J. Psychol.* 1942. Vol. XIII, 3–19.

40. Stagner, R. "Studies of Aggressive Social Attitudes. II Changes from Peace to War," *J. soc. Psychol.* 1944. Vol. XX, 121–8.

41. Wright, M. E. "Constructiveness of Play as Affected by Group Organization and Frustration," *Char. and Pers.* 1942. Vol. XI, 40–9.

42. Zander, A. F. "A Study of Experimental Frustration," *Psychol. Mon.* 1944. Vol. LVI, 3, 38.

CHAPTER IX

SOME PSYCHOLOGICAL STUDIES OF THE GERMAN CHARACTER

by H. V. Dicks

N

THE CONCEPT OF NATIONAL CHARACTER

THE purpose of this chapter is to direct the reader's attention through the medium of some actual systematic field work to an aspect of social study which has often been ignored by historians when considering the phenomena of political behaviour, and by many students of the intercourse between national or ethnic groups. This is the psychological aspect, using the term 'psychological' in the strict sense of an objective, scientific discipline applied to the experience and behaviour of human beings. Lest mention of this omission on the part of the political scientist, the statesman and the diplomat be taken as a criticism, it is only fair to add that this process of *ignoring* was the inevitable result of the psychologist's own *ignorance* of the nature of those forces, which, in the last analysis, are the prime movers of history—namely, the needs and strivings of individual human beings.

It is not perhaps widely enough appreciated that psychology has in the last few decades advanced to a point at which the student of politics can no longer reproach us with utter lack of understanding of his field. A very brief exposition of the point of view, of the concepts, from which this paper is written, may help to substantiate this claim and so make the later contents more acceptable. The subject matter is intended to be more of an example of a method of study than a complete exposition of the psychology of a national group.

Three lines of study have gradually converged to enable us to attack the problem of 'national character' with methods which are slowly approaching the canons of the science.

1. *The psycho-analytic study* of the individual personality and of its clinical abnormalities has enabled us to deduce certain laws of mental structure and function, and to interpret the relative parts played by inborn tendencies and biological needs (love, hunger, sex, etc.) on the one hand, and by the cultural heritage transmitted by educative influence on the other hand, in the shaping of human behaviour and its many tensions and conflicts—perhaps the very warp and woof of civilization itself.

195

In this respect, as in many another field of natural science and medicine, it was the initial study of the abnormal which laid bare the processes of normal function and enlarged our powers of control and prediction.

2. *The statistical method* applied to social science and to biology has enabled us to assign degrees of reliability and significance to observed data of behaviour, as in surveys of opinion and in factor analysis based on samples of population which, without such mathematical help, would have been regarded as much too small for purposes of scientific evidence.

3. *Social anthropology*, as exemplified by such field workers as Malinowski, Benedict and Margaret Mead, has demonstrated the feasibility of describing and interpreting the total behaviour, customs and beliefs of self-contained simple communities in terms of the above-mentioned interplay between instinctual needs and the force of group tradition, 'mores' and taboos brought to bear upon the rearing of the children of the community. As G. Gorer has said in his paper to the British Association (1947):[1]

"In various parts of the world—most spectacularly in New Guinea, and in the forests of West Africa—there are numerous independent small societies, many with less than a thousand members, often separated by only twenty or thirty miles, maybe just a wide river, from one another, of the same physical stock, sharing similar climates, diets, and technological development, and yet contrasting more strongly in many ways than any two societies in Europe; by every scientific criterion these groups are complete societies; apart from the level of technological development, and all that entails in the way of social differentiation and specialization, they possess the same types of institutions as our own society. And these societies differ most markedly from one another: one may be warlike, head-hunters or cannibals, raiding their peaceful neighbours who never consider retaliation; one may be hard-working, striving all through their adult life to amass fortunes in whatever valuables the society prizes and honouring above all their successful traders. . . . Even when the same institutions are shared by two or more societies they may be used for quite different ends. Thus, for example, many tribes in New Guinea have the *tamberan* cult, a male society involving the use of masks and bull-roarers; in some societies this cult is used to frighten the women and uninitiated children and keep them in subjection; in others it is phrased as

[1]"The Scientific Study of National Character"—unpublished.

the protection of the women and children from supernatural dangers which the men undertake in a spirit of self-sacrifice."

Geographical and physical environment, no doubt, impose limits on what is possible to a human group and what traits it must cultivate in order to survive, but within those limits human adaptation is flexible and capable of being moulded into every conceivable kind of behaviour pattern. From the process of institutionalized moulding by the social forces acting upon the children of a given community there results a *basic personality*. This may be defined as the sum of characteristics found to recur regularly in representatives of a given cultural group and resulting from exposure to similar influences and early experiences. It is that part of the human being which corresponds to the common cultural inheritance, the 'collective' man or woman, in virtue of which he or she can take for granted certain typical ways of dealing with other members of the group by the behavioural 'shorthand' of custom and accepted practice. This part of the personality may be said to constitute the 'national character', which enables outside observers to recognize a person as belonging to his cultural group: e.g. a Frenchman, an American, despite class and economic difference. It is not the whole individual, but rather the basis on which individuality is built. For purposes of simplification class and economic differences are here left out of account. These would, however, have to be seriously considered in a full study of any given society.

There is no reason to think that the complex behaviour patterns which mark the individuality of ethnic or cultural groups and make of them distinctive societies, are inherited; only the raw material, the basic requirements and strivings of human nature probably are inborn and perhaps much the same for all mankind, although there may be quantitative differences. Nor is there any *a priori* reason why anthropological method, enriched by clinical psychological studies, should not be equally applicable to complex modern societies, though until the Second World War nobody had attempted such a task.

Gorer further says:

"The conduct of the war raised in an urgent fashion problems of exactly the nature I have been outlining—problems of national character, of understanding why certain nations were acting in the way they did, so as to understand and forestall them. Germany, and even more Japan, were acting irrationally and incomprehensibly by our standards; understanding them became an urgent military necessity, not only for psychological warfare—though that was important—but also for strategical and tactical reasons, to find out how to induce them to surrender, and having surrendered to give information; or, in the case of occupied countries, how to induce them to create and maintain a resistance movement, and so on. In an endeavour to further the war effort, a small number of anthropologists and psychiatrists were willing to risk their scientific reputations in an attempt to give an objective description of the characters of our enemies. . . ."

MOTIVATIONS OF GERMAN BEHAVIOUR

The present writer was among this small band, and was assigned in 1942 to a transit camp for recently captured German prisoners of war, bringing with him his clinical experience, a good knowledge of German and Germans and the above described notions about social psychology and anthropology.

Scope and Methods of the Study

The main effort during the period in question was directed to a running survey of enemy morale, for which a schedule of interviewing was used which enabled my colleagues and myself to plot fluctuations in German prisoners' expectations and pre-occupations during various phases of the war. From this part of the work we derived our data on the distribution of political attitudes among German soldiers, to which fuller reference will be made in a moment.

A second piece of work consisted in a delineation of the human relationships and morale structure within the German Armed Forces, as seen through the eyes of a British Army psychiatrist. This aspect is not directly dealt with in this chapter.

These duties involved many informal conversations with prisoners of various ranks and arms, the study of captured documents and comparisons with the insights of intelligence officers. It resulted in a large number of studies of Germans of all kinds in which a broad picture of the general recurring regularities of German behaviour became fairly clear. It was at this point that the statement "Character moulds institutions but institutions perpetuate character" became meaningful.

The constant contact with German prisoners forced the question whether the degree of fanaticism with which the typical and now well-known Nazi beliefs were held was not associated with certain peculiarities of individuals—perhaps at that stage thought of as a character disorder, even a form of madness.

To test this assumption, a list of clinical-psychological criteria was drawn up in the light of which a statistically adequate number of German prisoners of war were to be examined, as it were, under a higher power of magnification. These criteria or points of description of the personality were some among those commonly used in the assessment of any human being brought before a psychiatrist for clinical diagnosis or investigation. They will be described in greater detail presently.

The point of the investigation was to secure at least a limited number of fairly detailed personality studies of Germans, and to compare these records of their psychological profile and life history with their political ideology, the latter if possible to be assessed by independent investigators.

Interpretation of German Behaviour

Let us first glance at the broad picture of German behaviour which emerged as the result of many talks and of a kind of mass observation technique among prisoners of war. Our typical German is earnest, industrious, meticulous, over-respectful to authority, docile and kow-towing, tense and over-polite, but a little martinet and unpleasantly ferocious in his dealings with those he can dominate. His anxiety to know his place in the social hierarchy, his touchy insistence on paying and receiving due respect to title and rank, his love of uniformity and regimentation and his incapacity to cope with the unexpected are also familiar. His queer sentimental far-away romanticism, his brooding search for the depths strike a discordant note in this picture of striving efficiency. We are jarred too by his rigidity of outlook, by his intellectual blinkers, and by his cavalier (in both senses) treatment of his womenfolk, the contempt, and the polite veneer with which he attempted to camouflage it. And lastly, in this thumbnail sketch, his martial swagger—his nationalist arrogance and self-adulation especially when in the mass, and his resentful jealous accusations of all his neighbours of evil designs against his innocent nation and incomparable Fatherland, so wrongfully mis-understood and so uniquely great. Democracy, the essence of which is peaceful government by discussion among equals, found little response in German hearts during the short period when it was officially the rule of the country: because factional strife and rivalry, heat, one might say emotional anarchy destroyed it, despite all that the reasonable men could do—and there are reasonable Germans.

My interpretation of how the Germans came to behave in this

fashion must be limited to the psychological findings in the present generation, how the character is transmitted by the family. How the pattern originated and grew must be left for the social historian to determine. But this much is sure: it cannot be attributed to any special inheritance, any more than can the British love of liberty or the French love of logic.

For this interpretation of German male behaviour some basic assumptions were made, like those the anthropologists used. These are simple: The child is father to the man. The man brings up his child in his likeness, and the child tries to please his parents. The child, therefore, adopts and perhaps even intensifies the kind of behaviour which is traditionally handed on to it, because that will help it to gain approval and success in its community. The more stereotyped, intolerant and one-sided this approved pattern of conduct becomes, the more will the extreme representatives of that behaviour succeed and the less chance will aberrant or contrary conduct have; the more it must be camouflaged or repressed. The approved pattern, on the other hand, becomes the 'done thing', and percolates through from the *élite* to ever larger circles of those who look for a model and guide.

Let us start with submissiveness. It is easy to see how a little German boy might be overawed, when faced with a father who dominates the home and believes in harshness, in moulding his children in his image. The German father, with his own need to kow-tow at his work, traditionally expects to be kow-towed to in the home. The German mother is not the social equal of the father— her values, her influence are not allowed to preponderate. She does not provide the full counterweight of tenderness and love. She does not shield her children from the father but rather helps to build up his prestige in their eyes both by her own meekness and by precept derived from her own embeddedness in the prevailing pattern and standards. Many of our prisoners have confirmed this strong patriarchal flavour of their home life and have taken it for granted. "Oh, Mother was good—but, of course, Father made all decisions." Or again— a wounded air force prisoner related with real resentment an episode in which a British hospital sister had sharply ordered him to bed: "We Germans are proud. We don't let ourselves be bullied round by old women. I am outraged!"

The typical result is a repression of the tender tie with the devoted, despised but idealized mother, and a cowed acceptance of paternal attitudes: to be obedient, to conceal that one wants to be a cry-baby—one must be big and manly and loud-voiced. From this conflict follow several important developments. The first is the persistence of an unconscious over-attachment to the mother, which prevents a balanced maturing both of independence and of the capacity to love.

This open or concealed mother-fixation, as M. Hicklin[1] points out, has a drawback: "it ties the son in his ideal very closely to the home, and he may feel, as many German men do, that no one can rival mother as a wife. They may, therefore, either disdain their own wives, or regard them as beings from another world, in order not to enter them into competition with their mothers. This split between an ideal and a real wife (or mother) leads to conflict, and when the external situation also becomes unstable, unfaithfulness, discord and broken homes may result".

Hence comes much of that sentimental longing for a lost happiness and promised land, hence the emotional difficulties of adolescence, the introspective, tormented self-dissection, the devaluation of women too. Much of the tender feeling is displaced to mother-symbols, such as the home country which is thought of, like oneself, as helplessly shamed, in the grip of the bully, the same bully to whom one has to submit.

This immaturity leads to that curious mixture of submission and aggressiveness which has been mentioned. Father-symbols are all those above one, towards whom one must aspire, whom one must please. But, like the public school 'fag' who dreams of one day becoming a prefect, the German's secret resentment at having to knuckle under turns into a need to treat those who are weaker than himself in the way that the father authority has dealt with himself: there grows a desire to mould, control, bully and dominate. To have power to the German means to be strong like daddy.

It does not follow that all German fathers are bullies. Much of the same effect can be produced by secondary educational influences—school, public ethos, military service and the like, in which authority figures are unconsciously revalued by individuals as father-symbols. Indeed the mothers themselves foster this authoritarian view of fathers in their children even when they are the effective educators.

I think this insight explains much of the love of hierarchy, of knowing one's place, of insistence on rank and title, that was so characteristic of German social institutions. It was a strong factor in the love of military life and discipline, that perfect expression of a

[1]Hicklin, Margot: in a "Survey of German Youth" (privately circulated), 1946.

o

hierarchical pattern for wielding collective power, for being respected, and for strutting. To make submission palatable, it was idealized. To curb one's self-will, to subordinate oneself in blind obedience became the hall-mark of a fine soldierly character. To exact this sort of discipline from others was the duty of a leader (cf. 'Herrennatur'). The greater the leader, the nobler the act of devoted submission, the oath of faithfulness unto death and all that kind of romantic gush. Authority symbols were not to be questioned. The father-leader is powerful and responsible. He is everyone's ideal to copy. Each within his station is but a 'little man' who is only transmitting Führer-power to still lesser men. This was a very common statement, among all ranks from private to general: "What could I do, I am only a little man"—a refrain even heard at Nuremberg.

It is not hard to see that such emphasis on submission and on dominance (under the authoritarian system) does grave injury to character. There is a residue of unexpressed, frustrated rage or hate which has to be disposed of in the economy of the personality, because energy is indestructible. Deflected by custom and taboo from its primary object—the father and all his symbols in the nation—this hate manifests itself in other ways. Some of it, as has been said, provides the urge to bully all those who are weaker—this was the standard, approved way, the 'done thing' among Germans. Some of it remained repressed, but betrayed itself as a sense of inferiority, of inability to control oneself; a dread of the unknown, of inner anarchy, as depicted in the legend of Siegfried and his weak spot. A typical saying was: "We Germans are weak; we need a strong leader to control us or we should quarrel among ourselves—democracy is not for us". And this in the same breath as an arrogant assumption of Nazi victory. These protestations of manful loyalty and strength were in fact a sort of 'moral corset' against the fear of weakness and treachery.

T. H. Marshall, in a broadcast on this theme,[1] has emphasized this feature of the German character-conflict:

"It is remarkable how often this theme of division and discord figures in accounts of the German character. Sometimes it is the relations between Germans that are cited to illustrate it—the jealousies of the states that formed the German Reich, the bitter rivalry between political parties, the sharp division between social classes. But sometimes the emphasis is on the conflict within the individual German—between realism and romance, between the

[1]Published in *The Listener*, 21st August, 1947, p. 287.

urge to obey and the desire to dominate, between worship of heroism and the love of domesticity.

The territory we knew as Germany had been occupied for centuries by a multitude of small states and petty dukedoms, forming a pattern so complex and kaleidoscopic in its changes that it was hardly possible to show it on a map. Harmony between local and national loyalties seemed unattainable, because the local loyalties were themselves unstable and shifting, while the national loyalty was not attached to any effective central power, but only to an idea—the idea of a great people with a culture to cherish and a mission to fulfil. When the idea was clothed with power by Bismarck there was a clash between the local patriotism that resisted unity and the Germanism that accepted it. And the mission remained unfulfilled; it was always just out of reach, like a mirage in the desert."

It was unfortunately the Prussian warrior-caste, the lordly officials and the arrogant Junkers who brought unity and order to this ethnic group, as the result of a successful war of aggression. Perhaps the Prussian tradition of discipline, and rigid hierarchy was accepted because it supplied the moral corset to the emotional, impressionable, 'soft-skinned' Germans. It became fashionable for the *élite* to assume the manner and philosophy of Machtpolitik, Herrenvolk, and ruthlessness—as a psychological counterweight to inner conflict and lack of self-confidence which are the soil in which the bully is nurtured. These traits, it must be remembered, were not the result of a lost war, but were widespread before the First World War—a time of rising prosperity and influence.

The peculiar mixture of national self-glorification and sense of mission, begun in the studies of thinkers, on one hand, and of self-pity as a simple, exploited, 'ever-so-good' people not so cynically sophisticated as the perfidious foreigner on the other hand, began to spill over into the field of international politics. Being thought bad or weak is intolerable to Germans as a whole. Since their self-respect is so brittle, so easily disturbed, they inflate it partly by their insistence on status, on their so-called honour. This status anxiety leads to over-valuation, both of the individual by himself and of the national group. Germans as individuals and as members of their group, *vis-à-vis* foreigners, are very touchy so far as status and 'honour' are concerned. Anyone who has lived in Germany could verify the tenseness and rank-consciousness of German society in which the inferiors accept their subordinate positions and in turn exact similar subordination from those still lower in the social scale. This same tendency has led to over-emphasis of the idea of group power and dignity, especially in relation to weaker and therefore despised nations. This need to feel great and strong has been well exploited by German nationalist propaganda. The German is stirred by the sense of might and order, of belonging to a mighty national organism about which he has created a legend of invincibility; it helps him personally to feel stronger by such an identification.

Thus the motivations for nationalism, militarism and an aggressive foreign policy have deep roots in the psychological compensations and reactions of Germans generated in the prevalent educational patterns of their *élite* and of those who aped that *élite* and fostered such attitudes in their sons. To quote T. H. Marshall again:

"I remember clearly attending a local rally of the Hitler Youth in 1937. It was a drab and uninspiring gathering of docile and bewildered boys, in uniform, of course, who were subjected to a passionate tirade by a young leader who told them of the great deeds done in their name by the German heroes of the past. And I thought they hardly dared look into their own hearts and face the comparison with the models set before them. Yet that was what they were being urged to do—to contemplate and admire their own innate greatness, to lift themselves up by their own shoe-strings. As I came away I felt it must be very hard work to be German."

Nazism especially exploited some of these tendencies and systematized into a political code of behaviour another germane complex which was never far below the surface of the German character. This is the tendency to psychological projection. Germans have great difficulty in accepting in themselves considerable charges of smouldering hatred against the paternal authority. Therefore, at a time when economic and social conditions had produced a general feeling of dissatisfaction with authorities—now felt to be bad—a revolution was averted by the widest possible use of these projection mechanisms; guilt tension was relieved by being directed on to outside scapegoats who were regarded as the only disturbers of the peace. Aggressive rebellious forces could be attributed to the agency of wicked outsiders, and the belief that all within the fold were good sons was thereby restored. Two such scapegoat symbols were ready to hand—the Jews and the Bolsheviks. To' these was ascribed all 'inner weakness', the emasculation of German resistance in 1918 and much more besides. The success of these scapegoats can only be attributed to the average German's intolerance of his own aggressive tendencies and to the need of keeping the national *amour-propre* inviolate. The average German is extremely touchy and squeamish about brutality and goes to great trouble to provide excuses and to repudiate evidence of brutal traits in his group. This side of the German has been very clearly illustrated at the Nuremberg trials in the elaborate attempts at whitewashing their conduct. The notion of being surrounded by envious rich powers who wanted to keep Germany impotent, or destroy her at the behest of the Jewish-Bolshevik conspiracy, became one of the great theme-songs of Nazi propaganda, and was found to be widely and fanatically believed by something like 30 per cent of Hitler's soldiers down to 1944. The individual German has felt so small and helpless in his personal relations with his father that he has tended to project this situation into his national destiny. He has been eager and gratified to find any elements of reality which have corresponded to this phantasy. For that reason the Nazis before the war harped so much on the injustice of the Treaty of Versailles or on any signs of Soviet militarization. It is, of course, also true that paranoid behaviour at last results in defensive measures on the part of the neighbours and so to some extent provides later real confirmation of the initially persecutory fears.

This ambivalence or duality which pervades so many Germans of the present day has undoubtedly contributed to giving a paranoid flavour, to put it mildly, to the Nazi movement. Their blatant assertion of national superiority and uniqueness, coupled with the compulsion to see internal and external enemies everywhere, resulting finally in their 'justified' acts of aggression and brutality, are clinical facts in evidence of this statement. This paranoid behaviour could be interpreted in terms of psycho-pathology as being founded on the stifled wish to be the favoured and irresponsible baby, and on the unconscious rejection of paternal authority and order which they had so overwhelmingly to accept in their own society. The resultant unconscious frustration-rage and its attendant guilt feelings were projected on to the many scapegoat symbols, and led to all the persecution for internal treason and all the heresy hunting, characteristic of the later Nazi period, when external successes waned and the duplicity towards authority became more marked. There seems little doubt that the clique of leading Nazis were not simply exploiting this national psychological structure in a cunningly rational way, but that they were themselves deeply emotionally involved in this paranoid dynamic. Only in this way can we account for their supreme mis-judgments of reality situations, in such matters as the power potentials of the free world or the reactions of other nations to their bullying, which ultimately led them with somnambulistic sureness to defeat. This lack of insight and perspective is consistent with the gift for painstaking organization and planning of detail, itself a function of the need for order and exactitude as a defence against the deeper inner anarchy and division which has been so amply demonstrated in German behaviour over the last fifteen years, when one clique of Nazi bosses was plotting against another and the scramble for power was barely masked by the defiant shouts of solidarity and unity of Goebbels's propaganda machine. We see in this incapacity for objective thinking, in this imprisonment in their own mental imagery and theory-making, in an almost dreamlike detachment from reality, a fairly typical German trait, observable at all levels from the savant to the party fanatic.

The temptation to enlarge unduly upon this analysis must be resisted. One more feature—perhaps the most puzzling—must be mentioned. It is related both to submissiveness and to the duplicity which have been discussed. Germans tend to turn against their own country when its power shows signs of weakening, or when they are under a new authority. It was remarked by the Italians how German troops, after fighting excellently, showed not a gradual waning of morale, but crumpled up suddenly and surrendered, meekly and docilely. The comparison of feminine yielding to a strong suitor after a sham fight for chastity has been used by many observers in regard to this phenomenon. It seemed as if beneath the martial armour there was a passive streak which suddenly betrayed itself—with a complete break in loyalty to their cause and their alleged soldierly ideals. There was only eagerness to be thought well of by their new masters—the captors—to show how 'good' they were. Those who 'protested too much', that is, the arrogant, tough and swaggering, had a thicker armour. In them their passive streak seemed to require a self-immolation. They went out to seek death, and not having found it they had to make such nuisances of themselves as to invite punishment. Then they could dramatize themselves as suffering for their loyalty and noble steadfastness. T. H. Marshall's view of the Germans' unrealism is fully borne out by these studies. Germany has to act the drama of her destiny in which the others have their allotted parts—follow a certain phantasy of herself to its logical extreme— then suddenly she turns round as in a dream, and is very hurt because others have not appreciated this narcissus-like gazing at the great and romantic urges of the German 'depths', this schizophrenic preoccupation with their dream. It is thus that the mentally sick commit crimes through phantasies of 'destiny', 'liberation' and projection of responsibility. It is as if their national egoism, arrogance and trampling on the rights of others evokes a deeply repressed sense of guilt which ultimately expresses itself as self-destruction. After an orgy of self-assertive effort comes the anti-climax of defeat and humiliation. This unbalanced swing between opposites can be seen even in German vital statistics. In 1938 the officially published rates for homicide and suicide were four times as high as in Britain.

So much for a general and very incomplete account of the German basic personality and some of its resultant behaviour patterns.

THE NAZIS[1]

What meaning was to be assigned to the emergence of the Nazi within this pattern? Was his a special kind of character type, or was he the logical extreme—the basic German in pure culture—of the national type? What were his distinguishing traits, and what proportion of the population did he represent? Let us deal with the last question first.

Distribution. The running opinion surveys which were made on random samples of German prisoners of war led to a practical, operationally useful classification of them into five political categories (in which F. is short for both Fanatic and Fascist):

F. I. Fanatical, whole-hearted Nazis (the 'hard core').

F. II. Believers with reservations (the camp followers and near-Nazis).

F. III. Unpolitical men. (The 'herd man'—submissive, politically unthinking, pre-occupied with personal problems and interests.)

F. IV. The divided (often emotionally anti-Nazi but loyal because of 'national unity' and fear).

F. V. Active, convinced anti-Nazis. (Comprising a wide variety of persons—the sort of people who would have composed a resistance movement in other countries.)

A Nazi for this purpose was defined as a person within the jurisdiction of the Reich who subscribed with sincerity and emotional conviction to the major items of the well-known programme of the NSDAP and its affiliated organs.

[1]This portion of the paper is dealt with in technical detail in a forthcoming paper in "Human Relations" vol. III, No. 2 (1950).

The categories may be roughly delineated as follows:

(a) *Fanatical Nazis*: usually under thirty-five and of lower middle class, with an admixture of intellectuals and working-class youths, initially arrogant, disdainful, convinced of victory, completely identified with the aims and personalities of Hitler, Goering and others, justifying all the acts of the regime, holding race-superiority views, professing their faith and loyalty with dramatic conviction. Thuringians, Bavarians and Western Germans predominated over Berliners, Prussians and citizens of the great sea ports.

(b) *Believers with reservations*: more nearly identical with former 'German nationalists', often of better education than the fanatics, and thus ready to admit certain shortcomings of the Nazi regime, but on the grounds of inefficiency or as due to temporary revolutionary or wartime causes, rather than on ethical or political grounds. Regular soldiers, intellectuals, business men, but also working-class men were found in this category. The veneer of western culture was usually thicker than in the zealots.

(c) *Unpolitical men*: minor civil servants, small artisans and country folk made up this category, which was concerned with personal problems, security, order and daily worries. A typical and frequent saying of this sort of person was, "We've had the Kaiser, and the Republic, and now the Führer, but we still have to work hard to get our cows milked".

(d) *The divided men*: were those in conflict, disillusioned, who had often voted for Hitler because of the promise of economic benefits and order, but who had a general emotional bias against Nazism and war. They were, like the 'believers with reservations', a transitional group, with considerable two-way traffic with that category according to the state of the war.

(e) *The anti-Nazis*: these were the men who had maintained constant opposition in feeling, thought and sometimes deed, to the regime on religious, ethical, political or individualist grounds. The group comprised many social types, from working-class trade unionists and Marxists, Catholic adherents of 'the Centre', and intellectual Liberals to aristocratic Conservatives. The young sons of such people were a not inconsiderable ingredient. Despite their heterogeneity they showed certain common features—a rejection of nazism and a valuation of individuality.

The classification was in every case made only after personal interview and close study, not on the basis of formal membership of this or that Nazi Party organization.

The figures for September 1944, for instance, when the war was going against Germany but was not yet obviously lost in the awareness of the rank and file, and when the new German terror weapons were making their mark, disclosed an almost regular Gaussian distribution curve:

In a sample of 600 men there were—

Fanatics	11	per cent
Believers with reservations	25	,,
Unpoliticals	40	,,
Divided men	15	,,
Anti-Nazis	9	,,

In fact, the first, last and unpolitical categories remained remarkably constant between 1942 (pre-Stalingrad and pre-El Alamein) and the end of hostilities. Changes occurred chiefly in the numbers of the two intermediate groups. It will be seen that in all at least 35 per cent of the population of the Wehrmacht were active supporters of Nazi-militarist ideas and policies, even so late as 1944. If men below the age of twenty-eight were taken separately, this proportion rose to nearer 70 per cent.

Detailed Study of Nazi Personalities

In an attempt to answer the question as to what manner of men Nazis were and how they differed from the other part of the population, 138 men—a sample judged statistically adequate by people who knew about sampling—were subjected to detailed psychological examination.

While not representative of the exact composition of the Wehrmacht or its distribution of ideologies, the group in fact included people from eighteen to fifty-five years old, at various economic levels, and from private to lieutenant-colonel in rank; from farm labourer to university lecturer in the educational scale, with a sprinkling of regular soldiers especially among the naval fraction of the sample.

The method of examination consisted of prolonged personal interviews in a quiet room, an informal atmosphere being maintained; in not a few instances several interviews, the average time per man being about two hours. No psychiatric or medical status was disclosed, care being taken to represent oneself as a kind of welfare officer interested in the prisoners as men.

So far as their political views were concerned, these were obtained by the method just indicated, usually by another observer and confirmed by a conference or collation of reports from yet other observers.

The technical psychological data were in every case obtained and recorded by me personally. They may be divided into:

1. Background data, i.e. items obtained from the past history of the man;
2. Personality traits as exhibited during the interview, independently of the past history, in so far as any psychiatric examination can separate these two chief components in an evaluation of a human being.

I. *Background data* included details of service, rank, educational and socio-economic status, parental religion, regional and urban or rural origins and domicile.

A more personal background study was recorded under the headings of:

(*i*) Relations between father and mother, especially with regard to dominance of either in the family; (*ii*) the atmosphere of harshness or toleration in the home; (*iii*) patterns of guilt inculcation; (*iv*) the relation of the subject to his father, past and present and as mirrored in his later feelings about father figures; (*v*) the relation of the subject to his mother, as shown in the later fate of this part of his feeling life.

II. *Personality traits.* These were defined as aspects of mental behaviour discernible to a psychiatrist in a subject during the examination or while under survey at the camp. These traits were drawn up on empirical grounds after pilot interviews (notably after the prolonged study of Rudolf Hess). They are all to some extent overlapping, dovetailing or complementary, and theoretically dependent on the vicissitudes of the conflicts arising from the primary emotional relationships within the family. In these assessments quantitative expression was given by a clinically judged three-point scale, which reads:

(1) Gross presence of trait;
(2) Perceptibly heightened amount of trait;
(3) Normal limits or absence of a trait, as was most suitable.

For brevity, and because they are well-known psychological working concepts, these traits will simply be listed, with comment only on exceptional features:

Ambivalence, split libido, homosexual trends, narcissism, inferiority feelings, projection, clinical anxiety, hypochondriasis, depression/elation, schizoid trends, sadism.

In the case of the last-named, sadism, it was necessary to adopt a special score, not based on the simple three-point scale. Sadistic trends were recorded as falling under two main headings.

1. Anti-social, with three sub-categories:
(a) Overt, direct (i.e. bestiality, cruelty, delight in killing, etc.);
(b) Aggressive, harsh, domineering attitudes (a milder slightly more socialized degree, e.g. the 'Prussian N.C.O.' type);
(c) Indifference—calm acceptance of brutal behaviour in others.
2. Social reaction-formations to, or sublimations of sadism:
(d) Average, normal aggressivity (loves a fight, stands up for himself but lacks viciousness);
(e) Gentle, submissive, over-conciliatory attitudes;
(f) Horror, condemnation of, and guilt over sadism of others.

These were ranked in ascending degrees of moral self-scrutiny, (d) being considered the most 'normal' quality by the standards of a British clinician.

The datum of adherence to a church was recorded separately, although also entering in some cases into other data.

We had five categories:
1. Staunch active protestant.
2. Staunch active Catholic.
3. Easy-going indifference.
4. Atheism and rational agnosticism.
5. 'Gottgläubig', i.e. an adherent of Hitler's pseudo-religious ideas.

My hypothesis had been that the Nazi might be a person who was afflicted with a character disorder distinguished by psychological immaturity, which Fromm[1] had called the sado-masochistic or authoritarian character. It was assumed that such a character would have had particular trouble over his infantile love needs and his frustration rage, that he might have resolved this conflict under German conditions of upbringing by a strong father-identification with resulting ambivalence, split feelings towards women, heightened homosexual and narcissan trends with powerful sadistic urges, over-compensated inferiority feelings and a tendency to attribute his guilt feelings to outside people and symbols, in order to guard his ego from guilt. The experiment of comparing the frequency of occurrence or intensity of certain character-traits with the five classes of F rating could now be made. F I and II were taken as 'Nazis', F III, IV and V as 'non-Nazis'.

The results were subjected to statistical methods of checking their validity by Dr. Edward A. Shils, of the University of Chicago. We found that not all the postulated traits fitted; some expectations

[1] Fromm, E. *The Fear of Freedom*. Kegan Paul, 1941.

were disappointed. But an interesting picture emerged. As in all matters of living organisms, the distribution of traits was not sharply polarized as black and white, but rather spread out along a graded scale. But at the Nazi end of the scale a combination of traits was found strongly marked, which was either absent or replaced by other traits at the non-Nazi end of the scale.

F I and F II showed a significant concentration of the following sets of attitudes: (1) an undue acceptance of paternal authority and leader-worship with a resultant docility towards those above and an expected right to dominate those below, that is, authoritarianism. (2) An exaggerated shame about, and a contemptuous rejection of, tender relationships in the family, and hence in social life generally, i.e. a taboo on the gentle, affectionate side of life, in some instances coupled with a sentimental idealization of the mother. (3) An over-valuation of masculinity and gang solidarity, associated with personal and social depreciation of women, that is, 'social homosexuality'. (4) A tendency to read their own motivations or characteristics into the behaviour or intentions of others, that is, to seek scapegoats and to deny personal or group guilt or badness, while emphasizing other people's badness and their own rightness. This resulted in suspiciousness, bitter fanatical intolerance and a sense of being innocently persecuted and surrounded by hostile neighbours. (5) The acceptance of brutality and resort to force in order to achieve domination over others, which was always justified on the grounds of the inferiority or worthlessness of the other groups or persons: sadism. (6) A rejection of Christianity in the more orthodox sense in favour of pseudo-religious beliefs or doctrinaire atheism. (7) A proneness to react with neurotic anxiety to situations where he is not at ease: unconscious guilt and inferiority.

These were the main features in the personalities of the men who were the pacemakers in the German community: emphasis on stern, manful, soldierly glory; on the Führer principle; on being a unique, misunderstood people surrounded by scheming jealous enemies; on Jewish and Bolshevik scapegoats; on the natural subordination of the weaker, lesser breeds, including women; on the rightness of ruthlessness and mercilessness. But these ideas found a response among many more because of the psychological readiness to believe them, created in the German community by the force of traditional rearing. In the non-Nazis, in contrast, the features just mentioned were not marked. Certain other traits were statistically prominent: a high valuation of women and a capacity for tender relationships; anti-father attitudes towards authority with consequent insistence on individual freedom, and either sincere adherence to one of the great religions or else an easy-going indifference.

The statistical results as here stated present a somewhat over-simplified picture. It seemed to be a question not only of siding with or opposing an *actual*, personal father, but of acceptance or rejection of a 'collective' harsh image of paternal authority. The technical discussion on this piece of symbolism would lead us too far. It appears that the *cliché*, the stereotype of father as the basic symbol of all authority is involved, and that this is a bad one in the case of Nazi or nationalist jingo personalities.

The ideological aspects of Nazi behaviour are so well known as to require no elaboration in this chapter. They can, however, be deduced fairly easily from the outline of German character which has been given here. The categories used were psycho-analytic—other terms could have been substituted.

It appears then, that the Nazi is not a separate species of human being, but harbours in concentrated form some of the most distorted characteristics of the basic 'political' personality of Germany.

No studies could be made of German women by the present writer.

If we may assume that character runs true to form, that character is deeply rooted, then we have to expect that some 10 to 30 per cent of younger German males (and the younger the age, the higher was the degree of nazification) will have strong tendencies to deny guilt or responsibility; to harbour anti-Allied and even generally destructive attitudes, in order to hide the passive yielding streak in their natures and to hold on to their nationalist-militarist superman phantasies. This intransigent attitude perhaps motivates many an act of semi-anarchic, semi-sabotaging destructiveness against Allied order and property now known to be sporadically common in Germany. Some of them threatened during interviews as prisoners that should Germany lose the war, they would turn themselves into 'werewolves' or become 'Bolshevik terrorists'. We also know that thousands of these youths wander about in bands, unable or unwilling to form new social values or take part in constructive efforts.

This sort of response has been most strikingly outlined by the German war-writer E. v. Salomon in his *Die Geächteten* ("The Outlaws"). In Chapter XX ("Kern and I") he gives the views of the post-1918 'Free Corps' type of disappointed, spiritually bankrupt ex-officer nationalist, the murderer of Rathenau:

"Between them (the Weimar leaders who tried to restore Germany) and us no agreement is possible; for they are no longer capable of the final sacrifice . . . that (power) it is our task to destroy . . . that power . . . in the nation who have allowed their Teutonism to be submerged in a flood of western culture. They are surprised that the Germans continue to be feared! It is not they who are feared—it is . . . us!

I couldn't bear it if once again something great were to rise out of the chaotic, insane age in which we live . . . we are not fighting to make the nation happy—we are fighting to force it to tread the path of its destiny. But I will not tolerate that this man (Rathenau—whose greatness the speaker had earlier enviously conceded—H.V.D.) should once again inspire the nation with a faith. . . ."

And again:

"I did not survive it (9th November, 1918). As honour demanded, on 9th November I blew out my brains. . . . What survived is another thing. Since that day I have lost my ego. . . . I died for the nation . . . were it otherwise, I could not bear it . . . my actions (frantic underground and free corps activity against the French occupation, Fehm-murder, sabotage, etc. H.V.D.) are the sole motive force within me. . . . This force is destructive—hence I destroy. Who sups with the devil, must have a long spoon. I know that I shall perish in the moment in which this power no longer has any use for me. . . . Nothing is left to me except to reconcile myself to the noble suffering imposed on me by fate."

These quotations illustrate a thinly veiled death-wish which staves off suicide only through mad destructive activity in the service of a very poorly idealized ego-centric jealousy, dog-in-the-manger sulking and obstinacy. The lust of suffering, the pseudo-manly self-dramatization and denial of the right of others to happiness because one's own wish-world has collapsed, is clearly illustrated. There is clear evidence of a sense of guilt and personal damnation, recalling both the Faust story and the conduct of an obstinate naughty baby.

It is fair to point out that such a man has, but denies, a sense of values, he kicks against the pricks. Once converted, he is possibly one of the best focus-points of social change. The practical question of who is going to put in the time and effort at 'saving' these souls makes it likely, however, that this type of man is bent on destruction—first of things and people—and then of himself. After the First World War just such men formed the 'Old Fighter' vanguard of the Nazi movement. We need hardly be in doubt as to the likely course of action of such people (far more of them deeply resentful and hurt after the late war) if Allied control should weaken, or a general threat to peace offer opportunities for further military glory in any kind of armed force.

CONCLUSION

An attempt has been made in this chapter to give some account of the essentials of work done by the present writer and some of his collaborators on the German character. Only a very condensed picture has been given with many corroborative links in the evidence omitted.

No high degree of scientific polish is claimed for this piece of field work. Rather should it be regarded as the illustration of a method by which the clinical psychologist with experience of personality study can contribute depth and content to a sector of research into national character and political psychology. It avoids the meaningless question as to whether the ideology makes the character or the character evolves the ideology. Clearly there are birds of a feather whose characteristic personal attitudes fit in best with the 'Zeitgeist' of a given culture and who tend to rise to the position of an *élite*. In such a position they will influence and intensify the political ideas and their resultant institutions and practices in conformity with their characterological needs.

With due caution we may perhaps draw from this study some more general conclusions about the kind of socio-psychological conditions likely to dispose a modern national group to warlike behaviour. The reader will, it is hoped, have gathered that it has not been our purpose to pillory the Germans, as if they were the sole white nation to harbour the mentality we found typical of Nazis. The sabre-rattling, arrogant, politically obscurantist, bigoted and xenophobic personality exists among us all, with his lack of insight and his profoundly irrational, prejudice-ridden interpretation of political phenomena in terms indicative of his own personal weakness and a consequent desire for the violent solution of conflict situations between groups.

It is too early yet to say whether in the light of psycho-analytic research the Marxist view will have to be modified, according to which the war-mentality results from 'bourgeois' authoritarianism inherent in the capitalist structure of society, especially during its period of decay. This would presumably mean that a capitalist *élite*, aided by the greater number of 'petty bourgeois' who identify them-selves with it by virtue of being 'owners' or 'individual traders', etc., would be bound to defend their status and threatened profits by psychological reactions leading to demands for greater, easier or forcible markets, hence for military and political power ('imperialism'), stand to authoritarian measures along repressive, patriarchal lines against the upward struggle of the proletariat. According to this view, the *élite*, in such a situation of menace 'from below', would endeavour to deflect the patricidal jealousy of the 'have-nots' from its 'real goal' towards outgroups, such as foreign peoples or systems. The climate and behaviour pattern of such a society, at least in the ranks of its ruling circles or cliques, would thus support and encourage penal, educational and other social practices and institutions favouring the preservation and strengthening of the kind of trends we have found, in their logical extreme, to be characteristic at least of German Nazis.

Certain it would seem to be that a desperate economic situation, at least in Germany, favoured the emergence of personality types ready to exploit it in the above sense, and that the type existed in that country in sufficiently large numbers to determine the course of history. We have as yet no data comparable even to this modest study, by which we could try to estimate the war-mindedness of other important national or ideological groups upon whom the peace of the world now depends.

The methods exist: we have the techniques of the questionnaire, of mass-observation, and of the intensive study of sample groups by individual interview, perhaps supplemented in favourable con-ditions by such test-procedures as the Rorschach or the Thematic Apperception Test.

We may conclude with another quotation from Gorer's paper to the British Association:

"These results and others like them were obtained under the stress and difficulties of war, with inadequate working conditions, and with unsatisfactory scientific safeguards and criteria. They were crude approximations; there was neither time nor opportunity to take into account variables which—we were perfectly well aware—should have been taken into account, differences of social and economic class, differences of region, and so on. Even so, the results were extremely suggestive.

With a few notable exceptions, academic sociologists, historians and political scientists have ignored the differing national characters of the societies they were discussing, either acting on the assumption that the only differences were individual differences, which cancelled out in a sufficiently large mass; or else that human beings in their social lives were guided overwhelmingly by reason and more or less intelligent self-interest. Practical politicians and economists almost invariably act on the assumption that all humanity act in the same way as the society they are accustomed to. Even an intuitive psychologist of genius, such as Hitler, was, we may be thankful, finally destroyed by this basic underlying assumption.

I should like to suggest that it is this ignorance or ignoring of national character differences which keep politics, both national and international, a kind of guessing game with infinitely more wrong than right answers. No party and no school has a record to be proud of.

I think that there would be general agreement that the most urgent task facing us today, whether as scientists or as citizens, is the understanding of our own and other societies. Physical science has developed so disproportionately to social science that we are literally threatened with extinction unless we learn to understand, and so control, the people who have the possibility of setting the enormous destructive forces in motion. I suggest that the study of national character is one tool, so far practically undeveloped, for achieving this aim.

Do not misunderstand me. I do not wish for a moment to suggest that a study of national character will be able to displace, or should displace, any of the older established disciplines—history, economics, political science, sociology and the like. What I think it could do is bring these sciences nearer to reality by taking into systematic account the fact that members of different societies have their characters developed differently due to the fact that the rules of child-rearing, the values and goals, the experiences which individuals undergo, vary systematically from society to society, with the result that members of different societies are driven by different motives and needs, conscious or unconscious, interpret the universe differently, avoid different fears, and seek different satisfactions. We cannot transform society—whether we wish to establish a world state, make the United Nations work, re-educate the Germans or the Japanese, or re-educate ourselves—except in so far as we understand it; and I suggest that in the concept of national character, and in its scientific study, as rigorous as the present development of the apposite disciplines will allow, we have a potential tool for such an understanding."

P

Acknowledgment

I am indebted to Mr. Gorer for permission to use quotations from an unpublished paper, "The Scientific Study of National Character" (1947), and to the B.B.C. for permission to incorporate portions of broadcasts by Professor T. H. Marshall and by myself, published in *The Listener*. My thanks are also due to the War Office for giving me opportunities to conduct these studies, and to many technical and 'lay' friends in the British and U.S. armies, who assisted in them.

CHAPTER X

THREATS AND SECURITY

by L. F. Richardson

THE DIVERSE EFFECTS OF THREATS

THE reader has probably heard a mother say to her child: "Stop that noise, or I'll smack you". Did the child in fact become quiet?

A threat from one person, or group of people, to another person or group has occasionally produced very little immediate effect, being received with contempt. Effects, when conspicuous, may be classified as submission at one extreme, negotiation or avoidance in the middle, and retaliation at the other extreme. The following incidents are classified in that manner; otherwise they are purposely miscellaneous.

Contempt

EXAMPLE 1. About fifty states, organized as the League of Nations, tried in 1935 and 1936, by appeals and by cutting off supplies, to restrain Mussolini's Italy from making war on Abyssinia. At the time Mussolini disregarded the League, and went on with the conquest of Abyssinia. He did not however forget. Four years later in his speech to the Italian people on the occasion of Italy's declaration of war against Britain and France, Mussolini said, "The events of quite recent history can be summarized in these words—half promises, constant threats, blackmail and finally, as the crown of this ignoble edifice, the League siege of the fifty-two States".[1]

Submission

EXAMPLE 2.[2] In 1906 the British Government had a disagreement with the Sultan of Turkey about the exact location of the frontier between Egypt and Turkish Palestine. A British battleship was sent on 3rd May with an ultimatum, and thereupon the Sultan accepted the British view. Some resentment may perhaps have lingered, for after the First World War had been going on for three months Turkey joined the side opposite to Britain.

EXAMPLE 3. In August 1945 the Japanese, having suffered several

[1]*Glasgow Herald*, 11th June, 1940.
[2]*Ency. Brit.* XIV, ed. 14. 2, 156. Grey, Viscount, 1925, *Twenty-Five Years*. Hodder and Stoughton, London.

221

years of war, having lost by defeat their Italian and German allies, being newly attacked by Russia, having had two atomic bombs dropped on them, and being threatened with more of the same, surrendered unconditionally.

Negotiation Followed by Submission

EXAMPLE 4.[1] After the Germans annexed Austria on 13th March, 1938, the German minority in Czechoslovakia began to agitate for self-government, and both the German and Czech Governments moved troops towards their common frontier. On 13th August there began German Army manœuvres on an unprecedented scale. On 6th September France called up reservists. In September the cession of the Sudetenland by Czechoslovakia to Germany was discussed, to the accompaniment of threats by Hitler on 12th, the partial mobilization of France on 24th, and the mobilization of Czechoslovakia and of the British Navy on 27th. Finally, at Munich on the 29th the French and British agreed to advise the Czechs to submit to the German demand for the Sudetenland, partly because its population spoke German, and partly because of the German threat to take it by armed force. Intense resentment at this humiliation lingered.

Negotiation Followed by a Bargain

EXAMPLE 5.[2] In the spring of 1911 French troops entered Fez, in Morocco, the German Government protesting. On 1st July, 1911, the German Government notified those of France and Britain that a German gunboat was being dispatched to Agadir on the southern coast of Morocco in order there to protect some German firms from the local tribesmen. The French and British interpreted the movement of the gunboat as a threat against themselves, like a 'thumping of the diplomatic table'. On 21st July Mr. Lloyd George made a speech containing the sentence "I say emphatically that peace at that price would be humiliation intolerable for a great country like ours to endure". Much indignation was expressed in the newspapers of France, Britain and Germany. Negotiations ensued. By 4th November France and Germany had agreed on a rearrangement of their West African territories and rights. The arms race continued.

[1] *Keesing's Contemporary Archives.* Bristol.
[2] *Ency. Brit.,* XIV, ed. 14. **23**, 349, 352. Morel, E. D., 1915, *Ten Years of Secret Diplomacy,* National Labour Press, London. Grey, Viscount, 1925, *Twenty-Five Years,* Hodder and Stoughton, London.

Avoidance

EXAMPLE 6. The normal behaviour of the armed personnel guarding any frontier in time of peace is to avoid crossing the frontier lest they should be attacked.

EXAMPLE 7. During 1941 British shipping mostly went eastward via the Cape of Good Hope avoiding the Mediteranean where the enemy threat was too strong.

EXAMPLE 8. Criminals are usually said to avoid the police: that is, when the criminals are decidedly outnumbered by the police.

Retaliation

EXAMPLE 9. After the Agadir incident had been settled by the Franco-German Agreement of 4th November, 1911, the 'defence' expenditures of both France and Germany nevertheless continued to increase. See the tabular statement on page 227.

EXAMPLE 10. Within six weeks after the Munich Agreement of 29th September, 1938, rearmament was proceeding more rapidly in France,[1] Britain,[2] Germany[3] and U.S.A.[4]

EXAMPLE 11. On 5th November, 1940, the British armed merchantship *Jervis Bay*, being charged with the defence of a convoy, saw a German pocket-battleship threatening it. The *Jervis Bay*, although of obviously lesser power, attacked the battleship, and continued to fight until sunk, thus distracting the battleship's attention from the convoy, and giving the latter a chance to escape.

EXAMPLE 12. On 10th November, 1941, Mr. Winston Churchill warned the Japanese that "should the United States become involved in war with Japan the British declaration will follow within the hour". This formidable threat did not deter the Japanese from attacking Pearl Harbour within a month.

These miscellaneous illustrations may serve to remind the reader of many others. Is there any understandable regularity about the wider phenomena which they represent? The present question is about what happens in fact; the other very important question as to whether the fact is ethically good or bad, is here left aside. Some conclusions emerge:

[1] Athlone broadcast, 5th October and 12th October.
[2] *Parliamentary Debates*, 3rd to 6th October.
[3] *Glasgow Herald*, 10th October.
[4] *Glasgow Herald*, 7th November.

(*a*) People, when threatened, do not always behave with coldly calculated self-interest. They sometimes fight back, taking extreme risks. (Examples 11 and 12.)

(*b*) There is a notable distinction between fresh and tired nations, in the sense that a formidable threat to a fresh nation was followed by retaliation (Example 12) whereas an even more severe threat to the same nation, when tired, produced submission. (Example 3.)

(*c*) A group of people, having a more or less reasonable claim, has sometimes quickly obtained by a threat of violence, more than it otherwise would. But that may not have been the end of the matter. (Examples 2 and 4.)

(*d*) There have often been two contrasted effects, one immediate, the other delayed. An immediate effect of·contempt or submission or negotiation or avoidance has been followed by resentful plans for retaliation at some later opportunity. (Example 1, Example 2, Examples 4 and 10, Examples 5 and 9.)

(*e*) What nowadays is euphemistically called national 'defence', in fact always includes preparations for attack, and thus constitutes a threat to some other group of people. This type of 'defence' is based on the assumption that threats directed towards other people will produce in them either submission, or negotiation, or avoidance; and it neglects the possibility that contempt or retaliation may be produced instead. Yet in fact the usual effect between comparable nations is retaliation by counter-preparations, thus leading on by way of an arms race towards another war.

SCHISMOGENESIS

In his study of the Iatmul tribe in New Guinea, Gregory Bateson[1] noticed a custom whereby, at a meeting in the ceremonial hall two men would boast alternately, each provoking the other to make bolder claims, until they reached extravagant extremes.

He also noticed a process whereby a man would have some control over a woman. Then her acceptance of his leadership would encourage him to become domineering. This in turn made her submissive. Then he became more domineering and she became more abject, the process running to abnormal extremes.

Bateson called both these processes 'schismogenesis', which may be translated as 'the manner of formation of cleavages'. When both parties developed the same behaviour, for example, both boasting,

[1]Bateson, G., 1935, in the periodical *Man*, p. 199. Bateson, G., 1936, *Naven*, University Press, Cambridge.

Bateson called the schismogenesis 'symmetrical'. When the parties developed contrasted behaviour, say, one domineering and the other submissive, he called the schismogenesis 'complementary'. In this terminology an arms race between two nations is properly described as a case of symmetrical schismogenesis.

In the year 1912 Germany was allied with Austria-Hungary, while France was allied with Czarist Russia. Britain was loosely attached to the latter group, thus forming the Triple Entente, while Italy was nominally attached to the former group, thus making the Triple Alliance. The warlike preparations of the Alliance and of the Entente were both increasing. The usual explanation was then, and perhaps still is, that the motives of the two sides were quite different, for we were only doing what was right, proper and necessary for our own defence, whilst they were disturbing the peace by indulging in wild schemes and extravagant ambitions. There are several distinct contrasts in that omnibus statement. Firstly that their conduct was morally bad, ours morally good. About so national a dispute it would be difficult to say anything that the world as a whole would accept. But there is another alleged contrast as to which there is some hope of general agreement. It was asserted in the years 1912-14 that their motives were fixed and independent of our behaviour, whereas our motives were a response to their behaviour and were varied accordingly. In 1914 Bertrand Russell[1] (now Earl Russell) put forward the contrary view that the motives of the two sides were essentially the same, for each was afraid of the other; and it was this fear which caused each side to increase its armaments as a defence against the other. Russell's pamphlet came at a time when a common boast in the British newspapers was that the British people 'knew no fear'. Several conspicuous heroes have since explained that they achieved their aims in spite of fear. When we analyse arms races it is, however, unnecessary to mention fear, or any other emotion; for an arms race can be recognized by the characteristic outward behaviour, which is shown in the diagram on page 228. The valuable part of Russell's doctrine was not his emphasis on fear, but his emphasis on mutual stimulation.

This view has been restated by another philosopher, C. E. M. Joad:[2]

". . . if, as they maintain, the best way to preserve peace is to prepare war, it is not altogether clear why all nations should regard the armaments of other nations as a menace to peace.

[1]Russell, B. A. W., 1914, "War the Offspring of Fear," Union of Democratic Control, London.

[2]Joad, C. E. M., 1939, Why War? Penguin Special, p. 69.

However, they do so regard them and are accordingly stimulated to increase their armaments to overtop the armaments by which they conceive themselves to be threatened. . . . These increased arms being in their turn regarded as a menace by nation A whose allegedly defensive armaments have provoked them, are used by nation A as a pretext for accumulating yet greater armaments wherewith to defend itself against the menace. These yet greater armaments are in their turn interpreted by neighbouring nations as constituting a menace to themselves and so on. . . ."

This statement is, I think, a true and very clear description but needs two amendments. The competition is not usually between every nation and every other nation, but rather between two sides; so that a nation looks with moderate favour on the armaments of other nations on its own side, and with strong dislike on those of the opposite side. Joad's description applies to an arms race which has become noticeable. Motives other than defence may have been important in starting the arms race.

It may be well to translate these ideas into the phraseology of 'operational research' which began to be used during the Second World War. Professor C. H. Waddington[1] explains that "The special characteristic which differentiates operational research from other branches of applied science is that it takes as the phenomenon to be studied the whole executive problem and not the individual technical parts. . . ." Surely the maintenance of world peace is an executive problem large enough to be called an operation and to require an appropriate background of operational research. This book is a contribution thereto. Sir Charles Goodeve,[2] in a survey of operational research, distinguishes between 'self-compensating and self-aggravating systems', and he mentions, as an example of the latter, the system composed of the public and of the store-keepers; a system such that a rumour of scarcity can make a real scarcity. In this phraseology it can be said that a system of two great powers, not in the presence of any common enemy, is a 'self-aggravating system' such that a rumour of war can make a real war.

It will be shown in the next section that arms races are best described in quantitative terms; but, for those who do not like mathematics, Bateson's word 'schismogenesis' may serve as an acceptable summary of a process which otherwise requires a long verbal description such as those given by Russell, Bateson, or Joad.

[1] Waddington, C. H., in *Nature*, Vol. CLXI, p. 404.
[2] Goodeve, Sir Charles in *Nature*, Vol. CLXI, p. 384.

THE QUANTITATIVE THEORY OF ARMS RACES

The facts for the years 1909 to 1914 are interesting. The 'defence' budgets of France Germany and Russia were taken from a digest by Per Jacobsson;[1] those for Austria-Hungary from the *Statesman's Year Books*. To make them comparable, they were all reduced to sterling. In those years the exchange rates between national currencies were held steady by the shipment of gold, so that the conversion to sterling is easy and definite.

Because France was allied to Russia it is reasonable to consider the total of their 'defence' expenditures. Let it be U. For a similar reason let V be the total for Germany and Austria-Hungary. In the accompanying diagram the rate of increase of $(U + V)$ is plotted against $(U + V)$. See page 228.

The accuracy with which the four observed points are fitted by a straight line is remarkable, especially as one of the co-ordinates is a difference. Similar diagrams drawn for other years, for other countries, and from other sources of information, are not so straight; but still they are straight enough to suggest that the explanation of the phenomenon is hardly likely to be found in the caprice of a few national leaders; the financial facts suggest either regular planning, or the regularity which results from the average of many opinions.

The main feature shown by the diagram is that the more these nations spent, the more rapidly did they increase their expenditure. Athletic races are not like that, for in them the speed of the contestants does not increase so markedly with the distance that they have run.

TABLE I. *The arms race of* 1909-14
Defence budgets expressed in millions of £ sterling

	1909	1910	1911	1912	1913
France	48·6	50·9	57·1	63·2	74·7
Russia	66·7	68·5	70·7	81·8	92·0
Germany . . .	63·1	62·0	62·5	68·2	95·4
Austria-Hungary .	20·8	23·4	24·6	25·5	26·9
Total = $U + V$.	199·2	204·8	214·9	238·7	289·0
Time rate = $\Delta(U + V)/\Delta t$		5·6	10·1	23·8	50·3
$(U + V)$ at same date . .		202·0	209·8	226·8	263·8

Here Δ signifies 'take the annual increase of' whatever symbol follows next.

From Monog. Supplt. No. 23 of *Brit. Journ. Psychol.*, by permission of the British Psychological Society.

[1]Jacobsson, Per (1929?). *Armaments Expenditures of the World*, published by the *Economist*, London.

The sloping line when produced backwards cuts the horizontal, where $\Delta(U + V)/\Delta t$ vanishes, at the point where $U + V = 194$ million £. This point may suitably be called a point of equilibrium. To explain how it could be a point of equilibrium we can suppose that the total expenditure of 194 million was regarded as that which would have been so ordinary as not to constitute any special threat.

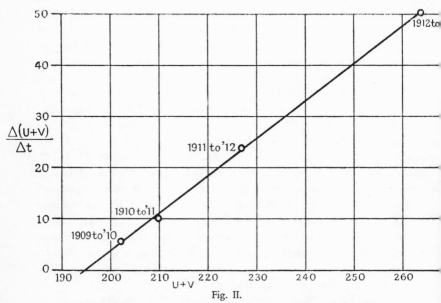

Fig. II.

The financial facts in the table at the foot of page 227 are here plotted.

It was a theory[1] which led L. F. Richardson to make a diagram having those co-ordinates $U + V$ and $\Delta(U + V)/\Delta t$. This theory will now be explained. The opening phase of the First World War afforded a violent illustration of Russell's doctrine of mutuality, for it was evident that warlike activity, and the accompanying hatred, were both growing by tit for tat, alias mutual reprisals. Tit for tat is a jerky alternation; but apart from details, the general drift of

[1]Richardson, L. F., 1919, *Mathematical Psychology of War*. In British copyright libraries. The diagram first appeared in *Nature* of 1938, Vol. CXLII, p. 792.

mutual reprisals was given a smoothed quantitative expression in the statement that the rate of increase of the warlike activity of each side was proportional to the warlike activity of the other side. This statement is equivalent to the following pair of simultaneous differential equations

$$\frac{dx}{dt} = ky, \qquad \frac{dy}{dt} = lx \qquad (1)\ (2)$$

where t is the time, x is the warlike activity of one side, y that of the other side, k and l are positive constants, dx/dt is the excellent notation of Leibniz for the time rate of increase of x, and dy/dt is the time rate of increase of y. In accordance with modern custom, the fraction-line is set sloping when it occurs in a line of words. If k were equal to l, then the relation of x to y would be the same as the relation of y to x, so that the system of x and y would be strictly mutual. Strict mutuality is, however, not specially interesting. The essential idea is that k and l, whether equal or not, are both positive. They are called '*defence coefficients*' because they represent a pugnacious response to threats.

The reader may here object that anything so simple as the pair of equations (1) and (2) is hardly likely to be true description of anything so complicated as the politics of an arms race. In reply appeal must be made to a working rule known as Occam's Razor whereby the simplest possible descriptions are to be used until they are proved to be inadequate.

The meaning of (1) and (2) will be further illustrated by deducing from them some simple consequences. If at any time both x and y were zero, it follows according to (1) and (2) that x and y would always remain zero. This is a mathematical expression of the idea of permanent peace by all-round total disarmament. Criticism of that idea will follow, but for the present let us continue to study the meaning of equations (1) and (2). Suppose that x and y being zero, the tranquillity were disturbed by one of the nations making some very slightly threatening gesture, so that y became slightly positive. According to (1) x would then begin to grow. According to (2) as soon as x had become, positive, y would begin to grow further. The larger x and y had become the faster would they increase. Thus the system defined by (1) and (2) represents a possible equilibrium at the point where x and y are both zero, but this equilibrium is unstable, because any slight deviation from it tends to increase. If any historian or politician reads these words, I beg him or her to notice that in the mechanical sense, which is used here, stability is not the same as equilibrium; for on the contrary stable and unstable are adjectives qualifying equilibrium. Thus an equilibrium is said to be stable, or to have stability, if a small disturbance tends to die away; whereas an equilibrium is said to be unstable, or to have instability, if a small disturbance tends to increase. In this mechanical sense the system defined by (1) and (2) has instability. It describes a schismogenesis. "It is an old proverb," wrote William Penn in 1693. "*Maxima bella ex levissimis causis*: The greatest Feuds have had the smallest Beginnings."

One advantage of expressing a concept in mathematics is that deductions can then be made by reliable techniques. Thus in (1) and (2) the nations appear as entangled with one another, for each equation involves both x and y. These variables can, however, be separated by repeating the operation d/dt which signifies 'take the time rate of'.

Thus from (1) it follows that $\dfrac{d}{dt}\left(\dfrac{dx}{dt}\right) = k\dfrac{dy}{dt}$

Simultaneously from (2) $k\dfrac{dy}{dt} = klx$

On elimination of dy/dt between these two equations there remains

an equation which does not involve y, namely $\dfrac{d}{dt}\left(\dfrac{dx}{dt}\right) = klx.$ \hfill (3)

Similarly $\dfrac{d}{dt}\left(\dfrac{dy}{dt}\right) = kly$ \hfill (4)

In (3) and (4) each nation appears as if sovereign and independent, managing its own affairs, until we notice that the constant kl is a property of the two nations jointly.

Another advantage of a mathematical statement is that it is so definite that it might be definitely wrong; and if it is found to be wrong, there is a plenteous choice of amendments ready in the mathematicians' stock of formulæ. Some verbal statements have not this merit; they are so vague that they could hardly be wrong, and are correspondingly useless.

The formulae (1) and (2) do indeed require amendment, for they contain no representation of any restraining influences; whereas it is well known that, after a war, the victorious side, no longer feeling threatened by its defeated enemy, proceeds to reduce its armed forces in order to save expenditure, and because the young men are desired at home. The simplest mathematical representation of disarmament by a victor is

$$\frac{dx}{dt} = -ax$$ \hfill (5)

where a is a positive constant. For, so long as x is positive, equation (5) asserts that dx/dt is negative, so that x is decreasing. Equation (5) is commonly used in physics to describe fading away. In accountancy, depreciation at a fixed annual percentage is a rule closely similar to (5). As a matter of fact[1] (5) is a good description of the disarmaments of Britain, France, U.S.A., or Italy during the years just after the First World War. In equation (5), which represents disarmament of the victor, there is no mention of y, because the defeated nation no longer threatens. It seems reasonable to suppose that restraining influences of the type represented by (5) are also felt by both of the nations during an arms race, so that equations (1) and (2) should be amended so as to become

$$\frac{dx}{dt} = ky - ax, \qquad \frac{dy}{dt} = lx - \beta y \qquad (6), (7)$$

in which β is another positive constant. At first[2] a and β were called 'fatigue and expense coefficients', but a shorter and equally suitable name is *restraint coefficients*. These restraining influences may, or may not, be sufficient to render the equilibrium stable. The interaction is easily seen in the special, but important, case of similar nations, such that $a = \beta$, and $k = l$. For then the subtraction of (7) from (6) gives

$$\frac{d(x-y)}{dt} = -(k+a)(x-y) \qquad (8)$$

In this $(k+a)$ is always positive. If at any time $(x-y)$ is positive, equation (8) shows that then $(x-y)$ is decreasing; and that moreover $(x-y)$ will continue to decrease until it vanishes, leaving $x = y$. If on the contrary $(x-y)$ is initially negative, (8) shows that $(x-y)$ will increase towards zero. Thus there is a stable drift from either side towards equality of x with y. That is more or less in accord with the historical facts about arms races between nations which can be regarded as similar.

To see the other aspect, let (7) be added to (6) giving

$$\frac{d(x+y)}{dt} = (k-a)(x+y) \qquad (9)$$

The meaning of (9) can be discussed in the same manner as that of (8). The result is that $(x+y)$ will drift towards zero if $(k-a)$ is negative, that is if $a > k$. We may then say that restraint overpowers 'defence', and that the system is thoroughly stable. Unfortunately

---

[1](*See* 3 on page 234).
[2]Richardson, L. F., in *Nature* of 18th May, 1935, p. 830.

that is not what has happened in Europe in the present century. The other case is that in which $k > a$ so that 'defence' overpowers restraint, and $(x + y)$ drifts away from zero. That is like an arms race. When $k > a$, the system is stable as to $(x - y)$, but unstable as to $(x + y)$. It is the instability which has the disastrous consequences. The owner of a ship which has capsized by rolling over sideways can derive little comfort from the knowledge that it was perfectly stable for pitching fore and aft. People who trust in the balance of power should note this combination of stability with instability.

If at any time x and y were both zero, it would follow from (6) and (7) that x and y would always remain zero. So that the introduction of the restraining terms still leaves the theoretical possibility of permanent peace by universal total disarmament. Small-scale experiments on absence of armament have been tried with success between Norway and Sweden, between Canada and U.S.A., between the early settlers in Pennsylvania and the Red Indians. The experiment of a general world-wide absence of arms has never been tried. Many people doubt if it would result in permanent peace; for, they say, grievances and ambitions would cause various groups to acquire arms in order to assert their rights, or to domineer over their unarmed neighbours. The theory is easily amended to meet this objection. Let two constants g and h be inserted respectively into (6) and (7) thus

$$\frac{dx}{dt} = ky - ax + g; \qquad \frac{dy}{dt} = lx - \beta y + h \qquad (10), (11)$$

If x and y were at any time both zero, then would $dx/dt = g$, and $dy/dt = h$, which do not indicate a permanent condition.

There may be still an equilibrium, but it is not at the point $x = 0$, $y = 0$. To find the new point of equilibrium let $dx/dt = 0$, and $dy/dt = 0$. Then by (10) and (11)

$$0 = ky - ax + g; \quad 0 = lx - \beta y + h \qquad (12), (13).$$

These equations represent two straight lines in the plane of x and y. If these lines are not parallel, their intersection is the point of equilibrium. It may be stable or unstable.

The assertion that the defence-coefficients k and l are positive is equivalent to supposing that the effect of threats is always retaliation. The reader may object that in the opening section of this chapter other effects were also mentioned, namely, contempt, submission, negotiation, or avoidance. The most important of these objections relates to submission, because it is the direct opposite of retaliation. The answer is that the scope of the present theory is restricted to the interaction of groups which style themselves powers, which are proud of their so-called sovereignty and independence, are proud of their armed might, and are not exhausted by combat. This theory is not about victory and defeat. In different circumstances k or l might be negative. A theory of submissiveness showing this has been published.[1] As to contempt, negotiation, or avoidance, they have sometimes gone on concurrently with an arms race, as in Examples (1), (5) and (9), (4) and (10) of the diverse effects of threats.

Let us now return to the 'defence' budgets of France, Russia, Germany and Austria-Hungary. The diagram on page 228 relates to the total $U + V$ of the warlike expenditures of the two opposing sides. The equilibrium point, at $U + V = 194$ millions sterling, presumably represents the expenditure which was excused as being customary for the maintenance of internal order, and harmless in view of the treaty situation. In the theory the treaty situation is represented by the constants g and h. Their effects can be regarded as included in the 194, together with the general goodwill between the nations. It appears suitable therefore to compare fact with theory by setting simultaneously $x + y = U + V - 194$, together with $g = 0$ and $h = 0$. (14), (15), (16) From (14) one derives

$$\frac{d(x + y)}{dt} = \frac{d(U + V)}{dt} \qquad (17)$$

The two opposing alliances were about of equal size and civilization, so that it seems permissible to simplify the formulae by setting $a = \beta$ and $k = l$. Addition of the formulae (10) and (11) then gives, as before in (9),

$$\frac{d(x + y)}{dt} = (k - a)\,(x + y) \qquad (18)$$

Now $x + y$ can be thoroughly eliminated from (18); from its first member by (17), and from its second member by (14), with the result that

$$\frac{d(U + V)}{dt} = (k - a)\,(U + V - 194) \qquad (19)$$

This is a statement about the expenditures of the nations in a form comparable with Fig. II on page 228. For $d(U + V)/dt$ is a close approximation to $\Delta(U + V)/\Delta t$. The assumed constancy of $k - a$ agrees with the fact that the sloping line on the diagram is straight. Moreover the

[1]See references 1 and 3 on page 234.

Q

absence from (6) and (7) of squares, reciprocals, or other more complicated functions, which was at first excused on the plea of simplicity, is now seen to be so far justified by comparison with historical fact. The slope of the line on the diagram, when compared with (19) gives

$$k - a = 0\cdot73 \text{ per year} \tag{20}$$

Further investigations of this sort have dealt with demobilization,[1,3] with the arms race of 1929–39 between nine nations,[1,3] with war-weariness and its fading,[3] with submissiveness in general,[1,3] and with the submission of the defeated in particular.[2,3]

All those investigations had to do with warlike preparations, an outward or behaviouristic manifestation. The best measure of it was found to be a nation's expenditure on defence divided, in the same currency, by the annual pay of a semi-skilled engineer. This conception may be called 'war-finance per salary" a phrase which can be packed into the new word 'warfinpersal'.

MOODS, FRIENDLY OR HOSTILE, PRIOR TO A WAR

What of the inner thoughts, emotions, and intentions which accompany the growth of warfinpersal? Lloyd George, who was Chancellor of the Exchequer in 1914, describes some of them in his *War Memoirs*, revised in 1938. He relates that although there had been naval rivalry between Britain and Germany during the previous six years, yet as late as 24th July, 1914, only a very small minority of Britons wished for war with Germany. Eleven days later the British nation had changed its mind. Another brilliant description of the moods occurs in H. G. Wells's novel *Mr. Britling Sees It Through*. The contrast between the comparatively slow growth of irritation over years, and the sudden outbreak of war, can be explained by the well-established concept of the subconscious. Suppose, for simplicity, that in a person there are only two mental levels, the overt and the subconscious, and that the moods in these levels are not necessarily the same. In Britain in the year 1906 the prevailing mood towards Germany was friendly openly, and friendly also in the subconscious. The arms race during 1908 to 1913 did not prevent the King from announcing annually to Parliament that "My relations with foreign powers continue to be friendly"; and the majority of British citizens

[1]Richardson, L. F., 1939, *Generalized Foreign Politics*. Monog. Supplt. No. 23 of the *British Journal of Psychology*.

[2]Richardson, L. F., 1944, letter in *Nature* of 19th August, p. 240.

[3]Richardson, L. F., 1947, *Arms and Insecurity* on 35 mm. punched safety microfilm, sold by the author.

continued to speak in friendly terms of their German acquaintances. It is reasonable to suppose, however, that during those same years there was a growing hostility to Germany in the British subconscious mind, caused by the arms race and by diplomatic crises. The hostile mood, having been thus slowly prepared in the subconscious, was ready suddenly to take open control at the beginning of August 1914. A quantitative theory of such changes of mood is offered by L. F. Richardson.[1] Here is a simplified specimen of that theory:

$$d\eta_1/dt = C_{12}\xi_1\eta_2$$

where η_1 is the fraction of the British population that was eager for war at time t, while η_2 is the corresponding fraction for Germany, C_{12} is a constant, and ξ_1 is the fraction of the British population that was in the susceptible mood: overtly friendly, but subconsciously hostile. An equation of this type is used in the theory of epidemics of disease[2] Eagerness for war can be regarded analogously as a mental disease infected into those in a susceptible mood by those who already have the disease in the opposing country. In this theory, as in Russell's *War the Offspring of Fear*, the relations between the two nations are regarded as mutual. Accordingly the same letter, ξ say, is used in relation to either, but is distinguished by suffix 1 for the British, suffix 2 for the Germany quantity. Also there is another equation obtainable from that above by interchanging the suffixes.

CONCLUSION

This chapter is not about wars and how to win them, but is about attempts to maintain peace by a show of armed strength. Is there any escape from the disastrous mutual stimulation by threat and counter-threat? Jonathan Griffin[3] argued that each nation should confine itself to pure defence which did not include any preparation for attack, while aggressive weapons should be controlled by a supra-national authority. The difficulty is that, when once a war has started, attack is more effective than defence. Gandhi's remarkable discipline and strategy of non-violent resistance is explained and discussed by Gregg.[4] The pacifying influence of intermarriage has been considered by Richardson.[5]

[1]Richardson, L. F., 1948, *Psychometrika*, Vol. XIII, pp. 147–74 and 197–232.
[2]Kermack, W. O., and McKendrick, A. G., 1927, *Proc. Roy. Soc. Lond. A* Vol. CXV, pp. 700–22.
[3]Griffin, J., 1936, *Alternative to Rearmament*, Macmillan, London.
[4]Gregg, R. B., 1936, *The Power of Non-Violence*, Routledge, London.
[5]Richardson, L. F., 1950, *The Eugenics Review*, Vol. XLII pp. 25-36.

CHAPTER **XI**

STATISTICS OF DEADLY QUARRELS

by L. F. Richardson

INTRODUCTION

THERE are many books by military historians dealing in one way or another with the general theme 'wars, and how to win them'. The theme of the present chapter is different, namely, 'wars, and how to take away the occasions for them', as far as this can be done by inquiring into general causes. But is there any scope for such an inquiry? Can there be any general causes that are not well known, and yet of any importance? Almost every individual in a belligerent nation explains the current war quite simply by giving particulars of the abominable wickedness of his enemies. Any further inquiry into general causes appears to a belligerent to be futile, comic, or disloyal. Of course an utterly contradictory explanation is accepted as obviously true by the people on the other side of the war; while the neutrals may express chilly cynicism. This contradiction and variety of explanation does provide a prima-facie case for further investigation. Any such inquiry should be so conducted as to afford a hope that critical individuals belonging to all nations will ultimately come to approve of it. National alliances and enmities vary from generation to generation. One obvious method of beginning a search for general causes is therefore to collect the facts from the whole world over a century or more. Thereby national prejudices are partly eliminated.

COLLECTIONS OF FACTS FROM THE WHOLE WORLD

Professor Quincy Wright[1] has published a collection of *Wars of Modern Civilization*, extending from A.D. 1482 to A.D. 1940, and including 278 wars, together with their dates of beginning and ending, the name of any treaty of peace, the names of the participating states, the number of battles, and a classification into four types of war. This extensive summary of fact is very valuable, for it provides a corrective to those frequent arguments which are based on the few wars which the debater happens to remember, or which happen to support his theory. Wright explains his selection by the statement that his list

[1]Wright, Q., 1942, *A Study of War*, Chicago University Press, Chicago.

"is intended to include all hostilities involving members of the family of nations, whether international, civil, colonial, or imperial, which were recognized as states of war in the legal sense or which involved over 50,000 troops. Some other incidents are included in which hostilities of considerable but lesser magnitude, not recognized at the time as legal states of war, led to important legal results such as the creation or extinction of states, territorial transfers, or changes of government".

Another world-wide collection has been made by L. F. Richardson for a shorter time interval, only A.D. 1820 onwards, but differently selected and classified. No attention was paid to legality or to important legal results, such concepts being regarded as varying too much with opinion. Instead attention was directed to deaths caused by quarrelling, with the idea that these are more objective than the rights and wrongs of the quarrel. The wide class of 'deadly quarrels' includes any quarrel that caused death to humans. This class was subdivided according to the number of deaths. For simplicity the deaths on the opposing sides were added together. The size of the subdivisions had to be suited to the uncertainty of the data. The casualties in some fightings are uncertain by a factor of three. It was found in practice that a scale which proceeded by factors of ten was suitable, in the sense that it was like a sieve which retained the reliable part of the data, but let the uncertainties pass through and away. Accordingly the first notion was to divide deadly quarrels into those which caused about 10,000,000 or 1,000,000 or 100,000 or 10,000 or 1,000 or 100 or 10 or 1 deaths. These numbers are more neatly written respectively as 10^7, 10^6, 10^5, 10^4, 10^3, 10^2, 10^1, 10^0 in which the index is the logarithm of the number of deaths. The subsequent discussion is abbreviated by the introduction of a technical term. *Let the 'magnitude' of any deadly quarrel be defined to be the logarithm, to the base ten, of the number of persons who died because of that quarrel.* The middles of the successive classes are then at magnitudes 7, 6, 5, 4, 3, 2, 1, 0. To make a clean cut between adjacent classes it is necessary to specify not the middles of the classes, but their edges. Let these edges be at 7·5, 6·5, 5·5, 4·5, 3·5, 2·5 . . . on the scale of magnitude. For example magnitude 3·5 lies between 3,162 and 3,163 deaths, magnitude 4·5 lies between 31,622 and 31,623 deaths, magnitude 5·5 lies between 316,227 and 316,228 deaths, and so on. Richardson's collection has not yet been published in extenso, but various extracts from it have appeared in print, and it will be available in microfilm. (1950, from the author).

These two world-wide collections provide the raw material for many investigations. Three, which have already been published by learned societies, are summarized below. Others relating to language, religion, and common government will be offered in microfilm.

THE DISTRIBUTION OF WARS IN TIME

This aspect of the collections is taken first, not because it is of the most immediate political interest, but almost for the opposite reason, namely, that it is restfully detached from current controversies.

Before beginning to build, I wish to clear three sorts of rubbish away from the site.

1. There is a saying that "If you take the date of the end of the Boer War and add to it the sum of the digits in the date, you obtain the date of the beginning of the next war, thus $1902 + 1 + 9 + 0 + 2 = 1914$". Also $1919 + 1 + 9 + 1 + 9 = 1939$. These are merely accidental coincidences. If the Christian calendar were reckoned from the birth of Christ in 4 B.C. then the first sum would be $1906 + 1 + 9 + 0 + 6 = 1922$, not $1914 + 4$.

2. There is a saying that "Every generation must have its war". This is an expression of a belief, perhaps well founded, in latent pugnacity. As a statistical idea, however, the duration of a generation is too vague to be serviceable.

3. There is an assertion of a fifty-year period in wars which is attributed by Wright (1942, p. 230) to Mewes in 1896. Wright mentions an explanation by Spengler of this supposed period, thus: "The warrior does not wish to fight again himself and prejudices his son against war, but the grandsons are taught to think of war as romantic". This is certainly an interesting suggestion, but it contradicts the other suggestion that "Every generation must have its war". Moreover the genuineness of the fifty-year period is challenged. Since 1896, when Mewes published, the statisticians have developed strict tests for periodicity (*see* for example Kendall's *Advanced Theory of Statistics*, Part II, 1946). These tests have discredited various periods that were formerly believed. In particular the alleged fifty-year period in wars is mentioned by Kendall[1] as an example of a lack of caution.

Having thus cleared the site, let us return to Wright's collection as to a quarry of building material.

The Distribution of Years in Their Relation to War and Peace

A list was made of the calendar years. Against each year was set a mark for every war that began in that year. Thus any year was

[1]Kendall, M. G., 1945, *J. Roy. Statistical Soc.*, **108**, 122.

characterized by the number, x, of wars that began in it. The number, y, of years having the character x was then counted. The results were as follows.[1]

YEARS FROM A.D. 1500, TO A.D. 1931 INCLUSIVE. WRIGHT'S COLLECTION.
Number, x, of outbreaks

in a year . .	0	1	2	3	4	>4	Totals
Number, y, of such years	223	142	48	15	4	0	432
Y, as defined below .	216·2	149·7	51·8	12·0	2·1	0·3	432·1

It is seen that there is some regularity about the progression of the numbers y. Moreover they agree roughly with the numbers Y. These are of interest because they are calculated from a well-known formula, called by the name of its discoverer the 'Poisson Distribution' and specified thus

$$Y = \frac{N\lambda^x}{(2\cdot7183)^\lambda \, x!}$$

in which N is the whole number of years, λ is the mean number of outbreaks per year, and $x!$ is called 'factorial x' and is equal respectively to 1, 1, 2, 6, 24, when x equals 0, 1, 2, 3, 4. Similar results were obtained from Richardson's collection both for the beginnings and for the ends of fatal quarrels in the range of magnitude extending from 3·5 to 4·5, thus:

Years A.D. 1820 to 1929 inclusive

x outbreaks in a year .	0	1	2	3	4	>4	Total
y for war . . .	65	35	6	4	0	0	110
Poisson . . .	64·3	34·5	9·3	1·7	0·2	0·0	110·0
y for peace . .	63	35	11	1	0	0	110
Poisson . . .	63·8	34·8	9·5	1·7	0·2	0·0	110·0

The numbers in the rows beginning with the word 'Poisson' were calculated from the formula already given, in which N and λ have the same *verbal* definitions as before, and therefore have appropriately altered *numerical* values. Such adjustable constants are called parameters.

If every fatal quarrel had the same duration, then the Poisson distribution for their beginnings would entail a Poisson distribution for their ends; but in fact there is no such rigid connection. The durations are scattered: Spanish America took fourteen years to break free from Spain, but the siege of Bharatpur was over in two months. Therefore the Poisson distributions for war and for peace may reasonably be regarded as separate facts.

Observed numbers hardly ever agree perfectly with the formulae

---

[1]Richardson, L. F., 1945, *J. Roy. Statistical Soc.*, **107,** 242.

that are accepted as representing them. In the paper cited[1] the disagreement with Wright's collection is examined by the χ^2 test and is shown to be unimportant. It should be noted, however, that the application of this standard χ^2 test involves the tacit assumption that there is such a thing as chance in history.

There is much available information about the Poisson distribution; about the theories from which it can be derived; and about the phenomena which are approximately described by it.[2] The latter include the distribution of equal time intervals classified according to the number of alpha particles emitted during each by a film of radioactive substance.

In order to bring the idea home, an experiment in cookery may be suggested. Take enough flour to make N buns. Add λN currants, where λ is a small number such as 3. Add also the other usual ingredients, and mix all thoroughly. Divide the mass into N equal portions, and bake them. When each bun is eaten, count carefully and record the number of currants which it contains. When the record is complete, count the number y of buns, each of which contains exactly x currants. Theory would suggest that y will be found to be nearly equal to Y, as given by the Poisson formula. I do not know whether the experiment has been tried.

A more abstract, but much more useful, summary of the relations, is to say that the Poisson distribution of years, follows logically from the hypothesis that there is the same very small probability of an outbreak of war, or of peace, somewhere on the globe on every day. In fact there is a seasonal variation, outbreaks of war having been commoner in summer than in winter, as Q. Wright shows. But when years are counted as wholes, this seasonal effect is averaged out; and then λ is such that the probability of a war beginning, or ending, during any short time dt years is λdt.

This explanation of the occurrence of wars is certainly far removed from such explanations as ordinarily appear in newspapers, including the protracted and critical negotiations, the inordinate ambition and the hideous perfidy of the opposing statesmen, and the suspect movements of their armed personnel. The two types of explanation are, however, not necessarily contradictory; they can be reconciled by

[1] *J. Roy. Statistical Soc.*, **107**, 242.

[2] Jeffreys, H., 1939, *Theory of Probability*, Oxford University Press. Kendall, M. G., 1943, *The Advanced Theory of Statistics*, Griffin, London. Shilling, W., 1947, *J. Amer. Statistical Assn.*, **42**, 407-24. Cramér, H., 1946, *Mathematical Methods of Statistics*, Princeton University Press.

saying that each can separately be true as far as it goes, but cannot be the whole truth. A similar diversity of explanation occurs in regard to marriage: on the one hand we have the impersonal and moderately constant marriage rate; on the other hand we have the intense and fluctuating personal emotions of a love-story; yet both types of description can be true.

Those who wish to abolish war need not be discouraged by the persistent recurrence which is described by the Poisson formula. The regularities observed in social phenomena are seldom like the unalterable laws of physical science. The statistics, if we had them, of the sale of snuff or of slaves, would presumably show a persistence during the eighteenth century; yet both habits have now ceased. The existence of a descriptive formula does not necessarily indicate an absence of human control, especially not when the agreement between formula and fact is imperfect. Nevertheless, the Poisson distribution does suggest that the abolition of war is not likely to be easy, and that the League of Nations and its successor the United Nations have taken on a difficult task. In some other fields of human endeavour there have been long lags between aspiration and achievement. For example Leonardo da Vinci drew in detail a flying machine of graceful appearance. But four centuries of mechanical research intervened before flight was achieved. Much of the research that afterwards was applied to aeroplanes was not at first made specifically for that object. So it may be with social science and the abolition of war.

The Poisson distribution is not predictive; it does not answer such questions as 'when will the present war end?' or 'when will the next war begin?' On the contrary the Poisson distribution draws attention to a persistent probability of change from peace to war, or from war to peace. Discontent with present weather has been cynically exaggerated in a comic rhyme:

> As a rule a man's a fool:
> When it's hot he wants it cool,
> When it's cool he wants it hot,
> Always wanting what is not.

A suggestion made by the Poisson law is that discontent with present circumstances underlies even the high purposes of peace and war. There is plenty of psychological evidence in support. This is not the place to attempt a general review of it; but two illustrations may serve as pointers. In 1877 Britain had not been engaged in any considerable war since the end of the conflict with China in 1860.

During the weeks of national excitement in 1877 preluding the dispatch of the British Mediterranean squadron to Gallipoli, in order to frustrate Russian designs on Constantinople, a bellicose music-hall song with the refrain:

'We don't want to fight, but, by Jingo, if we do:

We've got the men, we've got the ships, we've got the money too.'

was produced in London and instantly became very popular.[1]

Contrast this with the behaviour of the governments of Britain, China, USA, and USSR in 1944, after years of severe war, but with victory in sight, who then at Dumbarton Oaks officially described themselves as 'peace-loving'.[2]

Chance in history. The existence of a more or less constant λ, a probability per time of change, plainly directs our attention to chance in history. Thus the question which statisticians are accustomed to ask about any sample of people or things, namely "whether the sample is large enough to justify the conclusions which have been drawn from it" must also be asked about any set of wars.

Have wars become more frequent? In particular the discussion of any alleged trend towards more or fewer wars is a problem in sampling. No definite conclusion about trend can be drawn from the occurrence of two world wars in the present century, because the sample is too small. When, however, the sample was enlarged by the inclusion of all the wars in Wright's collection, and the time was divided into two equal intervals, the following result was obtained.

Dates of beginning	A.D. 1500 to 1715	A.D. 1716 to 1931
Numbers of wars	143	156

The increase from 143 to 156 can be explained away as a chance effect.

This was not so for all subdivisions of the time. When the interval from A.D. 1500 to A.D. 1931 was divided into eight consecutive parts of fifty-four years each, it was found that the fluctuation, from part to part, of the number of outbreaks in Wright's collection was too large to be explained away as chance. The extremes were fifty-four outbreaks from A.D. 1824 to 1877, and sixteen outbreaks from A.D. 1716 to 1769. Other irregular fluctuations of λ were found, although less definitely, for parts of twenty-seven and nine years.[3] All these results may, of course, depend on Wright's selection rules. The problem has been further studied by Moyal.[4]

[1]*Ency. Brit.*, XIV, ed. 13, 69.

[2]H.M. Stationery Office, London, Cmd. 6666.

[3]*J. Roy. Statistical Soc.*, 107, 246-7.

[4]Moyal, J. E., 1950. *J. Roy. Statistical Soc.*, 112, 446-9.

THE LARGER, THE FEWER

When the deadly quarrels in Richardson's collection were counted in unit ranges of magnitude, the following distribution was found.[1] The numbers are those of deadly quarrels which ended from A.D. 1820 to 1929 inclusive.

Ends of range of magnitude	$7 \pm \frac{1}{2}$	$6 \pm \frac{1}{2}$	$5 \pm \frac{1}{2}$	$4 \pm \frac{1}{2}$
Quarrel-dead at centre of range	10,000,000	1,000,000	100,000	10,000
Number of deadly quarrels	1	3	16	62

Although Wright's list is not classified by magnitudes, yet some support for the observation that the smaller incidents were the more numerous is provided by his remark (p. 636) that "A list of all revolutions, insurrections, interventions, punitive expeditions, pacifications, and explorations involving the use of armed force would probably be more than ten times as long as the present list". Deadly quarrels that cause few deaths are not in popular language called wars. The usage of the word 'war' is variable and indefinite; but perhaps on the average the customary boundary may be at about 3,000 deaths. From the scientific point of view it would be desirable to extend the above tabular statement to the ranges of magnitude ending at $3 \pm \frac{1}{2}$, $2 \pm \frac{1}{2}$, $1 \pm \frac{1}{2}$, by collecting the corresponding numbers of deadly quarrels from the whole world. There is plenty of evidence that such quarrels, involving about 1,000, or 100, or 10, deaths, have existed in large numbers. They are frequently reported in the radio news. Wright alludes to them in the quotation above. Many are briefly mentioned in history books. But it seems not to have been anyone's professional duty to record them systematically. For the range of magnitude between 3·5 and 2·5 I have made a card index for the years A.D. 1820 to 1929 which recently contained 174 incidents, but was still growing. This number 174, though an underestimate, notably exceeds 62 fatal quarrels in the next unit range of larger magnitude, and is thus in accordance with 'the larger the fewer'.

Between magnitudes 2·5 and 0·5 the world totals are unknown. Beyond this gap in the data are those fatal quarrels which caused 3, 2, or 1 deaths, which are mostly called murders, and which are recorded in criminal statistics. For the murders it is possible to make a rough

[1] Letter in *Nature* of 15th November, 1941.

estimate of the world total in the following manner. Different countries are first compared by expressing the murders per million of population during a year. This 'murder rate' has varied from 610 for Chile[1] in A.D. 1932, to 0·3 for Denmark[2] A.D. 1911–20. The larger countries had middling rates. From various sources, including a governmental report[3] it was estimated the the murder rate for the whole world was of the order of 32 in the interval A.D. 1820 to 1929. As the world population[4] averaged about 1,358 million for the same interval, it follows that the whole number of murders in the world was about

$$110 \times 32 \times 1358 = 5 \text{ million}$$

This far exceeds the number of small wars in the whole world during the same 110 years. Thus 'the larger, the fewer' is a true description of all the known facts about world totals of fatal quarrels.

In the gap where world totals are lacking there are local samples: one of banditry in Manchukuo,[5] and one of ganging in Chicago.[6] Before these can be compared with the world totals it is essential that they should be regrouped according to equal ranges of quarrel-dead or of magnitude; for the maxim 'the larger the fewer' relates to statistics arranged in either of those manners. When thus transformed the statistics of banditry and of ganging fit quite well with the gradation of the world totals, on certain assumptions. A thorough statistical discussion will be found elsewhere.[7]

The suggestion is that deadly quarrels of all magnitudes, from the world wars to the murders, are suitably considered together as forming one wide class, gradated as to magnitude and as to frequency of occurrence. This is a statistical chapter; and for that reason the other very important gradations, legal, social, and ethical, between a world war and a murder are not discussed here. The present conspectus of

[1]*Keesing's Contemporary Archives*, p. 1052, Bristol. Corrected by a factor of ten.

[2]Calvert, E. R., 1930, *Capital Punishment in the Twentieth Century*, Putnam's, London.

[3]*Select Committee on Capital Punishment*, 1931, H.M.S.O., London, for reference to which I am indebted to Mr. John Paton.

[4]Carr-Saunders, A. M., 1936, *World Population*, Clarendon Press, Oxford.

[5]*Japan and Manchukuo Year Book*, 1938, Tokio.

[6]Thrasher, F. M., 1927, *The Gang*, Chicago University Press.

[7]Richardson, L. F., 1948, *Journ. Amer. Statistical Assn.*, Vol. XLIII, pp. 523–46.

all deadly quarrels should be compared with psycho-analytic findings about personal and national aggressiveness which are explained in Chapter VI by Professor J. C. Flugel.

WHICH NATIONS WERE MOST INVOLVED?

This section resembles quinine: it has a bitter taste, but medicinal virtues. The participation of some well-known states in the 278 'wars of modern civilization' as listed by Wright is summarized and discussed by him.[1]

Over the whole time interval from A.D. 1480 to 1941 the numbers of wars in which the several nations participated were as follows: England (Great Britain) 78, France 71, Spain 64, Russia (USSR) 61, Empire (Austria) 52, Turkey 43, Poland 30, Sweden 26, Savoy (Italy) 25, Prussia (Germany) 23, Netherlands 23, Denmark 20, United States 13, China 11, Japan 9.

It may be felt that the year 1480 has not much relevance to present-day affairs. So here are the corresponding numbers for the interval A.D. 1850 to 1941, almost within living memory: Great Britain 20, France 18, Savoy (Italy) 12, Russia (USSR) 11, China 10, Spain 10, Turkey 10, Japan 9, Prussia (Germany) 8, USA 7, Austria 6, Poland 5, Netherlands 2, Denmark 2, Sweden 0.

It would be difficult to reconcile these numbers of wars in which the various nations have participated, with the claim made in 1945 by the Charter of the United Nations[2] to the effect that Britain, France, Russia, China, Turkey, and USA, were 'peace-loving' in contrast with Italy, Japan, and Germany. Some special interpretation of peace-lovingness would be necessary: such as either 'peace-loving-ness' at a particular date; or else that 'peace-loving' states participated in many wars in order to preserve world peace.

It would be yet more difficult to reconcile the participations found by Wright with the concentration of Lord Vansittart's invective against Germans, as though he thought that Germans were the chief, and the most persistent, cause of war.[3]

In fact no one nation participated in a majority of the wars in Wright's list. For the greatest participation was that of England (Great Britain) namely in seventy-eight wars; leaving 200 wars in

[1]Wright, Q., 1942, A Study of War, Chicago University Press, pp. 220–3 and 650.
[2]H.M. Stationery Office, London, Cmd. 6666, Articles 3 and 4 together with the list of states represented at the San Francisco Conference.
[3]Vansittart, Sir Robert (now Lord), 1941, Black Record, Hamish Hamilton, London.

which England did not participate. The distinction between aggression and defence is usually controversial. Nevertheless, it is plain that a nation cannot have been an aggressor in a war in which it did not participate. The conclusion is, therefore, that no one nation was the aggressor in more than 28 per cent of the wars in Wright's list. Aggression was widespread. This result for wars both civil and external agrees broadly with Sorokin's findings after his wide investigation of internal disturbance. He attended to Ancient Greece, Ancient Rome, and to the long interval A.D. 525 to 1925 in Europe. Having compared different nations in regard to internal violence, Sorokin concluded that 'these results are enough to dissipate the legend of "orderly" and "disorderly" peoples'. . . . 'All nations are orderly and disorderly according to the times'.[1] The diversity of the conscious attitudes of individuals is discussed in Chapter III, by Dr. H. J. Eysenck.

There does not appear to be much hope of forming a group of permanently peace-loving nations to keep the permanently aggressive nations in subjection; for the reason that peace-lovingness and aggressiveness are not permanent qualities of nations. Instead the facts support Ranyard West's[2] conception of an international order in which a majority of momentarily peace-loving nations, changing kaleidoscopically in its membership, may hope to restrain a changing minority of momentarily aggressive nations.

THE NUMBER OF GROUPS ON EACH SIDE OF A WAR[3]

Wars can be classified according to the number of organized groups of people on the two sides: for example, 1 government *versus* 1 set of insurgents, or 2 states *versus* 1 state, or 5 nations *versus* 3 nations, or in general r belligerent groups *versus* s belligerent groups. Then the number of wars of the type 'r *versus* s' can be counted, for each r and s, and the results can be written in a table of rows and columns. As there was no good reason for distinguishing 2 *versus* 1 from 1 *versus* 2 the observed number of wars of this type was bisected, and half of it was written in each of the two possible places; and so in general whenever r was not equal to s. This analysis was applied to both Wright's and Richardson's collections with the following results.

[1]Sorokin, Pitrim A., 1937, *Social and Cultural Dynamics*, American Book Co.
[2]West, R., 1942, *Conscience and Society*, Methuen, London.
[3]Being an abstract of L. F. Richardson's paper in the *Journal of the Royal Statistical Society*, **109**, 130–56.

Quarrels of Magnitudes greater than 3·5 which ended from A.D. 1820 to 1939 inclusive. Richardson's Collection

s	1	2	3	4	5	6
6	0·5	0	0	0	0	0
5	1	0·5	0	0	0	0
4	2·5	0·5	0·5	0	0	0
3	2·5	1	0	0·5	0	0
2	12	3	1	0·5	0·5	0
1	42	12	2·5	2·5	1	0·5
	1	2	3	4	5	6
			r			

There were also beyond the bounds of the above table: 2 wars of 7 versus 1; 1 war of 9 versus 1; 1 war of 15 versus 5; thus making a total of 91 wars.

Wars not Marked Civil in Wright's List from A.D. 1480 to 1941 inclusive

s	1	2	3	4	5	6
6	1	0·5	0	0	0	0
5	1·5	0·5	0·5	0	0	0
4	6	0	0·5	0	0	0
3	6	3	1	0·5	0·5	0
2	14	4	3	0	0·5	0·5
1	117	14	6	6	1·5	1
	1	2	3	4	5	6
			r			

There were also in Wright's list beyond the bounds of the above table one war of each of the following types: 7 versus 1, 8 versus 1, 11 versus 1, 16 versus 1, 20 versus 1, 7 versus 3, 8 versus 5, 20 versus 5, 33 versus 5, 35 versus 7, 9 versus 8, thus making a total of 200 wars.

The above two tables, though based on different definitions of war, have a strong resemblance. In both the commonest type is 1 versus 1, and the next commonest 2 versus 1. Both distributions are tolerably well fitted by the formula

$$(\text{number of wars of type } r \text{ versus } s) = 5\,\frac{(\text{whole number of wars})}{9\,(rs)^{2\cdot5}}$$

Professor M. S. Bartlett has pointed out to me that, according to this law, any cell-frequency is equal to the product of the marginal totals for its row and its column, divided by the total for the whole table; so that the variable r would be said to be 'statistically independent' of the variable s. Apart from this bit of insight, the formula is empirical: it describes the facts, but does not explain them. Although tables in rows and columns, including especially correlation tables, are a common feature of works on statistics, yet a frequency-distribution of this particular shape was certainly not well known. No ready-made theory, which might have illuminated the causes of wars, was available. So rival theories were made on purpose, under the guidance of the following leading ideas:

(i) International relations have not been so deterministic as to justify any theory which would offer to predict exactly what must happen at any date.

(ii) A theory, however, should indicate what probably would happen. It ought to agree with the historical facts collected from any sufficiently long interval, say, from 100 years or more.

(iii) That because a nation cannot be at war all by itself, therefore the probabilities of war must be attached to pairs of nations, and not to nations singly.

(iv) In the course of a century the same nation may have been peace-loving on several occasions, and aggressive on several others. These characteristics are not sufficiently permanent to form the basis of a long-term theory. Klingberg[1] has published a summary of the opinions of 220 outstanding students of international affairs about the chance of war between pairs of States. Considerable fluctuations of opinion occurred in a few years. It would be an instructive adventure to begin at the opposite extreme by first regarding all nations as of similar pugnacity, and later introducing only such discriminations between nations as are called for by the statistics of r versus s.

(v) That any type of war, such, for example, as 2 versus 1, comprises many mutually exclusive varieties of conceivable war, which could be specified by naming the two belligerents and the one. The number of such mutually exclusive varieties can be formulated; and so in general for r versus s.

(vi) A remarkable feature is that 1 versus 1 has been much the commonest type; and that in general the more complicated types have been rarer than the simpler types. This is a characteristic of lack of organization, of chaos. In the molecular chaos of a gas, collisions of molecules two in a bunch are much more frequent than collisions three in a bunch. Mathematically the characteristic of chaos is that the probability of a complicated event contains among its factors the probabilities of simpler events.

[1]Klingberg, F. L. 1941. *Psychometrika* **6**, 335-352.

(vii) These ideas combine to give an expression of the following form for the probability of a war of the type r versus s

(number of mutually exclusive varieties) $\times\ p^x \times (1 - p)^y$

where p is the probability of war between any pair of nations, x is the number of pairs that are in the war, and $(1 - p)^y$ is the probability that the neutrals would keep out. Any such theory may be called, in musical terminology, a variation on the theme by Bernoulli concerning the binomial distribution of probability.

These general ideas were developed in connection with successive special hypotheses until a combination was found which agreed with the facts. For some theories the appropriate facts were numbers of wars, for others durations of wars. It was quite interesting to notice the manner in which some hypotheses failed. The details can be seen in the original paper, to which the Roman numerals refer. In one theory (VIII) which is called 'a simple chaos between sixty nations' it is supposed for simplicity that p, the probability of war inside a pair of nations, is the same for all pairs and at all times. But it was impossible to find any number p that would agree with all parts of the distribution of durations of wars classified as r versus s. Most of the misfits could have been avoided if the number of nations in the world had been about six or ten instead of about sixty. The next three theories (IX, X, XI) are devices for reducing the number of nations in effective contact with one another. Thus in theory IX an approximate agreement would be achieved if there were in the world only about ten bellicose nations, all the others being permanently non-belligerent. It is, however, impossible to sort the nations into these two supposed categories; for the total number of names of belligerents, including names of insurgents, but not counting any name twice, was found to be, not ten, but 108, for the ninety-one wars that ended from A.D. 1820 to 1939 according to Richardson's list.

To circumvent this obstacle a different device (X) was next considered for reducing the effective number of belligerents. It was supposed that disputes had occurred in localities scattered at random over the globe so that altogether they concerned numerous possible belligerents; but that each dispute was localized so that it concerned only eight nations or other possible belligerent groups; and that the probability of war about that dispute was 0·35 for every pair that could be formed from the eight groups. These remarkably simple hypotheses led to a good agreement with the facts in Richardson's collection, provided $r + s \leq 8$. But the theory denied the possibility of any war involving more than eight belligerents, and so in particular that of the First World War.

The failure of these three theories (VIII, IX, X) showed the need for a more inclusive hypothesis designed to explain both the localization of most wars, and the occasional occurrence of long-range or world wars, in the era before aviation became dominant. Accordingly in theory XI the world was supposed for simplicity to consist of only three sorts of nations, namely eleven land-locked, forty-four local-coastal, and five powers capable of reaching any coast by sea. This hypothesis greatly complicated the mathematics; for different sorts of pairs of nations were contemplated, each with its appropriate, but at first unknown, probability of war. The probability of any event is here defined to be the fraction of time during which the event occurred in the course of any very long historical interval. For comparison, the historical data in Richardson's collection had to be rearranged as durations of wars. Moreover the former type 1 *versus* 1 had now to be divided into three subtypes namely:

A long-range power *versus* a long-range power;

A long-range power *versus* a short-range power;

A short-range power *versus* a short-range power;

and so on for the more complicated types. The classification became four-dimensional; the type r *versus* s being analysed into subtypes such as r_1 and r_2 *versus* s_1 and s_2.

The probabilities were deduced from the historical data. For type 1 *versus* 1 the deduction was definite and unique. For type 2 *versus* 1 the deduction was a compromise fitted to redundant data. For type 3 *versus* 1 various difficulties increased. The comparison of theory with fact was carried as far as type 2 *versus* 2. Beyond that the historical facts would be described statistically as 'outliers' in the sense that the classification of them contained many empty compartments with rare observations irregularly dispersed. Similar ragged appearances are usually to be seen in the outer regions of any diagram of observed frequencies. In particular the First World War, which was regarded as 15 *versus* 5, was isolated in the four-dimensional classification, being surrounded on all sides by many empty cells; one cannot easily say how many. A comparison of theory XI with the fact of the First World War would involve a difficult summation of probabilities over the outer regions of the classification, both empty and occupied. Theory XI certainly admits the possibility of such a war; but a quantitative study of outliers was not attempted.

The probability, x, of war between two long-range powers was found to be only of the order of 0·001. The probability, y, of war between a long- and a short-range power was found rather discordantly to be 0·002 or 0·015 or 0·009; on the average one may say that y was of the order 0·01, about ten times as great as x. The probability, z, of war between neighbouring powers was found to vary conspicuously with circumstances, thus:

Number, rs, of pairs of opposed belligerents			1	2	3	4
z			0·008	0·020	0·046	0·119?

On the average z was decidedly greater than y, and all the more so than x. That is to say *propinquity tended to war*.

Theory XII was an amendment to theory XI such that the variation of z with rs was simply accepted and explained as due to the infectiousness of fighting.

Theory XIII was called 'a uniform chaos modified only by infectiousness'; that is to say geographical barriers were ignored, and every nation was supposed (as also in theory VIII) to be in contact with every other nation. Aviation may make it so in future; but for the years before A.D. 1929 theory XIII definitely misfits the history. So one should return to theory XII which is called '*chaos restricted by geography and modified by infectiousness*'; for of all these theories it is the only one which has survived the test of quantitative comparison with historical fact. The possibility remains that someone may invent a different theory which may fit the facts as well or better.

Historians will doubtless be keenly aware of many relevant considerations which have been ignored in the foregoing batch of theories. But a theory is not necessarily to be despised for what it leaves out. This may be gathered from the history of the explanation of the moon's motion.[1] Sir Isaac Newton began the explanation by considering an idealized moon moving uniformly in a circle about the earth as centre. As a description that was crude, for Hipparchus in the second century B.C. had known better. Yet Newton's first simple explanation is so interesting that it is still regularly taught to physics students. It has also been fertile. In 1913 Bohr used it, along with brilliantly novel ideas, to explain the motion of an electron around the nucleus of an atom. Meanwhile a succession of astronomers have laboured to improve lunar theory. In the present century E. W.

[1] John Jackson in *Ency. Brit.*, XIV, ed. **15**, 780–1.

Brown put in all the relevant considerations. Brown's theory is so accurate that it is used in the computation of the *Nautical Almanac*. But, as Brown's theory involves 1,500 terms, it is not teachable to scientists in general.

BOOKS RECOMMENDED

1. Bartlett, F. C. (ed.). *The Study of Society*. 1939. (Kegan Paul, London.
2. Bovet, P. *The Fighting Instinct*. 1923. (Allen and Unwin, London).
3. Brown, J. F. *Psychology and the Social Order*. 1936. (McGraw-Hill, London.)
4. Chase, S. *The Proper Study of Mankind*. 1948. (Phoenix House, London.)
5. Cohen, J. *Human Nature, War and Society*. 1946. (Watts, London.)
6. Delaisi, F. *Political Myths and Economic Realities*. 1936. (Williams and Norgate, London.)
7. Durbin, E. F. M. and Bowlby, J. *Personal Aggressiveness and War*. 1939. (Kegan Paul, London.)
8. Flugel, J. C. *Population, Psychology and Peace*. 1947. (Watts, London.)
9. Flugel, J. C. Chap. XIX of *Man, Morals and Society*. 1945. (Duckworth.)
10. Glover, E. *War, Sadism and Pacifism*. 1933, revised and enlarged 1946. (Allen and Unwin.)
11. Hobson, J. A. *Imperialism*. 1902, revised 1938. Third edition 1949. (Allen and Unwin.)
12. Klineberg, O. *Social Psychology*. 1940. (Holt, New York.)
13. Kluckhohn, C. "Anthropological Research and World Peace." In Newcomb, T. M., and Hartley, E. L. (ed.) *Readings in Social Psychology*. 1947. (Holt, New York.)
14. Krech, D. and Crutchfield, R. S. *Theory and Problems of Social Psychology*. 1948. (McGraw-Hill, London.)
15. Montagu, Ashley. *On Being Human*. 1950. (Henry Schuman, New York.)
16. Murphy, G. *Human Nature and Enduring Peace*. 1945. (Reynal and Hitchcock, Boston.)
17. Overstreet, H. A. *The Mature Mind*. 1950. (Gollancz, London.)
18. Robbins, L. *The Economic Causes of War*. 1939. (Jonathan Cape, London.)
19. Social Science Research Council. *Public Reaction to the Atomic Bomb and World Affairs*. 1947. (Ithaca, Cornell University.)
20. Sombart, Werner. *Krieg und Kapitalismus*. 1913. (Verlag von Duncker und Humblot, Munich and Leipzig.)
21. Stagner, R. *War and Peace*. In Harriman, P. L. (ed.), *Encyclopaedia of Psychology*. 1946. (Philosophical Library, New York.)
22. Wright, Quincy. *A Study of War*, two vols. (University of Chicago Press, 1942, and Cambridge University Press, 1943.)

SUBJECT INDEX

INDEX OF NAMES